NON-LEAGUE FOOTBALL TABLES OF NORTH WEST ENGLAND 1889-2016

EDITOR
Michael Robinson

FOREWORD

Following the success of our 'Non-League Football Tables' series of books, the first of which was published in 2002, we have long considered introducing a number of regionalised titles about various football leagues both past and present. The first book in such a series, 'Non-League Football Tables of South West England 1892-2015' was finally published earlier this year and is still available for purchase at our address shown below, priced £11.99.

This second book of a planned series of six covers nine football leagues from the North West of England. The earliest of these commenced in 1889 and a number of the other leagues included continue to operate to this day.

The Leagues which currently form the apex of the 'Non-League Pyramid', namely the Football Conference (currently called the National League) and its three feeder leagues (Northern Premier, Southern Premier & Isthmian) will continue to be covered by our yearly 'Non-League Football Tables' books.

We are indebted to Mick Blakeman for providing tables for the various Leagues included in this book.

British Library Cataloguing in Publication Data
A catalogue record for this book is available from the British Library

ISBN: 978-1-86223-340-9

Printed in the UK by 4edge Ltd.

CONTENTS

LANCASHIRE LEAGUE 1889-1903

The Football League was formed in 1888 and proved to be an immediate success. Lancashire had long been in the forefront of the development of the professional game and many of the established clubs who had not initially been considered for Football League membership moved quickly to form their own league.

Bury took the lead role and, following a meeting held at the Saddle Hotel in Bolton during April 1889, it was proposed that a new Lancashire League should be formed as soon as humanly possible.

When membership of this new league was finalised, the following 14 clubs were the founder members:

Blackburn Park Road, Blackpool, Bury, Earlestown, Fleetwood Rangers, Heywood, Heywood Central, Higher Walton, Hyde, Nelson, Oswaldtwistle Rovers, Rossendale, Southport Central and West Manchester.

1889-90

Higher Walton	24	14	4	6	68	43	32
Bury	24	14	3	7	65	35	31
Heywood Central	24	14	2	8	64	38	30
Nelson	24	12	4	8	55	44	28
Blackpool	24	10	6	8	61	46	26
Southport Central	24	9	7	8	40	32	25
Heywood	24	10	5	9	54	49	25
Blackburn Park Road	24	8	6	10	44	47	22
West Manchester	24	9	4	11	44	70	22
Hyde	24	8	5	11	46	56	21
Oswaldtwistle Rovers	24	8	4	12	39	62	20
Fleetwood Rangers	24	7	5	12	35	51	19
Rossendale	24	4	3	17	37	79	11

Earlestown were expelled for a systematic defiance of the League's decisions concerning fixture dates. Their record was deleted when it stood as follows: 21   4   3   14   45   89   11
Hyde left to join The Combination and Blackburn Park Road also left.
Burnley Union Star joined from the North East Lancashire League.

1890-91

Bury	20	15	3	2	74	32	33
Blackpool	20	14	2	4	62	39	30
Heywood Central	20	13	3	4	77	34	29
Nelson	20	10	4	6	68	54	24
Heywood	20	8	4	8	42	54	20
Southport Central	20	8	3	9	43	55	19
Rossendale	20	8	1	11	42	43	17
Fleetwood Rangers	20	6	4	10	39	61	16
Higher Walton	20	6	3	11	45	57	15
West Manchester	20	3	4	13	41	70	10
Oswaldtwistle Rovers	20	1	5	14	25	59	7

Burnley Union Star resigned and disbanded at the end of February 1891 and their record was deleted: 18   3   2   13   26   60   8
Their stand was moved to Turf Moor, where it became the first covered stand on the Longside, opposite the Brunshaw Road side. It survived there until being replaced by a larger stand in 1896. Oswaldtwistle Rovers left to join the North East Lancashire League.
Witton joined from The Combination and South Shore joined, having never previously played in any league.

1891-92

Bury	22	20	0	2	76	21	40
Blackpool	22	16	3	3	77	32	35
Fleetwood Rangers	22	12	5	5	84	44	29
Rossendale	22	12	3	7	64	38	27
Southport Central	22	12	3	7	59	47	27
Nelson	22	10	4	8	82	63	24
Heywood Central	22	10	3	9	67	46	23
South Shore	22	5	7	10	51	69	17
Higher Walton	22	5	7	10	46	64	17
West Manchester	22	4	4	14	40	76	12
Witton	22	3	2	17	31	111	8
Heywood	22	1	3	18	23	89	5

Heywood and Witton left the league. Liverpool and Liverpool Caledonians both joined as newly formed clubs and Fairfield also joined.

1892-93

Liverpool	22	17	2	3	66	19	36
Blackpool	22	17	2	3	82	31	36
Bury	22	17	1	4	83	24	35
Fleetwood Rangers	22	10	5	7	47	51	25
West Manchester	22	10	4	8	68	55	24
Heywood Central	22	11	1	10	54	60	23
Rossendale	22	8	2	12	46	55	18
Southport Central	22	7	2	13	33	44	16
South Shore	22	5	6	11	46	66	16
Fairfield	22	5	6	11	34	53	16
Nelson	22	4	2	16	54	73	10
Higher Walton	22	3	3	16	28	110	9

Liverpool Caledonians went into liquidation and disbanded in December 1892. Their record was deleted: 6   3   2   1   14   11   8
Liverpool left to join the Football League Division Two and Higher Walton left to join the Preston & District League. Accrington joined from the Football League Division One and Barrow also joined.

1893-94

Blackpool	22	15	3	4	73	32	33
Bury	22	13	4	5	85	35	30
Southport Central	22	13	0	9	57	42	26
Accrington	22	11	4	7	51	39	26
Nelson	22	10	6	6	70	55	26
Fleetwood Rangers	22	10	2	10	52	49	22
West Manchester	22	9	3	10	43	52	21
South Shore	22	10	0	12	50	68	20
Fairfield	22	8	2	12	40	61	18
Rossendale	22	7	3	12	57	57	17
Heywood Central	22	7	2	13	38	80	14
Barrow/Bacup	22	2	5	15	39	85	9

Heywood Central had 2 points deducted for fielding an ineligible player. Barrow resigned from the League and disbanded on 20th November 1893 when their record stood as follows: 7   0   0   7   1   36   0
Clitheroe and Bacup of the North East Lancashire League both applied to take over their fixtures and it was Bacup who were elected. At the end of the season, Bury leftto join the Football League Division Two, Chorley joined from the Lancashire Alliance, Stockport County joined from The Combination and Clitheroe joined from the North East Lancashire League.

1894-95

Fairfield	26	17	3	6	68	32	37
Blackpool	26	16	2	8	89	34	34
Nelson	26	14	5	7	75	48	33
Southport Central	26	14	4	8	68	43	32
Fleetwood Rangers	26	13	6	7	62	49	32
Bacup	26	13	5	8	65	55	31
Chorley	26	11	3	12	69	56	25
West Manchester	26	10	5	11	61	63	25
Stockport County	26	10	5	11	53	69	25
South Shore	26	9	6	11	59	45	24
Rossendale	26	10	3	13	52	51	23
Accrington	26	10	2	14	62	63	22
Clitheroe	26	7	1	18	61	93	15
Heywood Central	26	3	0	23	28	171	6

Accrington left to join the Lancashire Combination and Heywood Central also left. Ashton North End and Stalybridge Rovers both joined from The Combination, Liverpool South End joined from the Liverpool & District League and Halliwell Rovers also joined.

1895-96

Nelson	30	22	4	4	105	39	48
Halliwell Rovers	30	18	3	9	86	55	39
Fairfield	30	17	5	8	65	42	39
Southport Central	30	17	4	9	72	51	38
Liverpool South End	30	15	3	12	63	53	33
Stalybridge Rovers	30	14	4	12	58	65	32
Bacup	30	11	9	10	79	61	31
Chorley	30	12	7	11	66	53	31
South Shore	30	13	5	12	57	60	31
Ashton North End	30	11	7	12	75	77	29
Rossendale	30	13	3	14	47	55	29
Stockport County	30	13	3	14	56	70	29
Blackpool	30	11	6	13	65	50	28
Fleetwood Rangers	30	8	5	17	53	68	21
West Manchester	30	6	1	23	34	109	13
Clitheroe	30	3	3	24	36	109	9

Blackpool left to join the Football League Division Two.
Oldham County joined from The Combination.

1896-97

Chorley	28	21	3	4	66	23	45
Fairfield	28	19	3	6	77	35	41
Halliwell Rovers	28	14	7	7	74	47	35
Southport Central	28	16	2	10	84	51	34
Clitheroe	28	15	4	9	54	35	34
Stalybridge Rovers	28	14	6	8	51	34	34
Oldham County	28	14	4	10	60	53	32
Nelson	28	13	5	10	66	38	31
Stockport County	28	15	1	12	52	42	31
Ashton North End	28	10	4	14	43	58	24
Bacup	28	6	6	16	46	67	18
West Manchester	28	7	4	17	40	67	18
Fleetwood Rangers	28	6	4	18	33	92	16
South Shore	28	6	3	19	45	73	15
Rossendale	28	5	2	21	37	113	12

Liverpool South End resigned during the first week of February 1897 due to financial problems and their record at the time was deleted when it stood as follows: 17   4   1   12   18   81   9
The club disbanded soon afterwards.
At the end of the season, Rossendale disbanded, Fleetwood Rangers left to join the Lancashire Combination and West Manchester also left. Horwich joined from the Lancashire Alliance, Middleton joined from The Combination, Rochdale joined from the Lancashire Combination and two newly formed clubs also joined, New Brighton Tower and Wigan County.

1897-98

New Brighton Tower	26	20	2	4	48	17	42
Nelson	26	17	3	6	72	33	37
Stockport County	26	15	4	7	60	27	34
Halliwell Rovers	26	15	4	7	71	38	34
Chorley	26	13	6	7	51	27	32
Ashton North End	26	12	6	8	50	47	30
Southport Central	26	13	3	10	51	41	29
Wigan County	26	11	5	10	52	41	27
Stalybridge Rovers	26	11	5	10	55	49	27
Middleton	26	11	4	11	58	75	26
South Shore	26	7	6	13	36	59	20
Rochdale	26	5	3	18	47	77	13
Clitheroe	26	2	3	21	20	84	7
Horwich	26	2	2	22	22	78	6

Fairfield resigned and disbanded on 9th October 1897 and their record was deleted when it stood as follows: 4   0   3   1   5   8   3
Oldham County resigned on 8th November 1897 and disbanded soon after. Their record was deleted: 9   2   0   7   8   22   4
Bacup resigned and disbanded on 19th February 1898 and their record was deleted when it stoof as follows: 20   4   6   10   28   41   14
At the end of the season, New Brighton Tower left to join the Football League Division Two and Clitheroe also left.
Crewe Alexandra and Rock Ferry both joined from The Combination.

1898-99

Chorley	24	17	5	2	42	17	39
Southport Central	24	12	8	4	41	18	32
Ashton North End	24	13	5	6	35	29	31
Crewe Alexandra	24	11	5	8	61	34	27
Stalybridge Rovers	24	12	3	9	53	53	27
Stockport County	24	12	2	10	48	42	26
Wigan County	24	8	8	8	57	36	24
Middleton	24	8	8	8	40	41	24
Rock Ferry/Haydock	24	10	0	14	43	48	20
Halliwell Rovers	24	6	5	13	31	42	17
Horwich	24	8	1	15	27	47	17
Rochdale	24	6	3	15	34	80	15
South Shore	24	5	3	16	28	53	13

Nelson resigned from the league and disbanded in January 1899 and their record was deleted: 10 5 2 3 25 21 12
They reformed during the summer and joined the North East Lancashire League in 1899-1900. Rock Ferry resigned and disbanded on 9th February 1899 when their record was: 14 6 0 8 29 33 12
Haydock joined from the Lancashire Alliance and took over their fixtures. At the end of the season, Ashton North End disbanded and Halliwell Rovers also left. Blackpool and Darwen both joined from the Football League Division Two, South Liverpool and White Star Wanderers both joined from The Combination and Earlestown joined from the Lancashire Alliance.

1899-1900

Stockport County	28	21	3	4	80	23	45
Stalybridge Rovers	28	16	8	4	61	23	40
Blackpool	28	16	6	6	79	36	38
Crewe Alexandra	28	16	4	8	87	48	36
Darwen	28	13	10	5	56	31	36
Chorley	28	15	6	7	49	28	36
Southport Central	28	14	5	9	49	32	33
White Star Wanderers	28	11	4	13	51	56	26
Rochdale	28	9	7	12	50	53	25
Haydock	28	9	5	14	40	57	23
Earlestown	28	7	5	16	40	64	19
Wigan County	28	5	8	15	26	59	18
South Liverpool	28	5	7	16	32	66	17
Horwich	28	5	6	17	27	70	16
Middleton	28	5	2	21	18	99	12

South Shore resigned and ceased to exist as a separate club after amalgamating with Blackpool on 11th December 1899. Their record was deleted when it stood as follows: 10 3 2 5 15 10 8
At the end of the season, Blackpool and Stockport County both left to join the Football League Division Two, White Star Wanderers left to join The Combination, Horwich and Wigan County both disbanded and Middleton and South Liverpool also left. Blackburn Rovers Reserves and Bolton Wanderers Reserves both joined from the Lancashire Combination, Nelson joined from the North East Lancashire Combination and Wigan United joined as a newly formed club.

1900-01

Stalybridge Rovers	20	15	3	2	55	14	33
Southport Central	20	15	3	2	49	15	33
Crewe Alexandra	20	12	2	6	45	23	26
Darwen	20	10	3	7	40	25	23
Blackburn Rovers Reserves	20	6	8	6	34	31	20
Nelson	20	8	4	8	33	35	20
Chorley	20	9	1	10	31	26	19
Earlestown	20	8	3	9	31	45	19
Bolton Wanderers Reserves	20	4	4	12	26	41	12
Wigan United	20	3	3	14	21	49	9
Haydock	20	2	2	16	12	73	6

Rochdale disbanded on 1st January 1901 and their record was deleted when it stood as follows: 6 2 0 4 6 19 4
At the end of the season, Blackburn Rovers Reserves, Bolton Wanderers Reserves and Nelson all left to join the Lancashire Combination and Crewe Alexandra left to join the Birmingham League. Barrow, Rochdale Town and St. Helens Town all joined as newly formed clubs, Prescot joined from the Lancashire Alliance, Workington joined from the Cumberland County League and Bacup also joined.

1901-02

Darwen	24	18	6	0	78	16	42
Southport Central	24	16	4	4	56	25	36
Wigan United	24	15	3	6	56	25	33
Earlestown	24	12	5	7	54	37	29
Stalybridge Rovers	24	11	4	9	36	29	26
St. Helens Town	24	11	3	10	42	43	25
Rochdale Town	24	10	3	11	48	46	23
Workington	24	9	4	11	57	50	22
Prescot	24	9	4	11	40	40	22
Barrow	24	8	3	13	52	58	19
Chorley	24	7	4	13	44	57	18
Bacup	24	4	3	17	31	81	11
Haydock	24	2	2	20	17	104	6

Haydock and Prescot both left the league.
St. Helens Recreation joined from the Lancashire Combination.

1902-03

Southport Central	22	17	2	3	49	18	36
Darwen	22	15	1	6	68	21	31
Barrow	22	14	3	5	45	24	31
Stalybridge Rovers	22	12	4	6	40	25	28
St. Helens Recreation	22	13	1	8	51	41	27
Workington	22	11	3	8	57	47	25
Rochdale Town	22	9	3	10	54	52	21
St. Helens Town	22	8	2	12	31	42	18
Earlestown	22	8	0	14	43	48	16
Chorley	22	7	2	13	38	50	16
Bacup	22	3	4	15	25	77	10
Wigan United	22	1	3	18	18	74	5

The Lancashire Combination formed a Second Division and 9 of the 12 Lancashire League clubs joined the new division. The 3 exceptions were Darwen who joined the Lancashire Combination First Division, Workington who joined the Cumberland County League and Wigan United who disbanded. The Lancashire League then closed down.

NORTH EAST LANCASHIRE LEAGUE 1889-1894

Lancashire was an early leader in the establishment of league football and the North East Lancashire League was also formed in 1889. There were 12 founder members but one of these – Padiham – resigned and disbanded before the season even started.

There were therefore only 11 clubs who actually took part in the league's first season. Those 11 were: Bell's Temperance (from Accrington), Brierfield, Burnley Union Star, Colne and District, Darwen Rovers, Haslingden, Haslingden Church Institute, Irwell Springs (from Bacup), Peel Bank Rovers (from Church), Ramsbottom and Rawtenstall.

1889-90

Brierfield	20	16	2	2	96	40	30
Irwell Springs	20	14	2	4	71	44	30
Burnley Union Star	20	13	3	4	64	34	29
Darwen Rovers	20	11	1	8	66	54	23
Peel Bank Rovers	20	8	3	9	59	66	19
Colne & District	20	7	5	8	42	56	19
Bell's Temperance	20	7	3	10	44	55	17
Rawtenstall	20	5	6	9	39	40	16
Ramsbottom	20	6	2	12	48	62	14
Haslingden Church Institute	20	4	3	13	29	61	11
Haslingden	20	3	2	15	28	74	6

Brierfield had 4 points deducted.
Haslingden had 2 points deducted.
Padiham resigned before the season started. Burnley Union Star moved to the Lancashire League and Haslingden were not re-elected. Clitheroe and the reserve sides of Accrington, Blackburn Rovers and Burnley all joined.

1890-91

Accrington Reserves	18	15	1	2	88	28	31
Rawtenstall	18	12	1	5	64	27	25
Burnley Reserves	18	11	3	4	65	37	25
Irwell Springs	18	10	2	6	48	33	22
Brierfield	18	7	5	6	69	46	17
Peel Bank Rovers	18	5	3	10	40	76	13
Haslingden Church Institute	18	5	3	10	28	63	13
Ramsbottom	18	5	1	12	38	71	11
Darwen Rovers	18	4	3	11	33	65	11
Clitheroe	18	4	2	12	36	63	10

Brierfield had 2 points deducted.
Bell's Temperance resigned from the league soon after the season started without playing any games.
Colne & District could not complete their fixtures and their record was deleted when it stood as follows:

	19	5	1	13	28	77	11

Blackburn Rovers Reserves also did not complete their fixtures and their record was deleted:

	17	7	2	8	44	41	16

They then moved to the Lancashire Combination.
Haslingden Church Institute also left the league.
Peel Bank Rovers changed their name to Church and Darwen Rovers were replaced by Darwen Reserves. Padiham and Bells Temperance rejoined. Oswaldtwistle Rovers joined from the Lancashire League.

1891-92

Accrington Reserves	22	17	1	4	82	27	35
Burnley Reserves	22	15	4	3	99	36	34
Oswaldtwistle Rovers	22	13	3	6	58	40	29
Darwen Reserves	22	13	2	7	95	38	28
Irwell Springs	22	12	2	8	66	66	26
Bell's Temperance	22	10	2	10	59	69	22
Rawtenstall	22	8	5	9	45	58	21
Clitheroe	22	10	0	12	64	59	20
Ramsbottom	22	6	3	13	52	61	15
Brierfield	22	7	1	14	39	76	15
Padiham	22	6	3	13	31	80	15
Church	22	1	2	19	27	79	4
					717	*689*	

Irwell Springs changed their name to Bacup. Darwen Reserves moved to the Lancashire Combination and Church also left. Peel Bank Rovers and Haslingden both rejoined.

1892-93

Burnley Reserves	22	16	6	0	119	22	38
Bacup	22	15	4	3	98	36	34
Brierfield	22	14	3	5	72	48	31
Oswaldtwistle Rovers	22	10	8	4	52	34	28
Clitheroe	22	11	4	7	61	41	26
Rawtenstall	22	9	5	8	52	55	23
Ramsbottom	22	10	3	9	64	82	23
Accrington Reserves	22	6	2	14	57	68	14
Bell's Temperance	22	4	6	12	42	61	14
Padiham	22	5	2	15	47	58	12
Haslingden	22	3	6	13	29	95	12
Peel Bank Rovers	22	4	1	17	32	104	9
					725	*704*	

Haslingden and Peel Bank Rovers both left the league.

1893-94

Burnley Reserves	18	17	1	0	140	16	35
Oswaldtwistle Rovers	18	11	2	5	45	35	24
Clitheroe	18	10	1	7	43	38	21
Bacup	11	9	0	2	50	16	18
Brierfield	16	8	1	7	59	45	17
Padiham	16	7	1	8	26	28	15
Bell's Temperance	17	6	1	10	45	54	13
Rawtenstall	18	6	0	12	48	56	12
Ramsbottom	16	5	0	11	26	85	10
Accrington Reserves	18	0	1	17	12	98	1
					494	*471*	

During November, Bacup moved to the Lancashire League to take over Barrow's fixtures and did not complete their North East Lancashire League fixtures.
At the end of the season, Burnley Reserves, Oswaldtwistle Rovers, Padiham, Bell's Temperance and Rawtenstall all joined the Lancashire Combination. Clitheroe joined the Lancashire League and the North East Lancashire League closed down.

THE COMBINATION 1890-1911

Following the successful introduction of the Football League in 1888, other areas were quick to copy the idea. Several leagues were operating in Lancashire in 1889-90 but none of them specifically catered for senior clubs in the Manchester district or in Cheshire where the game had been popular for many years.

In the spring of 1890, moves began to start a league centred on that area and, following a meeting in Manchester in May of that year, 12 clubs were proposed as potential members. The 12 clubs were:

Ardwick (reformed in 1894 as Manchester City), Burslem Port Vale, Bury, Chester, Gorton Villa, Halliwell, Heywood Central, Kidderminster, Leek, Northwich Victoria, South Shore and Witton.

However, Burslem Port Vale and Kidderminster were elected to the Midland League instead while Bury and Heywood Central preferred to remain in the Lancashire League. Halliwell and South Shore also declined to join and so suitable replacements had to be found.

On Tuesday 3rd June 1890, another meeting was held at the Brunswick Hotel, Piccadilly, Manchester where a revised list of members was drawn up. In addition to the 6 remaining members from the original list: Ardwick, Chester, Gorton Villa, Leek, Northwich Victoria and Witton, 6 further clubs were now proposed: Burton Swifts, Denton, Derby St. Luke's, Hyde, Macclesfield and Stafford County. Buxton and Manchester also attended the meeting but were not elected while Witton were elected despite not attending. Ardwick later withdrew and Wrexham who had also missed the meeting, were elected in their place.

Of the 12 founder members, only Hyde and Leek had previously experienced league football, Hyde having played in the Lancashire League in 1889-90 and Leek in the Midland League.

1890-91

Gorton Villa	16	10	2	4	47	26	22
Macclesfield	16	9	3	4	44	27	21
Chester	16	8	4	4	42	30	20
Burton Swifts	14	9	0	5	55	28	18
Denton	16	8	1	7	39	32	17
Northwich Victoria	16	5	7	4	28	30	17
Hyde	14	3	4	7	25	39	10
Wrexham	16	4	4	8	25	47	10
Leek	16	1	1	14	21	67	3

Wrexham had 2 points deducted for fielding an ineligible player.
Hyde refused to meet Burton Swifts to complete the outstanding games.
Derby St. Luke's, Stafford County and Witton all resigned during the season and their records were deleted when they each stood as follows:

Stafford County (club disbanded)	9	1	0	8	11	57	2
Derby St. Luke's	11	2	2	7	17	32	6
Witton	12	4	0	8	22	62	8

Witton moved to the Lancashire League in 1891-92.
Burton Swifts moved to the Football Alliance and Hyde also left the league.
Everton Reserves joined from the Liverpool & District League where they had been known as Everton Athletic.
Buxton, Chirk, Stoke Swifts (Stoke's reserve side) and Stockport County all joined having never previously played in any league.

1891-92

Everton Reserves	22	17	2	3	99	20	36
Northwich Victoria	22	15	1	6	84	25	31
Macclesfield	22	15	0	7	52	38	30
Stoke Swifts	22	13	1	8	49	29	27
Buxton	22	11	3	8	35	30	25
Wrexham	22	9	2	11	45	65	20
Chirk	22	7	5	10	48	56	19
Chester	22	8	3	11	52	61	19
Gorton Villa	22	8	3	11	41	51	19
Leek	22	8	0	14	46	62	16
Stockport County	22	7	2	13	29	44	16
Denton	22	2	2	18	25	124	6

Northwich Victoria moved to the Football League – Division Two and Denton also left. Nantwich joined from the Shropshire & District League and Dresden United also joined.

1892-93

Everton Reserves	22	18	2	2	107	13	38
Stoke Swifts	22	14	4	4	48	23	32
Chester	22	12	2	8	52	41	26
Chirk	22	10	3	9	63	43	23
Buxton	22	8	7	7	37	33	23
Stockport County	22	8	6	8	38	35	22
Dresden United	22	8	3	11	34	43	19
Wrexham	22	9	1	12	41	66	19
Macclesfield	22	6	6	10	45	55	18
Leek	22	6	3	13	31	60	15
Nantwich	22	6	3	13	36	81	15
Gorton Villa	22	6	2	14	29	68	14

Chirk moved to the Welsh Senior League and Gorton Villa also left.

1893-94

Everton Reserves	18	15	2	1	77	19	32
Stoke Swifts	18	10	1	7	57	31	21
Leek	18	9	2	7	32	27	20
Stockport County	18	7	6	5	33	32	20
Dresden United	18	7	5	6	34	28	19
Chester	18	6	6	6	24	26	18
Macclesfield	18	5	7	6	36	35	17
Wrexham	18	5	6	7	36	46	16
Buxton	18	5	4	9	28	41	14
Nantwich	18	1	1	16	12	84	3

Everton Reserves moved to the Lancashire Combination, Stockport County moved to the Lancashire League, Stoke Swifts moved to the Midland League, Wrexham moved to the Welsh Senior League and Nantwich moved to the South Cheshire League. Northwich Victoria joined from the Football League – Division Two, Ashton North End, Hurst Ramblers and Stalybridge Rovers all joined from The Federation, Glossop North End joined from the North Cheshire Junior League and Hanley Town also joined.

1894-95

Ashton North End	20	14	3	3	62	32	31
Glossop North End	20	14	2	4	49	19	30
Chester	20	12	2	6	53	35	26
Dresden United	20	9	7	4	52	25	25
Stalybridge Rovers	20	8	5	7	41	35	21
Macclesfield	20	8	3	9	44	38	19
Leek	20	7	4	9	36	47	18
Hurst Ramblers	20	7	1	12	35	61	15
Hanley Town	20	6	2	12	37	62	12
Buxton	20	4	3	13	22	48	11
Northwich Victoria	20	4	2	14	26	55	10

Hanley Town had 2 points deducted for fielding an ineligible player.
Ashton North End and Stalybridge Rovers both moved to the Lancashire League, Dresden United moved to the Midland League, Hurst Ramblers moved to the North Cheshire League and Hanley Town also left.
Everton Reserves joined from the Lancashire Combination and Oldham County joined as a newly formed club.

1895-96

Everton Reserves	14	11	2	1	54	12	24
Macclesfield	14	11	2	1	37	13	24
Glossop North End	14	9	3	2	33	13	21
Oldham County	14	5	1	8	24	39	11
Chester	14	4	2	8	27	29	10
Northwich Victoria	14	4	1	9	14	35	9
Leek	14	3	3	8	15	35	7
Buxton	14	1	2	11	15	43	4

Leek had 2 points deducted for fielding an ineligible player.
Glossop North End moved to the Midland League, Leek left moved to the North Staffordshire & District League and Oldham County moved to the Lancashire League. Crewe Alexandra joined from the Football League Division Two, Middleton joined from the Lancashire Alliance, Rock Ferry joined as a newly formed club, Wrexham joined from the Welsh Senior League and Barnton Rovers joined from the Cheshire Junior League.

1896-97

Everton Reserves	18	14	3	1	61	14	31
Rock Ferry	18	12	3	3	57	18	27
Chester	18	11	3	4	41	25	25
Northwich Victoria	18	8	2	8	31	41	18
Buxton	18	7	3	8	39	34	17
Wrexham	18	7	2	9	41	40	16
Middleton	18	7	3	8	40	32	15
Macclesfield	18	5	2	11	34	60	12
Crewe Alexandra	18	5	1	12	35	53	9
Barnton Rovers	18	2	2	14	18	80	4

Middleton, Crewe Alexandra and Barnton Rovers each had 2 points deducted for fielding ineligible players.
Macclesfield resigned from the league and disbanded. A separate junior club called Hallefield, who had been playing in a field off the Buxton Road in the Stockport & District League, moved into the Moss Rose ground. Hallefield eventually became today's Macclesfield Town.
Barnton Rovers moved to the Cheshire League and Middleton moved to the Lancashire League. Garston Copper Works, Tranmere Rovers and White Star Wanderers all joined from the Liverpool & District League, Chirk and Druids both joined from the Welsh Senior League, Stoke Swifts joined from the North Staffordshire & District League and Dresden United joined from the Midland League.

1897-98

Everton Reserves	24	15	5	4	65	25	35
Crewe Alexandra	24	12	6	6	53	34	30
Chirk	24	11	4	9	38	27	26
Wrexham	24	10	6	8	45	44	26
Stoke Swifts	24	10	5	9	42	35	25
Buxton	24	9	7	8	44	44	25
Rock Ferry	24	8	8	8	34	30	24
White Star Wanderers	24	8	7	9	41	42	23
Garston Copper Works	24	8	7	9	37	60	23
Druids	24	9	3	12	43	46	21
Chester	24	7	5	12	39	50	19
Tranmere Rovers	24	9	3	12	35	45	19
Northwich Victoria	24	6	2	16	40	74	14

Tranmere Rovers had 2 points deducted for fielding an ineligible player.
Dresden United resigned from the league and subsequently disbanded in January 1898 due to financial difficulties. Their record was deleted when it stood as follows: 12   1   2   9   11   26   4
Crewe Alexandra and Rock Ferry both moved to the Lancashire League, Northwich Victoria moved to the Cheshire League and Stoke Swifts moved to the North Staffordshire & District League. Bangor and Llandudno Swifts both joined from the North Wales Coast League, Liverpool Reserves joined from the Lancashire Combination, Oswestry United joined from the Shropshire & District League, Rhyl United joined as a new club after a merger of Rhyl Athletic and Rhyl Town and South Liverpool (previously known as African Royal) joined from the Liverpool & District Amateur League.

1898-99

Everton Reserves	28	23	4	1	112	18	50
Liverpool Reserves	28	21	3	4	87	22	45
Tranmere Rovers	28	15	4	9	54	33	34
Druids	28	16	1	11	64	31	33
Wrexham	28	15	3	10	55	48	33
Chester	28	13	5	10	60	57	31
Bangor	28	12	6	10	63	78	30
Chirk	28	12	3	13	44	48	27
Llandudno Swifts	28	12	3	13	48	58	27
White Star Wanderers	28	11	6	11	68	54	26
South Liverpool	28	9	4	15	36	52	22
Oswestry United	28	9	2	17	49	73	20
Buxton	28	7	2	19	43	102	16
Garston Copper Works	28	5	2	21	31	77	12
Rhyl United	28	6	0	22	35	98	12

White Star Wanderers had 2 points deducted for fielding an ineligible player.
Everton Reserves and Liverpool Reserves both left to join the Lancashire Combination, Llandudno Swifts left to join the North Wales Coast League, South Liverpool and White Star Wanderers both left to join the Lancashire League and Buxton left to join the Manchester League. Chester had to cease playing after losing their ground and failing to find another. Tranmere Rovers left to join the Lancashire Alliance and Garston Copper Works disbanded. A new junior club, Garston AFC, was formed as a replacement. Newtown joined from the Shropshire & District League, Birkenhead joined as a newly formed club and Aberystwyth Town also joined.

1899-1900

Chirk	16	10	4	2	36	12	24
Wrexham	16	11	1	4	58	25	23
Druids	16	9	3	4	38	22	21
Bangor	16	8	1	7	37	36	17
Birkenhead	16	4	5	7	27	37	13
Newtown	16	6	1	9	34	56	13
Aberystwyth Town	16	4	4	8	23	36	12
Oswestry United	16	5	2	9	30	38	10
Rhyl United	16	2	5	14	38	64	9

Oswestry United had 2 points deducted for fielding an ineligible player.
Druids moved to the Birmingham & District League and Aberystwyth Town and Newtown also left. White Star Wanderers joined from the Lancashire League, Buckley, Hudson's (Liverpool) and Newton-le-Willows all joined from the Liverpool & District Combination and Tranmere Rovers and Warrington both joined from the Lancashire Alliance.

1900-01

Wrexham	22	16	3	3	62	20	35
Rhyl United	22	15	2	5	49	33	32
Bangor	22	13	3	6	62	45	29
Oswestry United	22	10	8	4	57	28	28
Chirk	22	10	5	7	46	40	25
White Star Wanderers	22	8	6	8	45	40	22
Hudson's (Liverpool)	22	7	3	12	39	42	17
Tranmere Rovers	22	6	5	11	32	37	17
Birkenhead	22	6	4	12	37	52	16
Warrington	22	7	2	13	27	57	16
Buckley	22	6	4	12	32	68	16
Newton-le-Willows	22	4	6	12	24	64	11

Buckley, Hudson's (Liverpool) and Warrington all left the league.
Burslem Port Vale Reserves, Nantwich and Witton Albion all joined from the Cheshire League, Wellington Town joined from the Birmingham & District League and Chester reformed and joined after finding a new ground.

1901-02

Wrexham	26	17	7	2	80	21	41
Burslem Port Vale Reserves	26	14	7	5	61	43	33
Oswestry United	26	12	6	8	55	33	30
Nantwich	26	13	4	9	68	47	30
Wellington Town	26	11	5	10	39	36	27
Bangor	26	11	5	10	51	74	27
Birkenhead	26	9	8	9	42	40	26
Witton Albion	26	11	3	12	47	52	25
Newton-le-Willows	26	9	6	11	40	71	24
Tranmere Rovers	26	8	7	11	46	49	23
Rhyl United	26	6	8	12	45	53	20
White Star Wanderers	26	9	2	15	50	63	20
Chirk	26	8	1	17	48	69	17
Chester	26	6	7	13	46	67	17

Burslem Port Vale Reserves and Chester each had 2 points deducted for fielding an ineligible player.
Wellington Town moved to the Birmingham & District League. Rhyl United changed their name to Rhyl. Middlewich Athletic Rangers and Winsford United both joined from the Cheshire League.

1902-03

Wrexham	26	19	5	2	80	23	43
Nantwich	26	15	4	7	69	43	34
Birkenhead	26	15	4	7	53	36	34
Burslem Port Vale Reserves	26	12	7	7	63	35	31
Oswestry United	26	14	2	10	57	42	30
Witton Albion	26	11	8	7	52	49	30
Chester	26	9	8	9	48	49	26
Middlewich Athletic Rangers	26	9	8	9	43	62	26
Bangor	26	9	8	9	53	72	24
Winsford United	26	8	5	13	51	54	19
Newton-le-Willows	26	8	3	15	52	74	19
Rhyl	26	8	4	14	52	64	18
Tranmere Rovers	26	4	5	17	30	64	13
Chirk	26	4	3	19	34	70	11

Bangor, Rhyl and Winsford United each had 2 points deducted for fielding ineligible players.
White Star Wanderers resigned and disbanded in March 1903 and their record was deleted:

	19	9	1	9	30	34	19

Newton-le-Willows moved to the Lancashire Combination and Burslem Port Vale Reserves moved to the North Staffordshire & District League. Broughton United joined as a newly formed club.

1903-04

Birkenhead	24	17	3	4	49	22	37
Chester	24	15	3	6	65	29	33
Nantwich	24	14	3	7	60	30	31
Tranmere Rovers	24	14	1	9	54	42	29
Wrexham	24	12	4	8	54	34	28
Bangor	24	12	2	10	60	55	26
Oswestry United	24	11	2	11	42	55	24
Rhyl	24	10	1	13	52	52	21
Broughton United	24	8	3	13	38	55	19
Middlewich Athletic Rangers	24	7	5	12	40	63	19
Winsford United	24	6	6	12	40	46	18
Witton Albion	24	4	8	12	30	61	16
Chirk	24	3	5	16	36	76	11

Witton Albion moved to the Manchester League and Winsford United also left. Druids joined from the Birmingham & District League, Port Sunlight joined from the Wirral & District League and Whitchurch also joined.

1904-05

Wrexham	26	21	1	4	70	16	43
Chester	26	17	3	6	69	35	37
Broughton United	26	14	5	7	43	44	33
Nantwich	26	11	7	8	66	39	29
Port Sunlight	26	11	5	10	56	50	27
Tranmere Rovers	26	10	7	9	41	37	27
Rhyl	26	11	5	10	40	44	27
Whitchurch	26	11	4	11	60	58	26
Middlewich Athletic Rangers	26	10	2	14	44	55	22
Oswestry United	26	10	2	14	43	62	22
Birkenhead	26	7	6	13	35	47	20
Bangor	26	8	3	15	55	61	19
Druids	26	7	5	14	29	54	19
Chirk	26	4	5	17	32	81	13

Wrexham moved to the Birmingham & District League.
Crewe Alexandra Reserves and Glossop Reserves both joined.

1905-06

Whitchurch	28	18	5	5	87	32	41
Chester	28	16	4	8	72	29	36
Glossop Reserves	28	15	4	9	53	37	34
Druids	28	14	5	9	52	46	33
Tranmere Rovers	28	13	8	7	40	36	32
Crewe Alexandra Reserves	28	14	3	11	53	42	31
Nantwich	28	14	2	12	47	53	30
Port Sunlight	28	11	6	11	43	42	28
Oswestry United	28	13	1	14	72	56	27
Bangor	28	9	6	13	38	63	24
Rhyl	28	10	3	15	61	70	23
Chirk	28	8	7	13	48	71	23
Broughton United	28	11	2	15	46	61	22
Birkenhead	28	9	3	16	38	54	21
Middlewich Ath. R./Wigan Town	28	4	3	21	32	90	7

Broughton United and Tranmere Rovers each had 2 points deducted for fielding ineligible players.
Middlewich Athletic Rangers resigned and disbanded in January 1906 when their record stood as: 13   1   1   11   18   58   3
Wigan Town who were formed just a month earlier, took over their fixtures. Four points were deducted from the joint final record for the fielding of ineligible players.
Glossop Reserves and Port Sunlight both moved to the Lancashire Combination and Broughton United also left. Wrexham Victoria joined from the Wirral & District League and Wrexham Reserves also joined.

1906-07

Whitchurch	26	20	5	1	84	30	45
Chester	26	19	3	4	75	27	41
Wigan Town	26	12	6	8	44	45	30
Nantwich	26	12	3	11	49	46	27
Wrexham Reserves	26	11	4	11	50	45	26
Birkenhead	26	12	4	10	64	63	26
Crewe Alexandra Reserves	26	10	5	11	66	61	25
Tranmere Rovers	26	10	5	11	35	39	25
Oswestry United	26	9	6	11	49	41	24
Bangor	26	8	5	13	36	51	21
Chirk	26	8	4	14	39	61	20
Rhyl	26	8	2	16	38	64	18
Druids	26	6	6	14	29	70	18
Wrexham Victoria	26	8	0	18	29	44	16

Birkenhead had 2 points deducted for fielding an ineligible player.
Wigan Town moved to the Lancashire Combination and Wrexham Victoria also left. Connah's Quay & Shotton United and Welshpool both joined.

1907-08

Tranmere Rovers	26	20	4	2	83	21	44
Chester	26	21	2	3	87	29	44
Oswestry United	26	16	4	6	62	38	36
Crewe Alexandra Reserves	26	14	3	9	69	50	31
Whitchurch	26	13	4	9	66	42	30
Nantwich	26	12	5	9	65	57	29
Connah's Quay & Shotton United	26	13	3	10	55	57	29
Druids	26	9	5	12	53	58	23
Bangor	26	8	3	15	38	68	19
Chirk	26	9	0	17	41	63	18
Rhyl	26	7	2	17	49	80	16
Wrexham Reserves	26	6	4	16	42	74	16
Birkenhead	26	5	5	16	33	61	15
Welshpool	26	5	4	17	34	79	14

Middlewich and Saltney both joined.

1908-09

Chester	30	21	7	2	91	34	49
Saltney	30	16	9	5	93	42	41
Tranmere Rovers	30	15	5	10	86	48	35
Welshpool	30	13	8	9	63	53	34
Crewe Alexandra Reserves	30	13	7	10	95	56	33
Connah's Quay & Shotton United	30	13	7	10	60	63	33
Bangor	30	13	6	11	71	81	32
Nantwich	30	12	7	11	59	61	31
Oswestry United	30	13	4	13	74	55	30
Whitchurch	30	11	8	11	53	64	30
Wrexham Reserves	30	10	6	14	48	59	26
Chirk	30	9	8	13	48	62	26
Middlewich	30	8	8	14	67	84	24
Druids	30	10	4	16	51	74	24
Birkenhead	30	7	2	21	48	95	16
Rhyl	30	6	4	20	37	113	16

Welshpool left the league.
Denbigh Town joined from the North Wales Coast League.

1909-10

Crewe Alexandra Reserves	30	24	3	3	105	33	51
Saltney	30	22	4	4	81	32	48
Chester	30	20	2	8	85	47	42
Tranmere Rovers	30	18	2	10	92	50	38
Bangor	30	16	3	11	79	66	35
Whitchurch	30	16	3	11	61	53	35
Wrexham Reserves	30	15	5	10	64	58	35
Nantwich	30	14	4	12	57	56	32
Connah's Quay & Shotton United	30	14	1	15	65	67	29
Middlewich	30	12	3	15	58	61	27
Oswestry United	30	9	7	14	44	62	25
Rhyl	30	7	6	17	54	83	20
Chirk	30	8	3	19	57	91	19
Druids	30	7	3	20	44	83	17
Denbigh Town	30	6	4	20	52	93	16
Birkenhead/Brymbo Victoria	30	5	1	24	42	105	11

Birkenhead resigned and disbanded soon after playing their last ever game on 4th December 1909, a 6-1 defeat at home to Chester. At the time, their record stood as follows: 10   0   1   9   11   45   1
Brymbo Victoria took over Birkenhead's remaining fixtures.
Chester and Tranmere Rovers both moved to the Lancashire Combination, Crewe Alexandra Reserves and Nantwich both moved to the Manchester League, Chirk and Druids both moved to the Liverpool County Combination and Middlewich also left.
Chester Reserves and Flint both joined.

1910-11

Whitchurch	20	12	3	5	56	25	27
Bangor	20	12	3	5	72	38	27
Oswestry United	20	11	3	6	44	27	25
Brymbo Victoria	20	11	2	7	55	34	24
Wrexham Reserves	20	11	2	7	53	40	24
Chester Reserves	20	9	3	8	57	44	21
Saltney	20	8	2	10	50	43	18
Connah's Quay & Shotton United	20	7	3	10	35	35	17
Rhyl	20	8	1	11	33	65	17
Flint	20	6	2	12	32	76	14
Denbigh Town	20	2	2	16	24	84	6

Bangor, Denbigh Town and Rhyl all moved to the North Wales Coast League, Chester Reserves and Whitchurch both moved to the Manchester League, Wrexham Reserves moved to the West Cheshire League, Connah's Quay & Shotton United and Saltney both moved to the Liverpool County Combination, Flint moved to the Chester & District League, Oswestry United moved to the Lancashire Combination and Brymbo Victoria also left.

The Combination closed at the end of the season.

MANCHESTER LEAGUE 1890-1912

The Manchester League was formed in 1890 but in its first few years, it received little attention from the local press. League tables were rarely printed and those that were often contained errors. Considerable research has been done to try and find tables for every year but until extra sources are found, it will not be possible to complete this work. After the turn of the century though, the league's catchment area extended and amongst the clubs who played their first XI's in the competition were Oldham Athletic, Rochdale, Macclesfield, Northwich Victoria, Altrincham and Witton Albion. It was then much more widely reported, up to its closure in 1912.

Many of the published tables contained errors. Additional research has succeeded in correcting many of these, those figures that still do not balance are shown in italics.

1890-91

St. Bride's	17	13	2	2	57	15	28
Whalley Range	16	10	3	3	54	23	23
Lancashire College	15	10	2	3	41	23	22
Stretford	15	10	1	4	51	27	21
Tonge	17	9	3	5	46	23	21
St. Mark's	17	7	3	7	48	58	17
Press	16	7	0	9	32	36	12
Dalton	15	5	1	9	30	45	11
Stockport	16	2	0	14	16	38	4
West End	15	1	1	13	12	50	3
	159	*74*	*16*	*69*	*387*	*338*	*162*

Press had 2 points deducted for fielding an ineligible player. The remaining games are thought not to have been played.

1891-93

No record has been found of the league operating in 1891-92 or 1892-93 and, when it was reinstated in 1893-94, it was referred to as the "new Manchester League". The only one of the 1890-91 clubs to enter the league in 1893-94 were Stretford.

1893-94

Stretford	20	15	3	2	75	22	33
Talbot	20	14	4	2	70	23	32
Hulme	20	11	3	6	50	36	25
Rusholme	20	9	6	5	45	28	24
Harpurhey	20	10	0	10	50	40	20
Beswick /Old Trafford	20	6	7	7	25	27	19
Fallowfield	20	7	4	9	42	47	18
Didsbury	20	6	3	11	31	69	15
Manchester St. Mary's	20	6	2	12	28	52	14
Burnage	20	5	3	12	42	56	13
Broadheath	20	2	3	15	17	75	7

Beswick disbanded at the end of October and were replaced by Old Trafford. Beswick's record was:

	5	0	0	5	8	31	0

Another club, Beswick Rovers, also withdrew from the league in December and their record was deleted. Burnage left and Higher Crumpsall, Manchester Amateurs, Molyneux (Longsight) and Moss Side joined.

1894-95

Talbot	26	19	2	5	105	41	40
Stretford	26	16	6	4	62	27	38
Higher Crumpsall	26	17	3	6	84	42	37
Molyneux (Longsight)	26	15	5	6	76	42	35
Hulme	26	15	3	8	62	30	33
Manchester St. Mary's	26	12	4	10	58	54	28
Fallowfield	26	12	3	11	68	43	27
Rusholme	26	9	7	10	66	52	25
Broadheath	26	9	4	13	35	64	22
Moss Side	26	9	3	14	50	70	21
Harpurhey	26	7	6	13	48	50	20
Didsbury	26	9	1	16	38	75	19
Manchester Amateurs	26	7	1	18	24	101	15
Old Trafford	26	1	2	23	16	102	4
					792	*793*	

Didsbury, Higher Crumpsall, Manchester Amateurs and Old Trafford left the league. Ladybarn Lads Club, Levenshulme, Lymm and Reddish joined.

1895-96

Talbot	24	18	1	5	72	28	37
Fallowfield	24	17	2	5	74	27	36
Reddish	21	13	3	5	57	41	29
Stretford	24	13	1	10	65	39	27
Levenshulme	23	11	4	8	56	43	26
Rusholme	22	12	1	9	51	47	25
Harpurhey	21	10	3	8	66	49	23
Broadheath	21	9	1	11	46	59	19
Molyneux (Longsight)	18	8	3	7	34	48	19
Hulme	23	5	3	15	43	71	13
Lymm	23	4	5	14	29	74	13
Manchester St. Mary's	22	5	2	15	24	58	12
Moss Side	22	3	3	16	29	63	9
					646	*647*	

Ladybarn Lads Club withdrew and their record was deleted.
Molyneux (Longsight) also withdrew but their record remained.
Remaining games may not have been played.
Harpurhey left the league while Tonge joined from the Lancashire Alliance and Higher Crumpsall and Longsight also joined.

1896-97

Tonge were champions but no published tables have been found for this season. The table below has been compiled from results found and is in estimated finishing order only:

Tonge (Champions)	15	13	1	1	65	14	27
Levenshulme	12	9	2	1	39	11	20
Broadheath	22	14	5	3	73	32	33
Fallowfield	14	8	3	3	39	24	19
Reddish	15	9	2	4	46	22	20
Hulme	17	8	2	7	37	36	18
Lymm	21	9	3	9	44	45	21
Rusholme and New Mills	17	5	6	6	23	37	16
Talbot	17	4	6	7	35	41	14
Stretford	17	4	5	8	26	46	13
Higher Crumpsall	18	3	6	9	28	37	12
Longsight	12	3	1	8	15	40	7
Moss Side	14	2	2	10	21	48	6
Manchester St. Mary's	17	0	2	15	15	73	2

Rusholme withdrew from the league on 23rd March 1897 and their fixtures were taken over by New Mills.
Longsight and Manchester St. Mary's left and Eccles and Prestwich joined.

1897-98

Tonge were again champions but no published tables have been found for this season. The table below has been compiled from results found only:

Tonge (Champions)	21	16	3	2	88	25	35
Lymm	23	17	1	5	64	28	35
Talbot	21	12	4	5	51	26	28
Broadheath	21	13	2	6	65	38	28
Fallowfield	24	11	2	11	55	45	24
Stretford	20	10	2	8	50	39	22
Higher Crumpsall	19	9	2	8	42	35	20
Moss Side	23	8	4	11	44	54	20
Levenshulme	22	8	3	11	44	56	19
Reddish	21	8	3	10	28	52	19
Prestwich	24	8	2	14	36	87	18
Hulme	22	7	3	12	33	46	17
New Mills	23	6	2	15	27	57	14
Eccles	20	1	3	16	15	54	5

Eccles, Higher Crumpsall, Hulme, Levenshulme, New Mills and Reddish left. Marple, Newton Heath Athletic, Seedley, South-West Manchester and Urmston joined.

1898-99

The published final table listed only games played and points won as shown below:

	Played	Points
Newton Heath Athletic	22	37
Tonge	22	34
Broadheath	22	31
Lymm	22	26
Talbot	22	25
South-West Manchester	22	22
Prestwich	22	22
Seedley	22	19
Stretford	22	18
Fallowfield	22	13
Urmston	22	9
Moss Side	22	9
	264	*265*

Marple are thought to have had their record deleted after not completing their fixtures.

The latest published detail table found, dated 28th April 1899, is shown below:

Newton Heath Athletic	20	17	2	1	56	11	36
Tonge	19	13	3	3	61	33	29
Broadheath	19	12	3	4	50	20	27
Lymm	18	12	3	3	53	27	27
Talbot	19	9	4	6	40	26	22
Prestwich	21	8	4	9	47	46	20
South-West Manchester	20	6	6	8	25	35	18
Stretford	19	6	4	9	49	55	16
Seedley	18	6	1	11	38	57	13
Fallowfield	19	6	1	12	23	46	13
Urmston	19	3	5	11	28	47	11
Moss Side	20	4	2	14	22	56	10
Marple	15	1	2	12	19	52	4

Fallowfield and Seedley left the league.
Buxton joined from The Combination and Oughtrington Park, Sale Holmfield and St. Mary's Park (Walkden) also joined.

1899-1900

Tonge	26	23	2	1	110	16	48
Newton Heath Athletic	26	20	3	3	112	32	43
Broadheath	26	19	1	6	54	30	39
Buxton	24	12	7	5	58	51	31
Talbot	26	10	7	9	50	46	27
Lymm	26	9	7	10	54	61	25
South-West Manchester	26	10	5	11	40	57	25
Sale Holmfield	25	11	2	12	46	50	24
Stretford	26	7	7	12	41	51	21
Urmston	26	6	7	13	25	50	19
Prestwich	26	7	2	17	32	49	16
Oughtrington Park	25	6	4	15	30	57	16
Moss Side	26	6	4	16	32	62	16
St. Mary's Park (Walkden)	26	3	4	19	21	83	10
					705	*695*	

Two games were not played.
Moss Side, South-West Manchester, St. Mary's Park (Walkden) and Urmston left. Northwich Victoria joined from the Cheshire League, Macclesfield joined from the North Staffordshire League, Oldham Athletic joined from the Manchester Alliance, Middleton joined from the Lancashire League and Hyde joined from the Stockport & District League.

1900-01

Team							
Tonge	28	23	2	3	94	32	48
Northwich Victoria	28	20	4	4	75	36	44
Newton Heath Athletic	28	19	2	7	78	35	40
Sale Holmfield	28	15	5	8	66	41	35
Hyde	27	14	5	8	79	41	33
Broadheath	27	13	4	10	75	59	30
Talbot	28	12	6	10	48	44	30
Buxton	28	12	4	12	54	46	28
Macclesfield	28	10	3	15	60	75	23
Oughtrington Park	28	8	6	14	46	64	22
Oldham Athletic	28	9	4	15	40	68	22
Lymm	28	7	4	15	42	64	20
Stretford	28	7	6	15	36	66	20
Middleton	28	8	5	15	47	66	19
Prestwich	28	1	1	26	18	128	3
	418	178	61	177	858	865	417

Middleton had 2 points deducted for a breach of the rules.
Stretford moved to the Manchester Federation and Oughtrington Park and Prestwich also left. Berry's Association joined from the Lancashire Combination and Failsworth and Heywood also joined.

1901-02

Team							
Hyde	26	17	6	3	74	27	40
Newton Heath Athletic	26	17	6	3	76	26	40
Northwich Victoria	26	16	2	8	61	53	34
Sale Holmfield	26	13	7	6	61	37	33
Tonge	26	13	4	9	79	47	30
Oldham Athletic	26	13	4	9	59	46	30
Berry's Association	26	12	4	10	55	52	28
Failsworth	26	10	4	12	64	54	24
Talbot	26	11	2	13	47	50	24
Heywood	26	8	4	14	59	66	20
Buxton	26	7	6	13	43	70	20
Broadheath	26	6	6	14	40	72	18
Macclesfield	26	8	1	17	44	68	17
Lymm	26	2	2	22	24	118	6

Hyde beat Newton Heath Athletic in a championship play-off.
Middleton resigned during the season and their record was deleted.
Heywood moved to the Lancashire Combination and Lymm moved to the Manchester Federation. Levenshulme joined from the Manchester Federation, Denton joined from the North Cheshire League and Hooley Hill joined from the North Cheshire League.

1902-03

Team							
Northwich Victoria	26	20	4	2	60	22	44
Failsworth	26	16	3	7	87	42	35
Newton Heath Athletic	25	16	3	6	71	36	35
Oldham Athletic	26	15	4	7	57	31	34
Berry's Association	26	14	3	9	68	41	31
Hyde	26	14	1	11	70	47	29
Buxton	26	12	2	12	47	53	26
Sale Holmfield	26	9	6	11	46	63	24
Broadheath	26	9	5	12	43	55	23
Denton	24	8	4	12	41	53	20
Macclesfield	26	8	3	15	36	63	19
Tonge	26	6	7	13	25	68	19
Hooley Hill	25	5	2	18	40	62	12
Talbot	25	3	4	18	19	68	10
	359	155	51	153	710	704	361

Levenshulme disbanded on 4th February 1903 and their record was deleted when it stood as follows: 16 2 3 11 16 48 7
Broadheath changed their name to Altrincham. Talbot moved to the Manchester Federation. Stretford joined from the Manchester Federation and Glossop United and Hollinwood also joined.

1903-04

Team							
Berry's Association	28	19	2	7	91	42	40
Northwich Victoria	28	17	4	7	68	40	38
Oldham Athletic	28	15	7	6	71	41	37
Denton	28	13	7	8	72	47	33
Sale Holmfield	28	15	3	10	80	53	33
Newton Heath Athletic	28	14	4	10	62	51	32
Failsworth	28	13	5	10	75	49	31
Tonge	28	15	1	12	57	61	31
Altrincham	28	12	4	12	54	53	28
Hyde	28	11	4	13	59	57	26
Macclesfield	28	9	8	11	49	57	26
Glossop United	28	9	3	16	37	64	21
Hooley Hill	28	8	4	16	52	75	20
Buxton	28	7	1	20	46	72	15
Stretford	28	4	1	23	22	133	9

Hollinwood withdrew from the league and disbanded in mid-April. Their record was deleted: 25 2 1 22 32 135 5
Oldham Athletic moved to the Lancashire Combination. Witton Albion joined from The Combination and Oughtrington Park also joined.

1904-05

Team							
Altrincham	30	18	8	4	66	43	44
Buxton	30	16	6	8	63	40	38
Denton	30	16	5	9	83	49	37
Sale Holmfield	30	14	9	7	66	39	37
Tonge	30	11	14	5	60	33	36
Failsworth	30	14	8	8	63	41	36
Northwich Victoria	30	13	10	7	47	43	36
Berry's Association	30	13	6	11	61	55	32
Witton Albion	30	9	12	9	44	41	30
Macclesfield	30	7	11	12	48	55	25
Hyde	30	9	7	14	40	53	25
Hooley Hill	30	9	6	15	47	53	24
Newton Heath Athletic	30	8	6	16	53	72	22
Stretford	30	8	5	17	54	78	21
Glossop United / Heywood United	30	6	7	17	45	91	19
Oughtrington Park	30	8	2	20	47	101	18

Heywood United took over Glossop United's fixtures in mid-season.
Failsworth moved to the Lancashire Combination and Oughtrington Park also left the league. Pendlebury joined from the Manchester Federation and Salford United joined as a new club.

1905-06

Team							
Denton	30	22	1	7	88	38	45
Sale Holmfield	30	15	10	5	53	30	40
Altrincham	30	16	5	9	81	51	37
Northwich Victoria	30	17	3	10	67	58	37
Tonge	30	15	5	10	67	57	35
Macclesfield	30	15	4	11	58	58	34
Heywood United	30	14	5	11	62	58	33
Pendlebury	30	10	10	10	74	53	30
Witton Albion	30	10	8	12	47	45	28
Berry's Association	30	10	6	14	53	71	26
Buxton	30	9	7	14	36	46	25
Hyde	30	10	4	16	48	81	24
Hooley Hill	30	9	4	17	57	65	22
Salford United	30	10	2	18	54	74	22
Newton Heath Athletic	30	9	4	17	45	73	22
Stretford	30	7	6	17	45	77	20

Hyde moved to the Lancashire Combination and Chadderton joined.

1906-07

Altrincham	28	18	7	3	70	30	43
Macclesfield	28	19	4	5	75	39	42
Witton Albion	28	18	5	5	49	30	41
Sale Holmfield	28	13	8	7	53	38	34
Salford United	28	10	10	8	61	39	30
Northwich Victoria	28	12	6	10	59	51	30
Tonge	28	12	6	10	51	45	30
Denton	28	12	5	11	52	44	29
Pendlebury	28	10	9	9	57	51	29
Stretford	28	11	4	13	39	55	26
Berry's Association	28	7	7	14	40	66	21
Heywood United	28	8	4	16	54	63	20
Buxton	28	7	5	16	39	57	19
Hooley Hill	28	4	7	17	35	68	15
Newton Heath Athletic	28	3	5	20	32	90	11

Chadderton resigned during the season and their record was deleted.
Heywood United and Pendlebury both moved to the Lancashire
Combination.
Rochdale joined as a new club and Eccles Borough and Ramsbottom also
joined.

1907-08

Denton	30	21	5	4	108	48	47
Northwich Victoria	30	15	10	5	75	53	40
Eccles Borough	30	16	7	7	59	44	39
Macclesfield	30	16	5	9	63	39	37
Tonge	30	14	8	8	67	46	36
Altrincham	30	13	6	11	63	53	32
Witton Albion	30	12	8	10	52	54	32
Sale Holmfield	30	14	3	13	70	53	31
Ramsbottom	30	10	8	12	61	68	28
Rochdale	30	10	8	12	49	63	28
Buxton	30	10	7	13	35	52	27
Hooley Hill	30	8	9	13	56	59	25
Salford United	30	9	5	16	49	63	23
Berry's Association	30	9	5	16	46	66	23
Stretford	30	5	10	15	43	75	20
Newton Heath Athletic	30	3	6	21	33	88	12

Eccles Borough and Rochdale both moved to the Lancashire Combination
and Stretford also left. Tyldesley Albion joined from the Lancashire Alliance
and Hazel Grove and New Mills also joined.

1908-09

Macclesfield	30	18	6	6	78	43	42
Northwich Victoria	30	17	4	9	73	51	38
Altrincham	30	16	4	10	82	56	36
Tonge	30	16	3	11	54	45	35
New Mills	30	13	8	9	73	45	34
Hazel Grove	30	13	8	9	62	47	34
Sale Holmfield	29	15	3	11	65	56	33
Salford United	30	14	5	11	61	55	33
Witton Albion	30	13	5	12	67	59	31
Tyldesley Albion	30	12	6	12	74	67	30
Denton	30	11	7	12	70	67	29
Ramsbottom	30	12	5	13	61	81	29
Hooley Hill	30	11	6	13	57	54	28
Berry's Association	29	10	5	14	52	53	25
Buxton	30	7	4	19	38	74	18
Newton Heath Athletic	30	0	3	27	34	148	3

Hurst and Rusholme joined the league.

1909-10

Salford United	34	20	6	8	79	44	46
Hurst	34	19	8	7	70	41	46
Altrincham	34	20	5	9	82	41	45
Macclesfield	34	18	6	10	86	45	42
Tonge	34	20	2	12	66	41	42
Denton	34	18	6	10	75	60	42
Northwich Victoria	34	18	4	12	81	65	40
Tyldesley Albion	34	15	8	11	65	50	38
Witton Albion	34	15	6	13	74	71	36
Buxton	34	15	5	14	60	51	35
Hooley Hill	34	11	13	10	67	62	35
Berry's Association	34	14	5	15	58	67	33
Hazel Grove	34	11	9	14	58	69	31
New Mills	34	10	9	15	53	66	29
Ramsbottom	34	12	5	17	66	86	29
Rusholme	34	8	3	23	49	91	19
Sale Holmfield	34	4	6	24	28	93	14
Newton Heath Athletic	34	3	4	27	31	105	10

Salford United beat Hurst in a Championship Play-Off.

Denton left to continue in the Lancashire Combination, where they had
taken over Pendlebury's fixtures during the season. Newton Heath Athletic
moved to the Manchester Federation and Ramsbottom and Sale Holmfield
also left the league. Crewe Alexandra Reserves and Nantwich both joined
from The Combination.

1910-11

Macclesfield	30	20	8	2	61	30	48
Altrincham	30	19	4	7	81	38	42
Crewe Alexandra Reserves	30	17	8	5	74	36	42
Northwich Victoria	30	16	5	9	75	41	37
Tyldesley Albion	30	15	5	10	62	55	35
Hurst	30	14	4	12	69	66	32
Hazel Grove	30	11	10	9	47	52	32
Buxton	30	13	5	12	57	56	31
Witton Albion	30	11	7	12	68	64	29
Berry's Association	30	11	6	13	62	72	28
Rusholme	30	11	4	15	67	76	26
Hooley Hill	30	7	11	12	41	56	25
Nantwich	30	8	6	16	60	83	22
New Mills	30	6	6	18	49	71	18
Salford United	30	7	3	20	43	85	17
Tonge	30	5	6	19	42	76	16
					958	957	

Altrincham and Tyldesley Albion moved to the Lancashire Combination
and Berry's Association, New Mills, Salford United, Tonge and Rusholme
also left the league.
Chester Reserves joined from The Combination and Eccles Borough
Reserves, Rochdale Reserves and Stalybridge Celtic Reserves also joined.

1911-12

Hurst	24	18	4	2	82	30	40	
Northwich Victoria	24	14	5	5	51	32	33	
Witton Albion	24	13	5	6	58	32	31	
Macclesfield	24	12	5	7	51	34	29	
Eccles Borough Reserves	24	11	3	10	48	39	25	
Stalybridge Celtic Reserves	24	10	3	11	55	53	23	
Chester Reserves	24	10	3	11	40	50	23	
Nantwich	23	11	1	11	40	45	23	
Crewe Alexandra Reserves	23	10	1	12	39	47	21	
Hooley Hill	24	7	3	14	46	65	17	
Rochdale Reserves	24	6	4	14	45	70	16	
Buxton	22	5	4	13	30	66	14	
Hazel Grove	24	5	3	16	48	70	13	

Two games were not played.

The Manchester League closed in 1912.

Hurst, Northwich Victoria, Witton Albion, Macclesfield, Stalybridge Celtic Reserves, Nantwich and Rochdale Reserves all joined the Lancashire Combination and Crewe Alexandra Reserves joined the North Staffordshire League.

The Manchester League was reformed in 1920 but with lower status clubs.

LANCASHIRE COMBINATION 1891-1982

The immediate success of the Football League when it was founded in 1888 soon led to many other leagues being formed for those clubs not strong enough to gain entry to the top competition.

Lancashire was particularly quick in providing alternatives and many of the major towns where the game was popular soon had their own leagues. However the principle league for Lancashire clubs outside the Football League was the county-wide Lancashire League which was formed in 1889 and it was this competition to which non-League clubs in the county initially aspired.

However, the Lancashire League had an implacable policy of not allowing reserve sides to enter and this led to the formation of the Lancashire Combination. Blackburn Rovers, Bolton Wanderers and Preston North End were not to be thwarted in finding a suitable competition for their second string sides, so in 1891 and, with the willing help of a number of other clubs, the rival Lancashire Combination was formed.

The founder members were: Blackburn Rovers Reserves, Bolton Wanderers Reserves, Halliwell, Hindley, North Meols (Southport), Preston North End Reserves, Royton, Skelmersdale United and Stanley (Liverpool).

Blackburn Rovers Reserves had previously played in the North East Lancashire League, Hindley in the Lancashire Alliance and Stanley in the West Lancashire League in 1889-90. Any leagues that the other founder members may have previously played in have not been traced.

Many of the published tables contained errors. Additional research has succeeded in correcting many of these, those figures that still do not balance are shown in italics.

1891-92

Blackburn Rovers Reserves	14	10	3	1	44	17	23
Hindley	14	9	0	5	28	22	18
Royton	14	7	2	5	39	25	16
Bolton Wanderers Reserves	14	7	1	6	42	25	15
Preston North End Reserves	13	6	3	4	44	33	15
North Meols (Southport)	14	6	0	8	27	37	12
Skelmersdale United	13	3	1	9	26	53	7
Stanley (Liverpool)	14	1	2	11	13	51	4

One game was not played. Halliwell were expelled as they were unable to fulfil their fixtures. Their record was deleted.

Hindley moved to the Lancashire Alliance and Stanley (Liverpool) moved to the Liverpool & District League. Darwen Reserves joined from the North East Lancashire League, Tranmere Rovers joined from the Liverpool & District League and Ardwick Reserves, Newton Heath Reserves and Turton also joined.

1892-93

Blackburn Rovers Reserves	20	14	1	5	59	30	29
Darwen Reserves	20	11	3	6	84	42	25
Newton Heath Reserves	20	10	5	5	47	30	25
Bolton Wanderers Reserves	20	12	0	8	42	42	24
Turton	20	9	3	8	50	41	21
North Meols (Southport)	20	8	4	8	42	38	20
Royton	20	8	4	8	44	42	20
Ardwick Reserves	20	8	3	9	49	46	19
Preston North End Reserves	20	6	4	10	40	44	16
Skelmersdale United	20	5	2	13	28	78	12
Tranmere Rovers	20	4	1	15	30	81	9
					515	*514*	

North Meols (Southport) moved to the Lancashire Alliance and Skelmersdale United moved to the Liverpool & District League. Lostock Hall joined the league.

1893-94

	P	W	D	L	F	A	Pts
Blackburn Rovers Reserves	16	13	2	1	62	13	28
Bolton Wanderers Reserves	16	11	2	3	72	26	24
Darwen Reserves	14	8	1	5	47	22	17
Tranmere Rovers	16	6	2	8	30	54	14
Lostock Hall	14	6	1	7	49	43	13
Newton Heath Reserves	16	5	2	9	37	36	12
Turton	16	5	2	9	28	43	12
Preston North End Reserves	16	4	1	11	24	63	9
Ardwick Reserves	16	3	3	10	18	69	9
	130	61	16	63	367	369	128

Royton failed to fulfil their fixtures and were expelled from the league. Their record was susequently deleted.
The games between Darwen Reserves and Lostock Hall were cancelled.
Ardwick Reserves changed their name to Manchester City Reserves.
Tranmere Rovers moved to the Wirral & District League and Lostock Hall moved to the Lancashire Alliance.
Bell's Temperance, Burnley Reserves, Oswaldtwistle Rovers, Padiham and Rawtenstall all joined from the North East Lancashire League while Everton Reserves joined from The Combination.

1894-95

	P	W	D	L	F	A	Pts
Everton Reserves	24	20	3	1	137	33	43
Preston North End Reserves	24	16	2	6	84	34	34
Darwen Reserves	24	13	3	8	86	61	29
Oswaldtwistle Rovers	24	13	1	10	59	56	27
Rawtenstall	24	12	2	10	57	70	26
Bolton Wanderers Reserves	24	12	3	9	78	55	25
Burnley Reserves	24	10	4	10	64	45	24
Blackburn Rovers Reserves	24	10	2	12	45	49	22
Turton	24	10	2	12	48	69	22
Padiham	24	8	3	13	41	82	17
Newton Heath Reserves	24	5	8	11	41	75	16
Manchester City Reserves	24	6	1	17	50	95	13
Bell's Temperance	24	3	2	19	34	103	6
					824	827	

Bolton Wanderers Reserves, Padiham, Newton Heath Reserves and Bell's Temperance each had 2 points deducted for fielding ineligible players.
Everton Reserves moved to The Combination and Bell's Temperance also left the league. Accrington joined from the Lancashire League and Little Lever, Lostock Hall and Tonge all joined from the Lancashire Alliance. Bury Reserves also joined.

1895-96

	P	W	D	L	F	A	Pts
Preston North End Reserves	26	20	3	3	93	28	43
Blackburn Rovers Reserves	26	15	6	5	61	34	36
Newton Heath Reserves	26	14	2	10	61	57	30
Bolton Wanderers Reserves	26	13	3	10	66	47	29
Oswaldtwistle Rovers	26	12	5	9	53	42	29
Burnley Reserves	26	11	7	8	66	54	29
Turton	26	13	3	10	57	52	29
Bury Reserves	26	7	10	9	51	47	24
Manchester City Reserves	26	10	4	12	54	53	24
Little Lever	26	11	2	13	51	70	24
Padiham	26	9	5	12	51	58	23
Rawtenstall	26	10	2	14	41	65	22
Darwen Reserves	26	6	4	16	49	77	16
Lostock Hall	26	1	4	21	18	88	6

Accrington and Tonge failed to complete their fixtures and their records were excluded from the final table. Tonge joined the Manchester League in 1896-97 while Accrington disbanded. Little Lever and Lostock Hall both left. Rochdale joined as a newly formed club while Blackpool Reserves and Liverpool Reserves also joined.

1896-97

	P	W	D	L	F	A	Pts
Liverpool Reserves	28	23	1	4	78	30	47
Preston North End Reserves	28	18	6	4	82	34	42
Bury Reserves	28	15	5	8	70	36	35
Manchester City Reserves	28	17	1	10	75	40	35
Blackburn Rovers Reserves	28	15	5	8	59	44	35
Rochdale	28	16	2	10	79	54	34
Burnley Reserves	28	12	6	10	64	44	30
Turton	28	10	9	9	58	64	29
Bolton Wanderers Reserves	28	12	2	14	66	49	26
Padiham	28	9	8	11	55	56	26
Newton Heath Reserves	28	8	8	12	49	53	24
Darwen Reserves	28	9	5	14	65	89	23
Blackpool Reserves	28	7	3	18	41	88	17
Rawtenstall	28	3	3	22	33	113	9
Oswaldtwistle Rovers	28	3	2	23	27	105	8
						901	899

Rochdale moved to the Lancashire League and Rawtenstall moved to the North East Lancashire Combination. Blackburn Reserves and Oswaldtwistle Rovers also left. Fleetwood Rangers joined from the Lancashire League while Prescot and Skerton both joined from the Lancashire Alliance. Berry's Association and Blackburn Park Road also joined.

1897-98

	P	W	D	L	F	A	Pts
Preston North End Reserves	30	24	3	3	121	,26	51
Liverpool Reserves	30	20	1	9	100	48	41
Bury Reserves	30	17	4	9	70	43	38
Bolton Wanderers Reserves	30	15	5	10	69	51	35
Blackburn Rovers Reserves	30	14	7	9	67	51	35
Fleetwood Rangers	30	16	2	12	69	54	34
Manchester City Reserves	30	15	4	11	67	68	34
Turton	30	16	2	12	68	71	34
Newton Heath Reserves	30	14	2	14	65	42	30
Skerton	30	11	7	12	58	71	29
Berry's Association	30	12	4	14	71	78	28
Blackburn Park Road	30	9	5	16	54	90	23
Burnley Reserves	30	9	4	17	61	82	22
Padiham	30	10	2	18	51	79	22
Prescot	30	6	5	19	43	99	17
Darwen Reserves	30	3	1	26	37	116	7
						1071	1069

Liverpool Reserves moved to The Combination and Prescot to the Lancashire Alliance. Padiham and Darwen Reserves also left the league. Leyland joined from the Lancashire Alliance while Rossendale United joined as a new club which had been formed by a merger of two North East Lancashire Combination clubs, Rossendale and Rawtenstall. Hurst Ramblers also joined.

1898-99

	P	W	D	L	F	A	Pts
Preston North End Reserves	28	21	3	4	99	42	45
Manchester City Reserves	28	19	3	6	83	37	41
Bolton Wanderers Reserves	28	19	3	6	88	40	41
Burnley Reserves	28	17	5	6	75	30	39
Newton Heath Reserves	28	14	6	8	62	43	34
Blackburn Rovers Reserves	28	14	5	9	72	55	33
Berry's Association	28	14	4	10	71	53	32
Skerton	28	13	3	12	67	55	29
Turton	28	12	3	13	41	56	27
Hurst Ramblers	28	11	3	14	58	75	25
Bury Reserves	28	9	4	15	55	58	22
Blackburn Park Road	28	5	5	18	36	96	15
Leyland	28	5	4	19	28	70	14
Fleetwood Rangers	28	2	8	18	36	87	12
Rossendale United	28	4	4	20	25	99	12
		179	63	178			421

Rossendale United moved to the Central Lancashire League and Fleetwood Rangers disbanded. Everton Reserves and Liverpool Reserves joined from The Combination while Astley Bridge Wanderers and St. Helens Recreation joined from the Lancashire Alliance. Glossop Reserves also joined.

1899-1900

Liverpool Reserves	30	23	2	5	76	26	48
Preston North End Reserves	30	22	1	7	83	29	45
Everton Reserves	30	20	4	6	78	28	44
Burnley Reserves	30	18	4	8	66	49	40
Manchester City Reserves	30	18	4	8	63	49	40
Blackburn Rovers Reserves	30	14	4	12	78	48	32
Newton Heath Reserves	30	13	4	13	63	56	30
Berry's Association	30	10	8	12	49	60	28
Bury Reserves	30	12	2	16	54	56	26
Blackburn Park Road	30	9	7	14	48	65	25
Turton	30	8	7	15	41	72	23
Glossop Reserves	30	9	4	17	46	65	22
Bolton Wanderers Reserves	30	10	2	18	38	56	22
Leyland	30	5	9	16	31	74	19
Astley Bridge Wanderers	30	8	2	20	41	76	18
St. Helens Recreation	30	7	4	19	37	83	18

Hurst Ramblers and Skerton both disbanded during the season and their records were expunged. Blackburn Rovers Reserves and Bolton Wanderers Reserves both moved to the Lancashire League while Astley Bridge Wanderers also left. Accrington Stanley joined from the North East Lancashire Combination and Stockport County Reserves joined from the Central Lancashire League. New Brighton Tower Reserves, Oswaldtwistle Rovers and Padiham also joined.

1900-1901

Everton Reserves	34	29	2	3	114	22	60
Liverpool Reserves	34	28	4	2	117	29	60
Manchester City Reserves	34	22	4	8	108	60	48
Bury Reserves	34	19	5	10	64	55	43
St. Helens Recreation	34	16	8	10	79	60	40
Preston North End Reserves	34	16	6	12	89	61	38
New Brighton Tower Reserves	34	16	6	12	73	56	38
Stockport County Reserves	34	16	6	12	60	66	38
Accrington Stanley	34	17	2	15	55	51	36
Padiham	34	14	6	14	60	63	34
Burnley Reserves	34	13	7	14	61	56	33
Turton	34	10	5	19	44	84	25
Glossop Reserves	34	11	2	21	42	81	24
Berry's Association	34	9	3	22	55	92	21
Leyland	34	7	6	21	37	79	20
Blackburn Park Road	34	6	7	21	38	90	19
Oswaldtwistle Rovers	34	7	4	23	39	93	18
Newton Heath Reserves	34	5	7	22	40	78	17
						1175	*1176*

Berry's Association moved to the Manchester League while Blackburn Park Road, Leyland and New Brighton Tower Reserves also left the league. Rossendale United joined from the Central Lancashire League and Blackburn Rovers Reserves, Bolton Wanderers Reserves and Nelson all joined from the Lancashire League.

1901-02

Manchester City Reserves	34	29	0	5	125	30	58
Everton Reserves	34	24	3	7	86	35	51
Accrington Stanley	34	21	5	8	79	48	47
Bolton Wanderers Reserves	34	19	5	10	81	58	43
Liverpool Reserves	34	16	7	11	83	54	39
Bury Reserves	34	17	4	13	84	46	38
St. Helens Recreation	34	17	3	14	80	64	37
Preston North End Reserves	34	17	2	15	91	73	36
Nelson	34	13	7	14	60	64	33
Rossendale United	34	13	5	16	62	89	31
Oswaldtwistle Rovers	34	12	6	16	55	62	30
Turton	34	12	6	16	50	67	30
Blackburn Rovers Reserves	34	11	7	16	56	77	29
Newton Heath Reserves	34	11	5	18	54	97	27
Stockport County Reserves	34	10	6	18	63	77	26
Burnley Reserves	34	9	5	20	42	99	23
Padiham	34	5	9	20	36	85	19
Glossop Reserves	34	4	7	23	36	98	15

St. Helens Recreation refused to play a game against Nelson. Nelson were awarded a win and 2 points.
Newton Heath Reserves changed their name to Manchester United Reserves. St. Helens Recreation moved to the Lancashire League and Burnley Reserves moved to the North East Lancashire Combination. Glossop Reserves also left and Stockport County Reserves ceased playing in 1902-03 to enable a ground-share with Stockport RLFC. Heywood joined from the Manchester League while Black Lane Temperance, Heywood United and Trawden Forest also joined.

1902-03

Accrington Stanley	34	26	2	6	114	36	54
Manchester City Reserves	34	23	7	4	84	36	53
Bury Reserves	34	22	6	6	85	39	50
Manchester United Reserves	34	20	8	6	83	45	48
Bolton Wanderers Reserves	34	19	3	12	81	58	41
Everton Reserves	34	16	7	11	74	54	39
Liverpool Reserves	34	15	8	11	70	64	38
Blackburn Rovers Reserves	34	13	9	12	66	53	35
Padiham	34	15	4	15	71	70	34
Black Lane Temperance	34	12	4	18	50	79	28
Preston North End Reserves	34	11	5	18	68	80	27
Heywood	34	10	7	17	49	66	27
Oswaldtwistle Rovers	34	11	5	18	53	84	27
Trawden Forest	34	9	8	17	38	66	26
Rossendale United	34	10	6	18	49	87	26
Heywood United	34	7	9	18	46	72	23
Nelson	34	7	7	20	43	80	21
Turton	34	6	7	21	43	98	19
		612	*252*	*112*	*248*		*616*

Heywood United were suspended by the Lancashire F.A. for the whole of the 1903-04 season for making illegal payments to players. Darwen joined from the Lancashire League. Trawden Forest changed their name to Colne.

A Second Division was formed containing 18 clubs.

Nine of these came from the Lancashire League: Bacup, Barrow, Chorley, Earlestown, Rochdale Town, Southport Central, St. Helens Recreation, St. Helens Town and Stalybridge Rovers. There were also four from the Lancashire Alliance: Bolton St. Luke's, Brynn Central, Chorley St. George's and Skelmersdale United. The other five were: Ashton Town (a newly formed club), Clitheroe Central from the Blackburn Sunday School League, Hyde St. George's from the Manchester Federation, Newton-le-Willows from The Combination and Stockport County Reserves, who resumed after a season's inaction.

1903-04

Relegated clubs are shown in *italics*.
Promoted clubs are shown in **bold**.

Division One

Everton Reserves	34	26	6	2	114	32	58
Accrington Stanley	34	24	4	6	89	36	52
Manchester City Reserves	34	21	7	6	90	36	49
Manchester United Reserves	34	19	8	7	72	35	46
Darwen	34	19	7	8	79	45	45
Blackburn Rovers Reserves	34	17	6	11	75	64	40
Bury Reserves	34	17	5	12	81	66	39
Nelson	34	16	4	14	66	61	36
Liverpool Reserves	34	12	10	12	75	65	34
Rossendale United	34	13	7	14	45	57	33
Bolton Wanderers Reserves	34	13	6	15	79	58	32
Preston North End Reserves	34	11	10	13	70	59	32
Colne	34	11	4	19	59	78	26
Oswaldtwistle Rovers	*34*	*7*	*9*	*18*	*50*	*84*	*23*
Heywood	34	9	4	21	51	112	22
Turton	*34*	*6*	*6*	*22*	*57*	*108*	*18*
Padiham	*34*	*6*	*5*	*23*	*31*	*94*	*17*
Black Lane Temperance	34	3	6	25	39	132	12
	612	*250*	*114*	*248*			*614*

Heywood and Black Lane Temperance both left. Stockport County joined after failing to be re-elected to Division Two of the Football League.

Division Two

Southport Central	34	23	6	5	82	30	52
Earlestown	34	23	5	6	94	49	51
Stalybridge Rovers	34	19	8	7	79	39	46
Stockport County Reserves	34	21	3	10	81	60	45
St. Helens Town	34	16	9	9	64	52	41
Ashton Town	34	16	8	10	51	42	40
Hyde St. George's	34	15	9	10	59	50	39
Bolton St. Luke's	34	12	9	13	79	71	33
Barrow	34	12	9	13	51	54	33
Newton-le-Willows	34	13	6	15	71	69	32
St. Helens Recreation	34	12	8	14	47	47	32
Atherton Church House	34	13	3	18	62	72	29
Chorley	34	11	7	16	53	62	29
Brynn Central	34	13	3	18	62	80	29
Skelmersdale United	34	9	9	16	52	75	27
Clitheroe Central	34	11	3	20	63	89	25
Chorley St. George's	34	5	10	19	46	82	20
Bacup	34	5	3	26	36	109	13
	612	*249*	*118*	*245*			*616*

Atherton Church House joined from the Lancashire Alliance in December 1903 and took over the fixtures of Rochdale Town, who disbanded after playing 14 games, winning just 6 points.
Chorley St. George's, Stockport County Reserves and Clitheroe Central left. Lytham joined from the Lancashire Alliance, Oldham Athletic joined from the Manchester League and Workington joined from the Cumberland League. Blackpool Reserves also joined.

1904-05

Division One

Stockport County	34	21	7	6	63	27	49
Liverpool Reserves	34	18	6	10	88	54	42
Southport Central	34	17	8	9	59	41	42
Manchester United Reserves	34	19	1	14	74	50	39
Darwen	34	14	10	10	55	49	38
Manchester City Reserves	34	13	11	10	64	56	37
Accrington Stanley	34	16	5	13	57	55	37
Bury Reserves	34	15	5	14	58	63	35
Everton Reserves	34	13	8	13	49	41	34
Nelson	34	13	7	14	57	53	33
Bolton Wanderers Reserves	34	13	7	14	67	65	33
Preston North End Reserves	34	12	8	14	50	48	32
Rossendale United	34	12	8	14	54	68	32
Earlestown	34	12	5	17	50	71	29
Blackburn Rovers Reserves	34	11	6	17	53	75	28
Ashton Town	*34*	*7*	*11*	*16*	*36*	*50*	*25*
Stalybridge Rovers	34	10	4	20	34	63	24
St. Helens Town	*34*	*7*	*9*	*18*	*38*	*77*	*23*

Stockport County left after being elected to the Football League – Division Two. They were replaced by their reserves who moved from the Midland League.

Division Two

St. Helens Recreation	34	22	6	6	91	32	50
Barrow	34	22	2	10	73	43	46
Oldham Athletic	34	19	6	9	80	38	44
Atherton Church House	34	20	4	10	81	55	44
Brynn Central	34	17	8	9	69	44	42
Hyde St. George's	34	14	12	8	86	49	40
Oswaldtwistle Rovers	34	17	6	11	81	56	40
Chorley	34	15	7	12	68	56	37
Workington	34	15	7	12	56	60	37
Turton	34	15	6	13	80	69	36
Blackpool Reserves	34	13	6	15	62	63	32
Skelmersdale United	34	12	7	15	56	53	31
Colne	34	13	3	18	59	66	29
Padiham	34	11	7	16	53	85	29
Newton-le-Willows	34	7	7	20	54	84	21
Bacup	34	6	7	21	43	92	19
Bolton St. Luke's	34	7	4	23	38	98	18
Lytham	34	8	1	25	38	125	17

Lytham moved to the West Lancashire League while Bolton St. Luke's and Turton also left the league. Failsworth joined from the Manchester League. Burnley Reserves and Clitheroe Central both joined from the North East Lancashire Combination, Carlisle United joined from the Cumberland League, Lancaster joined as a newly formed club and Haslingden also joined.

1905-06

Division One

Accrington Stanley	38	22	10	6	88	33	54
Darwen	38	19	9	10	81	64	47
Manchester United Reserves	38	17	10	11	86	62	44
St. Helens Recreation	38	17	10	11	74	69	44
Bolton Wanderers Reserves	38	15	13	10	72	50	43
Liverpool Reserves	38	17	8	13	72	57	42
Bury Reserves	38	15	12	11	82	69	42
Everton Reserves	38	14	10	14	64	63	38
Blackburn Rovers Reserves	38	13	12	13	65	69	38
Stalybridge Rovers	38	14	10	14	50	71	38
Manchester City Reserves	38	14	9	15	72	63	37
Rossendale United	38	14	8	16	68	73	36
Nelson	38	16	4	18	66	76	36
Oldham Athletic	38	14	8	16	45	52	36
Preston North End Reserves	38	14	7	17	67	65	35
Barrow	38	14	7	17	57	78	35
Southport Central	38	11	10	17	70	96	32
Atherton Church House	38	11	9	18	55	72	31
Stockport County Reserves	*38*	*9*	*9*	*20*	*57*	*77*	*27*
Earlestown	*38*	*9*	*7*	*22*	*64*	*96*	*25*

Atherton Church House changed their name to Atherton.

1906-07

Division One

Oldham Athletic	38	26	5	7	105	33	57
Liverpool Reserves	38	25	7	6	108	64	57
Everton Reserves	38	24	5	9	90	47	53
Bury Reserves	38	19	9	10	90	57	47
Accrington Stanley	38	18	7	13	76	60	43
Manchester United Reserves	38	18	6	14	80	67	42
Darwen	38	17	8	13	60	55	42
Bolton Wanderers Reserves	38	17	7	14	66	52	41
Southport Central	38	14	13	11	50	50	41
Atherton	38	15	10	13	67	59	40
Blackpool Reserves	38	16	8	14	70	64	40
Manchester City Reserves	38	16	7	15	70	86	39
Rossendale United	38	13	10	15	71	70	36
St. Helens Recreation	38	15	6	17	75	75	36
Preston North End Reserves	38	15	3	20	81	86	33
Barrow	38	12	4	22	73	95	28
Blackburn Rovers Reserves	*38*	*11*	*5*	*22*	*67*	*85*	*27*
Nelson	*38*	*10*	*5*	*23*	*53*	*113*	*25*
Colne	*38*	*7*	*5*	*26*	*56*	*92*	*19*
Stalybridge Rovers	38	5	4	29	39	137	14

Oldham Athletic were elected to the Football League – Division Two and were replaced by their reserves. Stalybridge Rovers disbanded.

Division Two

Colne	**36**	**24**	**6**	**6**	**95**	**40**	**54**
Blackpool Reserves	**36**	**23**	**4**	**9**	**92**	**66**	**50**
Workington	36	21	7	8	102	50	49
St. Helens Town	36	17	10	9	51	39	44
Chorley	36	18	6	12	88	62	42
Failsworth	36	19	3	14	86	62	41
Brynn Central	36	16	9	11	76	55	41
Ashton Town	36	17	6	13	70	60	40
Clitheroe Central	36	16	5	15	86	58	37
Burnley Reserves	36	16	5	15	69	55	37
Lancaster	36	12	11	13	54	70	35
Skelmersdale United	36	14	6	16	75	77	34
Carlisle United	36	14	6	16	70	73	34
Padiham	36	14	2	20	63	82	30
Bacup	36	9	9	18	45	87	27
Oswaldtwistle Rovers	36	10	4	22	56	77	24
Newton-le-Willows	36	10	4	22	45	89	24
Haslingden	36	10	3	23	64	115	23
Hyde St. George's	36	7	4	25	50	118	18
						1337	*1335*	

Hyde St. George's merged with Hyde of the Manchester League with the merged club continuing in the Lancashire Combination as Hyde. Padiham left the league and Glossop Reserves and Port Sunlight both joined from The Combination.

Division Two

Carlisle United	**38**	**23**	**10**	**5**	**113**	**46**	**56**
Earlestown	**38**	**24**	**5**	**9**	**124**	**57**	**53**
Chorley	**38**	**23**	**5**	**10**	**96**	**60**	**51**
Workington	**38**	**23**	**3**	**12**	**100**	**52**	**49**
St. Helens Town	38	21	6	11	88	72	48
Bacup	38	21	5	12	109	63	47
Glossop Reserves	38	18	8	12	85	63	44
Burnley Reserves	38	20	2	16	93	68	42
Lancaster	38	15	8	15	60	64	38
Stockport County Reserves	38	14	9	15	71	58	37
Failsworth	38	12	11	15	77	90	35
Port Sunlight	38	14	6	18	64	74	34
Clitheroe Central	38	11	12	15	65	81	34
Brynn Central	38	13	8	17	48	67	34
Haslingden	38	15	3	20	70	85	33
Hyde	38	13	6	19	63	79	32
Newton-le-Willows	38	14	3	21	76	97	31
Oswaldtwistle Rovers	38	12	6	20	72	114	30
Ashton Town	38	6	7	25	40	107	19
Skelmersdale United	38	6	1	31	39	156	13

Port Sunlight, Skelmersdale United and Stockport County Reserves left. Wigan Town joined from The Combination while Heywood United and Pendlebury both joined from the Manchester League and Turton joined from the Lancashire Alliance.

1907-08

Division One

Everton Reserves	38	26	7	5	109	38	59
Carlisle United	38	23	8	7	79	55	54
Workington	38	20	8	10	68	47	48
Liverpool Reserves	38	20	7	11	81	57	47
Rossendale United	38	18	7	13	69	64	43
Southport Central	38	18	7	13	64	63	43
Accrington Stanley	38	16	9	13	77	66	41
Bury Reserves	38	17	6	15	83	72	40
Preston North End Reserves	38	16	8	14	60	53	40
Bolton Wanderers Reserves	38	17	4	17	69	57	38
Atherton	38	14	9	15	60	64	37
Oldham Athletic Reserves	38	15	6	17	74	70	36
Manchester United Reserves	38	14	7	17	58	54	35
St. Helens Recreation	38	14	6	18	67	73	34
Blackpool Reserves	38	12	8	18	47	71	32
Darwen	38	11	8	19	52	85	30
Manchester City Reserves	*38*	*11*	*7*	*20*	*55*	*70*	*29*
Chorley	*38*	*9*	*9*	*20*	*68*	*89*	*27*
Earlestown	*38*	*8*	*8*	*22*	*43*	*88*	*24*
Barrow	*38*	*8*	*7*	*23*	*55*	*102*	*23*

Division Two

Blackburn Rovers Reserves	**38**	**30**	**3**	**5**	**141**	**34**	**63**
Burnley Reserves	**38**	**26**	**4**	**8**	**130**	**52**	**56**
Colne	**38**	**23**	**10**	**5**	**123**	**50**	**56**
Nelson	**38**	**26**	**3**	**9**	**124**	**48**	**55**
St. Helens Town	38	23	7	8	100	71	53
Lancaster	38	22	8	8	80	47	52
Haslingden	38	22	2	14	87	63	46
Pendlebury	38	16	5	17	74	79	37
Ashton Town	38	16	4	18	63	89	36
Hyde	38	13	8	17	72	63	34
Bacup	38	14	6	18	63	89	34
Glossop Reserves	38	11	10	17	54	67	32
Heywood United	38	14	3	21	72	96	31
Brynn Central	38	11	8	19	44	64	30
Turton	38	13	4	21	68	107	30
Clitheroe Central	38	12	5	21	64	86	29
Oswaldtwistle Rovers	38	11	5	22	58	100	27
Failsworth	38	8	10	20	57	99	26
Wigan Town	38	9	5	24	43	104	23
Newton-le-Willows	38	3	4	31	29	138	10

Wigan Town disbanded. Failsworth and Newton-le-Willows also left. Eccles Borough and Rochdale joined from the Manchester League and Stockport County Reserves also joined.

1908-09

Division One

Everton Reserves	38	23	8	7	104	51	54
Liverpool Reserves	38	23	3	12	91	60	49
Oldham Athletic Reserves	38	22	3	13	75	45	47
St. Helens Recreation	38	20	7	11	73	60	47
Burnley Reserves	38	17	12	9	92	66	46
Carlisle United	38	18	8	12	79	70	44
Blackburn Rovers Reserves	38	15	10	13	85	61	40
Nelson	38	15	9	14	62	63	39
Bury Reserves	38	16	7	15	76	78	39
Bolton Wanderers Reserves	38	16	7	15	90	93	39
Manchester United Reserves	38	13	11	14	63	70	37
Accrington Stanley	38	15	6	17	88	87	36
Workington	38	14	8	16	69	79	36
Southport Central	38	13	8	17	61	67	34
Preston North End Reserves	38	13	7	18	74	60	33
Colne	38	14	5	19	68	97	33
Darwen	*38*	*13*	*5*	*20*	*41*	*85*	*31*
Rossendale United	*38*	*11*	*7*	*20*	*58*	*94*	*29*
Blackpool Reserves	*38*	*11*	*3*	*24*	*60*	*90*	*25*
Atherton	*38*	*8*	*6*	*24*	*61*	*94*	*22*

Division Two

Manchester City Reserves	**38**	**24**	**8**	**6**	**131**	**50**	**56**
Chorley	**38**	**25**	**2**	**11**	**125**	**58**	**52**
St. Helens Town	**38**	**23**	**6**	**9**	**98**	**53**	**52**
Hyde	**38**	**23**	**5**	**10**	**93**	**59**	**51**
Stockport County Reserves	38	21	8	9	101	47	50
Eccles Borough	38	22	6	10	86	46	50
Haslingden	38	19	7	12	102	79	45
Lancaster	38	17	6	15	71	66	40
Barrow	38	18	4	16	80	85	40
Rochdale	38	16	5	17	58	60	37
Glossop Reserves	38	15	5	18	72	70	35
Earlestown	38	16	3	19	65	90	35
Heywood United	38	14	6	18	76	99	34
Clitheroe Central	38	12	8	18	72	82	32
Ashton Town	38	10	12	16	53	72	32
Bacup	38	13	6	19	60	85	32
Turton	38	14	3	21	98	89	31
Pendlebury	38	9	6	23	54	111	24
Oswaldtwistle Rovers	38	8	3	27	42	137	19
Great Harwood	38	6	1	31	55	148	13

Great Harwood took over the fixtures of Brynn Central who disbanded. Oswaldtwistle Rovers left the league and Walkden Central joined.

1909-10

Division One

Everton Reserves	38	22	8	8	87	39	52
Bolton Wanderers Reserves	38	21	9	8	83	49	51
Accrington Stanley	38	20	7	11	71	62	47
Chorley	38	18	11	9	61	55	47
Bury Reserves	38	20	4	14	81	66	44
Manchester City Reserves	38	17	9	12	65	58	43
Carlisle United	38	14	11	13	69	60	39
Nelson	38	14	10	14	61	59	38
Burnley Reserves	38	13	11	14	66	69	37
Preston North End Reserves	38	15	6	17	53	54	36
Blackburn Rovers Reserves	38	14	8	16	59	77	36
Workington	38	14	8	16	67	58	36
Colne	38	13	9	16	69	68	35
Manchester United Reserves	38	15	5	18	71	75	35
Oldham Athletic Reserves	38	14	6	18	47	59	34
St. Helens Recreation	38	13	8	17	58	69	34
Liverpool Reserves	38	12	9	17	73	80	33
Southport Central	38	13	7	18	61	67	33
Hyde	*38*	*10*	*7*	*21*	*54*	*94*	*27*
St. Helens Town	*38*	*10*	*3*	*25*	*48*	*86*	*23*

Carlisle United and Workington both moved to the North Eastern League.

Division Two

Glossop Reserves	**38**	**29**	**5**	**4**	**120**	**35**	**63**
Stockport County Reserves	**38**	**28**	**4**	**6**	**133**	**41**	**60**
Blackpool Reserves	**38**	**27**	**5**	**6**	**118**	**31**	**59**
Rochdale	**38**	**23**	**8**	**7**	**92**	**33**	**54**
Haslingden	38	25	3	10	113	45	53
Rossendale United	38	21	4	13	105	69	46
Atherton	38	20	5	13	78	60	45
Earlestown	38	18	7	13	80	71	43
Heywood United	38	16	6	16	72	76	38
Eccles Borough	38	17	4	17	61	52	38
Darwen	38	15	6	17	71	68	36
Great Harwood	38	14	6	18	74	77	34
Ashton Town	38	12	9	17	67	84	33
Lancaster	38	13	6	19	71	88	32
Barrow	38	12	8	18	60	78	32
Bacup	38	11	1	26	63	111	23
Walkden Central	38	10	3	25	65	128	23
Clitheroe Central	38	9	4	25	52	101	22
Turton	38	7	7	24	49	98	21
Pendlebury / Denton	38	1	3	34	23	189	5

Denton moved from the Manchester League and took over Pendlebury's fixtures.

Clitheroe Central, Lancaster and Turton left the league.
Chester and Tranmere Rovers both joined from The Combination and
Fleetwood joined from the West Lancashire League. Hindley Central and
Padiham also joined.

1910-11

Division One

Rochdale	38	25	6	7	87	45	56
Everton Reserves	38	21	7	10	82	35	49
Bolton Wanderers Reserves	38	19	10	9	72	59	48
Liverpool Reserves	38	19	8	11	76	59	46
Blackburn Rovers Reserves	38	16	8	14	66	63	40
Colne	38	17	5	16	67	56	39
Accrington Stanley	38	15	8	15	82	78	38
Nelson	38	15	8	15	64	63	38
Manchester United Reserves	38	15	7	16	75	69	37
Chorley	38	11	15	12	55	60	37
Southport Central	38	11	15	12	55	61	37
Preston North End Reserves	38	14	9	15	43	55	37
St. Helens Recreation	38	15	6	17	66	57	36
Blackpool Reserves	38	14	8	16	52	62	36
Bury Reserves	38	14	7	17	61	67	35
Burnley Reserves	38	15	5	18	62	69	35
Glossop Reserves	38	14	7	17	49	62	35
Manchester City Reserves	38	11	9	18	49	76	31
Stockport County Reserves	38	7	12	19	42	78	26
Oldham Athletic Reserves	38	9	6	23	42	73	24

Chorley vs Liverpool Reserves was abandoned after 25 minutes on the last
day of the season with Liverpool leading 1-0. The result stood.
Blackburn Rovers Reserves, Blackpool Reserves, Bolton Wanderers
Reserves, Burnley Reserves, Bury Reserves, Everton Reserves, Glossop
Reserves, Liverpool Reserves, Manchester City Reserves, Manchester
United Reserves, Oldham Athletic Reserves, Preston North End Reserves,
Southport Central and Stockport County Reserves all left to form the
Central League.

Division Two

Haslingden	38	26	5	7	98	47	57
Barrow	38	27	2	9	102	47	56
Chester	38	26	4	8	104	51	56
St. Helens Town	38	25	4	9	89	38	54
Hyde	38	24	5	9	99	49	53
Bacup	38	17	12	9	98	70	46
Rossendale United	38	19	7	12	124	64	45
Denton	38	21	3	14	100	76	45
Earlestown	38	15	8	15	73	76	38
Walkden Central	38	14	9	15	72	71	37
Eccles Borough	38	13	9	16	67	81	35
Heywood United	38	14	6	18	75	73	34
Tranmere Reserves	38	14	6	18	60	69	34
Fleetwood	38	14	6	18	72	83	34
Great Harwood	38	12	6	20	54	78	30
Atherton	38	11	7	20	55	73	29
Darwen	38	13	3	22	59	91	29
Hindley Central	38	9	4	25	48	103	22
Padiham	38	5	5	28	31	120	15
Ashton Town	38	2	7	29	21	141	11

Ashton Town's fixtures were taken over by Tyldesley Albion who moved
from the Manchester League late in the season.
Oswestry United joined from The Combination, Stalybridge Celtic joined
from the Lancashire & Cheshire League and Altrincham and Macclesfield
both joined from the Manchester League. Lancaster Town, Portsmouth
Rovers and South Liverpool also joined.

1911-12

Division One

Rochdale	32	23	4	5	81	24	50
St. Helens Recreation	32	19	6	7	69	49	44
Hyde	32	17	5	10	68	41	39
Barrow	32	15	9	8	66	48	39
Colne	32	16	6	10	59	43	38
Chester	32	15	7	10	74	50	37
Chorley	32	14	7	11	50	43	35
Rossendale United	32	12	9	11	58	48	33
Accrington Stanley	32	12	6	14	70	66	30
Haslingden	32	11	8	13	54	53	30
Eccles Borough	32	12	6	14	49	51	30
Heywood United	32	11	5	16	40	68	27
St. Helens Town	32	9	8	15	45	56	26
Nelson	32	9	7	16	58	66	25
Denton	32	11	3	18	52	77	25
Walkden Central	32	6	7	19	37	74	19
Bacup	*32*	*6*	*5*	*21*	*41*	*114*	*17*

Earlestown disbanded in October 1911 and Heywood United were
promoted from Division Two to take over their fixtures.
Rochdale moved to the Central League.

Division Two

Stalybridge Celtic	30	23	2	5	110	39	48
Altrincham	30	23	2	5	92	37	48
Tranmere Rovers	30	18	6	6	83	41	42
Fleetwood	30	16	4	10	64	31	36
South Liverpool	30	17	2	11	85	49	36
Macclesfield	30	14	6	10	57	40	34
Padiham	30	14	4	12	58	61	32
Oswestry United	30	13	5	12	75	64	31
Tyldesley Albion	30	11	5	14	61	66	27
Hindley Central	30	12	3	15	67	69	27
Barnoldswick United	30	10	5	15	53	79	25
Atherton	30	11	3	16	49	77	25
Darwen	30	9	3	18	34	84	21
Great Harwood	30	7	5	18	50	72	19
Portsmouth Rovers	30	6	5	19	51	86	17
Lancaster Town	30	4	4	22	29	123	12

Barnoldswick United took over Heywood United's fixtures in October 1911.
Stalybridge Celtic moved to the Central League and Tyldesley Albion also
left the league. Hurst, Nantwich, Northwich Victoria, Rochdale Reserves,
Stalybridge Celtic Reserves and Witton Albion all joined from the
Manchester League.

1912-13

Division One

Eccles Borough	34	23	4	7	96	49	50
Accrington Stanley	34	21	3	10	75	54	45
Nelson	34	19	4	11	82	59	42
Chorley	34	18	5	11	67	51	41
Barrow	34	17	6	11	73	34	40
Tranmere Rovers	34	16	6	12	92	58	38
Chester	34	12	13	9	89	64	37
St. Helens Recreation	34	16	4	14	72	56	36
Fleetwood	34	14	7	13	71	69	35
Haslingden	34	16	2	16	77	78	34
Altrincham	34	13	6	15	81	84	32
Hyde	34	13	5	16	76	70	31
Walkden Central	34	13	5	16	54	80	31
St. Helens Town	34	12	5	17	49	75	29
Heywood United	34	13	3	18	76	100	28
Denton	*34*	*9*	*6*	*19*	*55*	*101*	*24*
Rossendale United	*34*	*8*	*7*	*19*	*63*	*105*	*23*
Colne	34	6	4	24	49	110	16

Colne and St. Helens Recreation both left the league.

Division Two

South Liverpool	34	24	5	5	94	24	53
Stalybridge Celtic Reserves	34	21	5	8	74	45	47
Atherton	34	20	7	7	87	59	47
Northwich Victoria	34	18	9	7	101	43	45
Hurst	34	19	6	9	93	62	44
Macclesfield	34	17	8	9	75	40	42
Hindley Central	34	17	6	11	89	56	40
Witton Albion	34	17	5	12	81	57	39
Great Harwood	34	16	7	11	62	62	39
Oswestry United	34	17	3	14	79	80	37
Padiham	34	14	4	16	61	76	32
Nantwich	34	12	7	15	64	70	31
Rochdale Reserves	34	10	5	19	52	63	25
Darwen	34	9	5	20	53	85	23
Barnoldswick United	34	7	6	21	50	99	20
Portsmouth Rovers	34	8	3	23	53	101	19
Bacup	34	8	1	25	43	116	17
Lancaster Town	34	3	6	25	27	100	12

Crewe Alexandra Reserves joined from the North Staffordshire League and Newton Heath Athletic also joined.

1913-14

Division One

Tranmere Rovers	34	25	4	5	85	32	54
Barrow	34	21	5	8	92	39	47
Northwich Victoria	34	21	5	8	65	36	47
Eccles Borough	34	19	5	10	70	49	43
Atherton	34	18	6	10	82	57	42
South Liverpool	34	17	7	10	78	62	41
Accrington Stanley	34	15	8	11	76	66	38
Hurst	34	12	8	14	58	54	32
Chorley	34	12	8	14	48	60	32
Nelson	34	14	4	16	47	64	32
Fleetwood	34	10	9	15	54	57	29
Chester	34	9	10	15	59	62	28
Altrincham	34	10	7	17	61	80	27
Hyde	34	10	7	17	59	82	27
Heywood United	*34*	*10*	*6*	*18*	*41*	*57*	*26*
Haslingden	*34*	*11*	*4*	*19*	*52*	*77*	*26*
St. Helens Town	34	9	8	17	47	83	26
Walkden Central	*34*	*5*	*5*	*24*	*40*	*97*	*15*

St. Helens Town left the league.

Division Two

Witton Albion	34	22	5	7	107	44	49
Macclesfield	34	21	4	9	79	39	46
Rossendale United	34	19	4	11	84	42	42
Denton	34	18	4	12	62	56	40
Great Harwood	34	18	3	13	74	56	39
Stalybridge Celtic Reserves	34	17	4	13	77	47	38
Lancaster Town	34	16	6	12	70	54	38
Darwen	34	15	6	13	66	65	36
Crewe Alexandra Reserves	34	14	7	13	60	50	35
Nantwich	34	15	4	15	75	75	34
Padiham	34	13	7	14	61	67	33
Oswestry United	34	14	4	16	47	60	32
Barnoldswick United	34	13	5	16	61	72	31
Hindley Central	34	11	6	17	61	83	28
Rochdale Reserves	34	11	5	18	44	72	27
Newton Heath Athletic	34	10	5	19	44	89	25
Portsmouth Rovers	34	11	2	21	52	81	24
Bacup	34	5	5	24	40	112	15

Barnoldswick United, Crewe Alexandra Reserves, Darwen, Hindley Central, Oswestry United and Stalybridge Celtic Reserves all left the league. Hebden Bridge joined from the Yorkshire Combination and Glossop Reserves also joined.

1914-15

Division One

Eccles Borough	32	18	8	6	77	41	44
Hurst	32	17	8	7	76	48	42
Tranmere Rovers	32	19	3	10	84	52	41
Macclesfield	32	19	3	10	68	49	41
Northwich Victoria	32	16	6	10	71	50	38
Accrington Stanley	32	15	7	10	75	59	37
Altrincham	32	15	4	13	68	55	34
Atherton	32	15	4	13	69	59	34
South Liverpool	32	13	7	12	72	67	33
Witton Albion	32	13	6	13	61	63	32
Nelson	32	13	4	15	66	64	30
Denton	32	13	2	17	72	98	28
Barrow	32	11	6	15	59	89	28
Fleetwood	32	9	5	18	65	94	23
Rossendale United	32	11	0	21	42	64	22
Hyde	32	8	5	19	65	93	21
Chorley	32	6	4	22	46	91	16

Chester withdrew from the league in March 1915 due to war-time difficulties and their record was deleted. After the war, they became founder members of the Cheshire League.

Division Two

Rochdale Reserves	24	15	4	5	53	22	34
Lancaster Town	24	16	1	7	78	31	33
Haslingden	24	13	5	6	52	34	31
Nantwich	24	12	5	7	64	43	29
Heywood United	24	12	5	7	55	44	29
Great Harwood	24	12	4	8	62	36	28
Newton Heath Athletic	24	11	3	10	40	51	25
Walkden Central	24	9	5	10	45	44	23
Padiham	24	10	2	12	43	45	22
Glossop Reserves	24	9	4	11	39	55	22
Portsmouth Rovers	24	7	3	14	49	68	17
Hebden Bridge	24	7	1	16	31	62	15
Bacup	24	1	2	21	21	97	4

Between 1915 and 1919, the league operated a series of supplementary competitions.

1915-16

Northern Division – First League

Accrington Stanley	18	12	4	2	48	20	28
Blackburn Trinity	18	10	4	4	45	27	24
Haslingden	18	8	4	6	42	31	20
Rossendale United	18	8	3	7	41	30	19
Chorley	18	8	3	7	26	32	19
Nelson	17	7	4	6	24	35	18
Padiham	18	7	3	8	35	30	17
Great Harwood	18	7	3	8	30	26	17
Leyland	17	6	1	10	43	49	13
Adlington	18	1	1	16	18	72	3

Nelson vs Leyland was not played due to bad weather.

Northern Division – Subsidiary Competition

Great Harwood	12	8	3	1	27	14	19
Blackburn Trinity	12	7	2	3	43	20	16
Leyland	12	7	2	3	30	25	16
Accrington Stanley	12	4	2	6	21	19	10
Padiham	12	4	1	7	20	29	9
Rossendale United	12	4	1	7	21	33	9
Nelson	12	2	1	9	13	35	5

Southern Division – First League

South Liverpool	18	11	2	5	53	26	24
Eccles Borough	18	11	2	5	44	26	24
Atherton	18	10	3	5	38	22	23
Hyde	18	11	1	6	47	28	23
Altrincham	18	9	2	7	36	35	20
Stalybridge Celtic	18	6	7	5	35	23	19
Tranmere Rovers	18	6	4	8	37	37	16
Walkden Central	18	6	1	11	30	62	13
Glossop Reserves	18	5	2	11	29	45	12
Denton	18	2	2	14	12	57	6

Southern Division – Subsidiary Competition

Stalybridge Celtic	18	12	1	5	46	24	25
Atherton	18	12	0	6	38	19	24
Eccles Borough	18	11	1	6	36	25	23
South Liverpool	18	10	1	7	35	16	21
Tranmere Rovers	18	9	2	7	36	28	20
Altrincham	18	7	3	8	28	29	17
Hyde	17	8	1	8	33	41	17
Warrington Town	18	7	1	10	38	37	15
Walkden Central	17	3	3	11	14	42	9
Glossop Reserves	18	3	1	14	22	65	7

Hyde vs Walkden Central was not played due to bad weather.

1916-17

Some games were not played due to bad weather or the lack of official permission.

First Competition

Hurst	19	13	4	2	52	24	30
Stalybridge Celtic	19	12	2	5	48	32	26
Tranmere Rovers	19	11	1	7	43	30	23
South Liverpool	17	9	2	6	37	22	20
Warrington Town	20	7	5	8	31	45	19
Atherton	18	7	4	7	29	34	18
Altrincham	17	8	1	8	41	30	17
Walkden Central	18	5	5	8	33	40	15
Eccles Borough	15	3	4	8	23	38	10
Barrow	14	3	2	9	23	32	8
Hyde	14	0	4	10	15	48	4

Second Competition

Tranmere Rovers	9	5	3	1	15	8	13
South Liverpool	11	5	2	4	21	14	12
Warrington Town	7	4	1	2	19	11	9
Altrincham	8	2	1	5	11	21	5
Stalybridge Celtic	4	1	1	2	3	5	3
Barrow	2	1	1	0	6	4	3
Atherton	3	1	1	1	1	3	3
Lancaster United	4	0	0	4	2	12	0

1917-18

South Liverpool	22	12	3	7	39	38	27
Tranmere Rovers	20	10	4	6	43	21	24
Brynn	16	7	6	3	26	25	20
St. Helens Association	14	3	1	10	15	34	7
Horwich RMI	12	2	2	8	17	22	6

1918-19

Liverpool Section

Tranmere Rovers	22	17	1	4	69	26	35
Prescot	22	16	0	6	53	34	32
South Liverpool	22	12	5	5	49	38	29
Liverpool Reserves	22	12	1	9	67	38	25
Runcorn	21	11	1	9	46	35	23
Bolton Wanderers Reserves	22	9	3	10	49	47	21
Garswood Hall	22	8	3	11	35	40	19
Brynn	20	8	3	9	30	38	19
Everton Reserves	22	9	0	13	35	61	18
Plank Lane	22	6	1	15	34	65	13
Horwich RMI	21	4	3	14	34	53	11
Blackpool RAMC	18	5	1	12	26	52	11

Manchester Section

Stalybridge Celtic	14	12	0	2	46	15	24
Mossley	14	10	2	2	28	18	22
Altrincham	14	9	2	3	46	16	20
Hurst	14	6	1	7	28	29	13
Monk's Hall	14	6	1	7	30	40	13
Witton Albion	12	3	0	9	14	22	6
Northwich Victoria	12	3	0	9	15	29	6
Marple	10	0	0	10	6	44	0

Auxiliary Section

Chorley	19	4	7	8	26	39	15
South Liverpool	10	5	3	2	26	14	13
Lancaster United	12	5	3	4	21	26	13
Tranmere Rovers	8	5	2	1	24	11	12
Rylands Recreation	23	4	4	15	31	76	12
Runcorn	4	4	0	0	15	0	8
Plank Lane	4	4	0	0	17	3	8
Garswood Hall	6	3	2	1	11	11	8
Brynn	6	3	1	2	22	8	7
Horwich RMI	6	2	3	1	17	10	7
Prescot	5	3	1	1	11	8	7
Monk's Hall	10	3	1	6	21	25	7
Everton Reserves	3	2	0	1	10	5	4
Bolton Wanderers Reserves	4	2	0	2	6	10	4
Liverpool Reserves	3	1	1	1	3	3	3
Barrow	5	1	1	3	9	10	3
Blackpool RAMC	4	0	1	3	4	15	1

When the league resumed normal operations at the end of the war, it reformed with a single division.

Of the pre-war First Division members, Accrington Stanley, Barrow, Chorley, Fleetwood, Hurst, Rossendale United and South Liverpool all continued in the league as did Eccles Borough, after changing their name to Eccles United. Tranmere Rovers joined the Central League instead and were replaced in the Lancashire Combination by their reserves. Nelson also joined the Central League. Altrincham, Macclesfield, Northwich Victoria and Witton Albion did not rejoin, instead becoming founder members of the Cheshire League. Atherton had not yet re-formed and neither Denton nor Hyde rejoined.

Of the pre-war Second Division members, Great Harwood, Lancaster Town and Rochdale Reserves continued in the league but Bacup, Haslingden, Hebden Bridge, Heywood United, Newton Heath Athletic, Padiham, Portsmouth Rovers and Walkden Central did not rejoin. Nantwich did not rejoin and became a founder member of the Cheshire League instead. Glossop joined the league after failing to be re-elected to the Football League and replaced their reserves.

There were five new members: Dick Kerr's – who joined as a newly formed club, Horwich RMI – who were members of the West Lancashire League before the war, plus Plank Lane, Prescot and Stalybridge Celtic Reserves.

1919-20

Chorley	34	25	2	7	101	30	52
Lancaster Town	34	21	6	7	83	38	48
Eccles United	34	19	6	9	86	46	44
Tranmere Rovers Reserves	34	20	4	10	91	62	44
Barrow	34	20	3	11	58	37	43
Horwich RMI	34	20	0	14	72	59	40
Accrington Stanley	34	18	4	12	86	73	40
Great Harwood	34	17	3	14	78	57	37
Hurst	34	16	4	14	72	57	36
Rossendale United	34	16	3	15	64	71	35
South Liverpool	34	15	4	15	67	69	34
Fleetwood	34	15	3	16	67	63	33
Glossop	34	15	2	17	59	74	32
Stalybridge Celtic Reserves	34	11	3	20	60	95	25
Plank Lane	34	8	5	21	46	101	21
Dick Kerr's	34	6	5	23	61	89	17
Prescot	34	8	1	25	41	106	17
Rochdale Reserves	34	5	4	25	32	97	14

Glossop left to become founder members of the re-formed Manchester League while Plank Lane, Prescot, Rochdale Reserves and Stalybridge Celtic Reserves also left. Tranmere Rovers Reserves left in October 1919 to take over the fixtures of Leeds City Reserves in the Central League after that club was disbanded by order of the Football Association.
Darwen joined having not having re-formed in time to play in the 1919-20 season, Morecambe joined as a newly formed club and Wigan Borough joined from the West Lancashire League. Atherton, Bacup Borough and Leyland also joined.

1920-21

Barrow	34	23	6	5	79	28	52
Eccles United	34	21	4	9	90	40	46
Fleetwood	34	21	2	11	86	51	44
Darwen	34	17	10	7	79	51	44
Lancaster Town	34	17	8	9	67	40	42
Accrington Stanley	34	16	9	9	63	41	41
Hurst	34	14	9	11	61	56	37
Chorley	34	15	7	12	47	44	37
Atherton	34	14	9	11	59	57	37
South Liverpool	34	14	5	15	70	75	33
Leyland	34	12	9	13	58	66	33
Great Harwood	34	11	11	12	42	51	33
Morecambe	34	10	5	19	58	83	25
Rossendale United	34	10	5	19	52	76	25
Dick Kerr's	34	9	6	19	65	89	24
Bacup Borough	34	8	6	20	42	75	22
Wigan Borough	34	6	8	20	41	79	20
Horwich RMI	34	4	9	21	34	91	17

Accrington Stanley, Barrow and Wigan Borough left after being elected to the new Division Three (North) of the Football League and South Liverpool disbanded. Skelmersdale United joined from the Liverpool County Combination and New Brighton joined as a newly formed club. Stockport County Reserves joined from the Central League and Rochdale Reserves also joined.

1921-22

Lancaster Town	34	22	7	5	67	33	51
Chorley	34	22	4	8	79	43	48
New Brighton	34	22	3	9	72	38	47
Darwen	34	21	3	10	75	51	45
Fleetwood	34	19	5	10	76	43	43
Stockport County Reserves	34	18	7	9	71	49	43
Bacup Borough	34	15	6	13	57	48	36
Eccles United	34	15	5	14	57	48	35
Atherton	34	15	5	14	52	48	35
Rossendale United	34	13	8	13	66	51	34
Leyland	34	13	7	14	55	69	33
Horwich RMI	34	12	6	16	45	59	30
Skelmersdale United	34	13	4	17	45	62	30
Morecambe	34	10	6	18	36	56	26
Hurst	34	11	3	20	50	82	25
Great Harwood	34	7	6	21	44	87	20
Rochdale Reserves	34	6	5	23	47	83	17
Dick Kerr's	34	4	6	24	38	82	14

Stockport County Reserves left the league and New Cross joined from the Manchester League.

1922-23

Chorley	34	19	9	6	78	38	47
Lancaster Town	34	17	10	7	55	30	44
Darwen	34	17	9	8	77	60	43
New Brighton	34	16	9	9	69	32	41
Rossendale United	34	19	3	12	85	55	41
Fleetwood	34	17	6	11	67	54	40
New Cross	34	16	7	11	66	51	39
Leyland	34	14	7	13	55	47	35
Atherton	34	12	9	13	62	58	33
Eccles United	34	14	5	15	59	56	33
Rochdale Reserves	34	13	7	14	50	64	33
Hurst	34	12	7	15	58	63	31
Bacup Borough	34	13	5	16	44	59	31
Skelmersdale United	34	12	4	18	54	84	28
Morecambe	34	9	8	17	41	60	26
Dick Kerr's	34	6	13	15	38	68	25
Horwich RMI	34	7	10	17	54	76	24
Great Harwood	34	5	8	21	32	89	18

Hurst moved to the Cheshire League and New Brighton moved to the Football League – Division Three (North). Accrington Stanley Reserves, Nelson Reserves, Southport Reserves and Wigan Borough Reserves joined. New Cross changed their name to Manchester North End.

1923-24

Fleetwood	38	29	4	5	100	40	62
Southport Reserves	38	21	6	11	71	59	48
Darwen	38	19	8	11	84	63	46
Horwich RMI	38	20	4	14	72	49	44
Rossendale United	38	18	8	12	69	56	44
Bacup Borough	38	19	4	15	84	70	42
Eccles United	38	19	4	15	78	72	42
Lancaster Town	38	17	8	13	61	67	42
Wigan Borough Reserves	38	16	9	13	76	54	41
Chorley	38	17	7	14	77	66	41
Manchester North End	38	17	7	14	71	63	41
Accrington Stanley Reserves	38	17	6	15	72	67	40
Atherton	38	17	5	16	56	44	39
Nelson Reserves	38	14	7	17	65	65	35
Morecambe	38	15	5	18	60	63	35
Leyland	38	10	9	19	55	75	29
Great Harwood	38	9	6	23	55	102	24
Dick Kerr's	38	8	7	23	48	89	23
Rochdale Reserves	38	9	3	26	69	94	21
Skelmersdale United	38	7	7	24	52	117	21

Manchester North End moved to the Cheshire League and Skelmersdale United moved to the Liverpool County Combination. Barnoldswick Town joined the league.

1924-25

Team	P	W	D	L	F	A	Pts
Morecambe	36	24	7	5	88	31	55
Rochdale Reserves	36	24	6	6	105	38	54
Darwen	36	17	11	8	64	35	45
Dick Kerr's	36	20	5	11	81	60	45
Atherton	36	19	7	10	62	40	45
Rossendale United	36	16	9	11	76	67	41
Fleetwood	36	14	11	11	74	59	39
Southport Reserves	36	15	8	13	60	46	38
Horwich RMI	36	14	8	14	74	60	36
Barnoldswick Town	36	15	5	16	72	84	35
Lancaster Town	36	13	8	15	60	54	34
Eccles United	36	13	7	16	68	90	33
Nelson Reserves	36	12	8	16	60	77	32
Bacup Borough	36	11	10	15	65	82	32
Accrington Stanley Reserves	36	12	7	17	71	61	31
Chorley	36	10	8	18	49	77	28
Wigan Borough Reserves	36	12	4	20	45	82	28
Great Harwood	36	7	4	25	38	104	18
Leyland	36	6	3	27	40	105	15

Eccles United moved to the Cheshire League while Leyland and Rochdale Reserves also left the league. Hindley Green Athletic joined from the Lancashire Alliance while Clitheroe, Colne Town and Preston North End "A" also joined.

1925-26

Team	P	W	D	L	F	A	Pts
Nelson Reserves	38	27	5	6	123	51	59
Morecambe	38	21	10	7	103	58	52
Rossendale United	38	23	4	11	119	89	50
Fleetwood	38	19	7	12	87	69	45
Bacup Borough	38	20	3	15	71	82	43
Dick Kerr's	38	18	6	14	100	70	42
Horwich RMI	38	19	3	16	87	84	41
Lancaster Town	38	17	6	15	107	81	40
Darwen	38	18	4	16	93	75	40
Atherton	38	17	5	16	85	79	39
Chorley	38	16	7	15	103	101	39
Southport Reserves	38	16	5	17	82	75	37
Hindley Green Athletic	38	16	5	17	92	101	37
Barnoldswick Town	38	15	5	18	90	112	35
Accrington Stanley Reserves	38	14	5	19	83	106	33
Colne Town	38	14	4	20	77	101	32
Preston North End "A"	38	12	6	20	73	94	30
Wigan Borough Reserves	38	11	7	20	74	102	29
Clitheroe	38	9	7	22	76	103	25
Great Harwood	38	5	2	31	50	142	12

1926-27

Team	P	W	D	L	F	A	Pts
Rossendale United	38	27	6	5	129	65	60
Chorley	38	25	9	4	111	45	59
Morecambe	38	23	4	11	105	58	50
Barnoldswick Town	38	21	6	11	125	79	48
Dick Kerr's	38	21	6	11	105	68	48
Accrington Stanley Reserves	38	19	9	10	109	75	47
Lancaster Town	38	21	5	12	96	76	47
Southport Reserves	38	20	3	15	93	82	43
Clitheroe	38	17	8	13	100	91	42
Horwich RMI	38	18	5	15	106	76	41
Darwen	38	15	6	17	89	98	36
Fleetwood	38	14	5	19	63	82	33
Bacup Borough	38	12	8	18	82	92	32
Nelson Reserves	38	12	7	19	72	90	31
Preston North End "A"	38	10	8	20	77	93	28
Atherton	38	12	4	22	76	122	28
Hindley Green Athletic	38	10	5	23	93	146	25
Wigan Borough Reserves	38	9	6	23	73	120	24
Colne Town	38	11	1	26	55	127	23
Great Harwood	38	5	5	28	55	129	15

Colne Town left the league.
Burscough Rangers joined from the Liverpool County Combination.

1927-28

Team	P	W	D	L	F	A	Pts
Chorley	38	28	3	7	128	49	59
Lancaster Town	38	26	3	9	148	58	55
Horwich RMI	38	23	9	6	111	61	55
Accrington Stanley Reserves	38	25	2	11	100	64	52
Rossendale United	38	21	7	10	110	60	49
Dick Kerr's	38	19	4	15	115	93	42
Clitheroe	38	17	8	13	86	81	42
Morecambe	38	17	6	15	92	72	40
Wigan Borough Reserves	38	16	8	14	79	72	40
Southport Reserves	38	16	7	15	94	91	39
Burscough Rangers	38	13	9	16	88	99	35
Great Harwood	38	12	9	17	97	128	33
Atherton	38	12	6	20	87	114	30
Preston North End "A"	38	10	10	18	80	108	30
Nelson Reserves	38	12	6	20	80	113	30
Fleetwood / Prescot Cables	38	12	6	20	63	128	30
Barnoldswick Town	38	12	3	23	77	114	27
Hindley Green Athletic	38	11	4	23	71	108	26
Darwen	38	10	6	22	68	104	26
Bacup Borough	38	7	6	25	52	109	20

Fleetwood resigned after playing 22 matches and Prescot Cables took over their fixtures. Hindley Green Athletic left and Manchester Central joined.

1928-29

Team	P	W	D	L	F	A	Pts
Chorley	38	29	3	6	125	52	61
Horwich RMI	38	24	2	12	152	87	50
Rossendale United	38	23	4	11	126	74	50
Prescot Cables	38	20	8	10	87	49	48
Lancaster Town	38	20	8	10	91	65	48
Clitheroe	38	21	4	13	93	79	46
Manchester Central	38	21	3	14	106	87	45
Southport Reserves	38	21	2	15	98	63	44
Accrington Stanley Reserves	38	19	5	14	77	72	43
Morecambe	38	20	2	16	89	73	42
Darwen	38	17	5	16	84	82	39
Burscough Rangers	38	15	9	14	66	78	39
Dick Kerr's	38	13	8	17	77	82	34
Atherton	38	13	3	22	80	109	29
Nelson Reserves	38	12	5	21	55	85	29
Bacup Borough	38	10	5	23	69	109	25
Wigan Borough Reserves	38	9	6	23	69	99	24
Barnoldswick Town	38	10	4	24	66	139	24
Preston North End "A"	38	8	4	26	67	126	20
Great Harwood	38	8	4	26	65	132	20

Preston North End "A" left the league.
Lytham joined from the West Lancashire League.

1929-30

Team	P	W	D	L	F	A	Pts
Lancaster Town	38	28	4	6	138	49	60
Manchester Central	38	25	9	4	99	38	59
Bacup Borough	38	24	3	11	101	82	51
Darwen	38	22	4	12	93	62	48
Chorley	38	19	9	10	89	53	47
Prescot Cables	38	21	5	12	93	56	47
Horwich RMI	38	20	6	12	112	70	46
Rossendale United	38	18	7	13	83	82	43
Dick Kerr's	38	18	5	15	87	70	41
Southport Reserves	38	17	6	15	94	74	40
Accrington Stanley Reserves	38	14	12	12	77	76	40
Nelson Reserves	38	15	8	15	86	82	38
Atherton	38	15	3	20	72	105	33
Morecambe	38	12	7	19	74	111	31
Wigan Borough Reserves	38	12	6	20	66	96	30
Burscough Rangers	38	12	4	22	71	92	28
Clitheroe	38	12	3	23	74	100	27
Barnoldswick Town	38	6	9	23	63	117	21
Lytham	38	6	6	26	56	120	18
Great Harwood	38	3	6	29	50	143	12

Atherton left the league and Rochdale Reserves joined.

1930-31

Darwen	38	23	7	8	116	55	53
Prescot Cables	38	22	6	10	112	56	50
Lytham	38	23	4	11	94	64	50
Lancaster Town	38	20	9	9	85	64	49
Horwich RMI	38	21	5	12	119	73	47
Barnoldswick Town	38	21	5	12	111	92	47
Dick Kerr's	38	20	6	12	102	71	46
Southport Reserves	38	21	4	13	94	70	46
Manchester Central	38	19	6	13	97	60	44
Chorley	38	15	9	14	86	68	39
Bacup Borough	38	17	4	17	93	105	38
Burscough Rangers	38	19	0	19	84	96	38
Accrington Stanley Reserves	38	16	5	17	83	99	37
Clitheroe	38	16	4	18	87	85	36
Rossendale United	38	15	6	17	80	89	36
Morecambe	38	12	8	18	76	97	32
Great Harwood	38	9	5	24	67	106	23
Wigan Borough Reserves	38	10	2	26	63	120	22
Nelson Reserves	38	8	3	27	72	119	19
Rochdale Reserves	38	4	0	34	62	194	8

Manchester Central moved to the Cheshire League and Rochdale Reserves also left the league. Nelson joined after failing to be re-elected to the Football League – Division Three (North) and replaced their reserves. Fleetwood joined from the West Lancashire League, having changed their name from Windsor Villa. Barrow Reserves also joined.

1931-32

Darwen	36	24	7	5	104	43	55
Prescot Cables	36	21	6	9	91	48	48
Barrow Reserves	36	19	8	9	87	45	46
Lancaster Town	36	18	9	9	77	52	45
Nelson	36	19	6	11	74	53	44
Rossendale United	36	18	6	12	86	74	42
Fleetwood	36	17	7	12	98	78	41
Southport Reserves	36	18	4	14	87	60	40
Chorley	36	17	5	14	85	71	39
Barnoldswick Town	36	13	10	13	68	78	36
Clitheroe	36	14	7	15	65	77	35
Lytham	36	13	7	16	77	93	33
Dick Kerr's	36	14	4	18	85	83	32
Bacup Borough	36	15	2	19	71	83	32
Great Harwood	36	13	5	18	68	80	31
Burscough Rangers	36	11	8	17	60	82	30
Horwich RMI	36	10	3	23	73	108	23
Morecambe	36	6	6	24	41	93	18
Accrington Stanley Reserves	36	5	4	27	40	136	14

Wigan Borough disbanded in November 1931 and their reserves' record was deleted. Rochdale Reserves joined the league.

1932-33

Chorley	38	28	6	4	113	44	62
Prescot Cables	38	25	3	10	127	66	53
Southport Reserves	38	22	6	10	96	61	50
Darwen	38	22	5	11	119	67	49
Fleetwood	38	21	7	10	97	58	49
Barrow Reserves	38	21	6	11	100	55	48
Horwich RMI	38	21	5	12	107	82	47
Lancaster Town	38	18	8	12	86	72	44
Clitheroe	38	18	4	16	95	73	40
Accrington Stanley Reserves	38	16	5	17	86	94	37
Nelson	38	14	8	16	83	81	36
Dick Kerr's	38	14	6	18	72	106	34
Lytham	38	13	7	18	94	116	33
Morecambe	38	11	10	17	68	84	32
Rossendale United	38	10	11	17	65	89	31
Rochdale Reserves	38	13	4	21	73	111	30
Great Harwood	38	12	4	22	86	114	28
Burscough Rangers	38	9	9	20	59	100	27
Bacup Borough	38	7	5	26	62	125	19
Barnoldswick Town	38	3	5	30	42	132	11

Prescot Cables moved to the Cheshire League and Burscough Rangers also left. Leyland Motors and Northern Nomads joined.

1933-34

Chorley	38	29	3	6	133	53	61
Fleetwood	38	27	4	7	109	60	58
Lancaster Town	38	23	8	7	130	71	54
Clitheroe	38	21	6	11	129	86	48
Darwen	38	20	7	11	122	72	47
Barrow Reserves	38	22	3	13	92	70	47
Southport Reserves	38	17	10	11	73	70	44
Nelson	38	16	8	14	97	86	40
Accrington Stanley Reserves	38	15	7	16	85	102	37
Bacup Borough	38	15	6	17	86	83	36
Dick Kerr's	38	14	7	17	76	79	35
Rochdale Reserves	38	14	6	18	69	81	34
Lytham	38	13	6	19	83	94	32
Rossendale United	38	13	6	19	70	98	32
Great Harwood	38	11	9	18	72	103	31
Horwich RMI	38	13	4	21	85	107	30
Leyland Motors	38	12	3	23	94	129	27
Morecambe	38	9	9	20	65	101	27
Northern Nomads	38	10	3	25	77	114	23
Barnoldswick Town	38	6	5	27	54	142	17

Barnoldswick Town left the league and New Brighton Reserves joined.

1934-35

Lancaster Town	38	28	4	6	143	60	60
Fleetwood	38	25	5	8	99	44	55
Chorley	38	25	2	11	94	54	52
Clitheroe	38	22	8	8	99	65	52
Rossendale United	38	22	6	10	103	65	50
Nelson	38	17	10	11	88	61	44
Darwen	38	19	6	13	119	83	44
Morecambe	38	17	5	16	63	60	39
Rochdale Reserves	38	15	8	15	86	82	38
Horwich RMI	38	16	3	19	91	88	35
New Brighton Reserves	38	14	7	17	79	97	35
Dick Kerr's	38	13	8	17	82	73	34
Bacup Borough	38	13	8	17	88	90	34
Southport Reserves	38	15	4	19	81	88	34
Barrow Reserves	38	12	10	16	65	78	34
Accrington Stanley Reserves	38	13	5	20	65	92	31
Northern Nomads	38	11	6	21	77	127	28
Lytham	38	10	3	25	58	117	23
Leyland Motors	38	8	4	26	66	142	20
Great Harwood	38	8	2	28	62	142	18

Marine joined from the Liverpool County Combination and South Liverpool joined as a newly formed club.#

1935-36

Lancaster Town	40	29	5	6	142	60	63
Barrow Reserves	40	30	2	8	138	53	62
Fleetwood	40	23	6	11	117	64	52
South Liverpool	40	22	4	14	93	71	48
Chorley	40	22	4	14	100	82	48
Morecambe	40	19	9	12	78	65	47
Clitheroe	40	19	8	13	123	103	46
Darwen	40	21	3	16	104	77	45
Bacup Borough	40	20	5	15	96	83	45
Nelson	40	16	9	15	86	84	41
New Brighton Reserves	40	17	5	18	111	98	39
Accrington Stanley Reserves	40	17	5	18	76	90	39
Leyland Motors	40	15	7	18	73	104	37
Marine	40	14	8	18	94	86	36
Horwich RMI	40	14	8	18	103	111	36
Northern Nomads	40	15	4	21	79	101	34
Southport Reserves	40	12	9	19	76	97	33
Rochdale Reserves	40	13	6	21	91	133	32
Rossendale United	40	10	9	21	77	108	29
Great Harwood	40	6	7	27	55	129	19
Lytham	40	2	5	33	46	159	9

ick Kerr's disbanded in December 1935 and their record was deleted.
Nelson moved to the Nelson, Colne & District League and Lytham moved to
the West Lancashire League. Droylsden joined from the Manchester
League and Prescot Cables joined from the Cheshire League.

1937-38

South Liverpool	42	33	3	6	177	53	69
Clitheroe	42	25	9	8	139	82	59
Oldham Athletic Reserves	42	26	6	10	131	62	58
Accrington Stanley Reserves	42	23	7	12	103	63	53
Lancaster City	42	21	11	10	93	72	53
Morecambe	42	21	10	11	90	70	52
Darwen	42	19	9	14	103	85	47
Prescot Cables	42	17	11	14	82	72	45
Rossendale United	42	18	7	17	74	73	43
Leyland Motors	42	16	10	16	82	99	42
Bacup Borough	42	15	11	16	82	88	41
New Brighton Reserves	42	16	9	17	78	89	41
Chorley	42	18	4	20	93	104	40
Droylsden	42	13	13	16	91	98	39
Southport Reserves	42	16	7	19	80	96	39
Marine	42	15	7	20	80	105	37
Fleetwood	42	13	8	21	91	94	34
Horwich RMI	42	14	5	23	92	123	33
Barrow Reserves	42	13	5	24	66	99	31
Great Harwood	42	10	8	24	66	89	28
Rochdale Reserves	42	9	5	28	62	128	23
Northern Nomads	42	8	1	33	42	153	17

Northern Nomads left the league and Bangor City joined from the
Birmingham League.

1936-37

South Liverpool	40	29	2	9	125	55	60
Accrington Stanley Reserves	40	26	7	7	108	52	59
Darwen	40	24	7	9	106	63	55
Barrow Reserves	40	21	8	11	100	72	50
Chorley	40	22	5	13	120	74	49
Clitheroe	40	20	9	11	122	85	49
Fleetwood	40	22	5	13	99	82	49
Marine	40	20	6	14	107	81	46
Lancaster Town	40	21	4	15	106	107	46
Morecambe	40	17	10	13	95	75	44
Southport Reserves	40	17	10	13	84	75	44
Bacup Borough	40	14	7	19	61	83	35
New Brighton Reserves	40	12	8	20	77	102	32
Leyland Motors	40	9	13	18	77	105	31
Horwich RMI	40	11	8	21	80	93	30
Great Harwood	40	10	10	20	80	115	30
Droylsden	40	13	3	24	88	118	29
Prescot Cables	40	11	7	22	70	112	29
Rossendale United	40	11	6	23	82	135	28
Rochdale Reserves	40	9	6	25	82	123	24
Northern Nomads	40	9	3	28	71	143	21

1940 1950

Lancaster Town changed their name to Lancaster City and Oldham Athletic
Reserves joined the league.

1938-39

South Liverpool	42	29	4	9	137	61	62
Bangor City	42	27	7	8	126	75	61
Clitheroe	42	25	7	10	121	74	57
Accrington Stanley Reserves	42	23	8	11	109	64	54
Chorley	42	23	7	12	118	62	53
Rossendale United	42	19	12	11	110	95	50
New Brighton Reserves	42	20	7	15	107	83	47
Marine	42	22	3	17	107	92	47
Oldham Athletic Reserves	42	18	10	14	108	94	46
Fleetwood	42	18	8	16	85	92	44
Lancaster City	42	19	6	17	95	103	44
Rochdale Reserves	42	17	9	16	91	90	43
Darwen	42	18	6	18	116	87	42
Leyland Motors	42	16	7	19	94	101	39
Morecambe	42	14	10	18	67	76	38
Barrow Reserves	42	16	5	21	87	116	37
Southport Reserves	42	14	8	20	81	99	36
Bacup Borough	42	13	6	23	81	99	32
Prescot Cables	42	12	7	23	79	131	31
Great Harwood	42	7	8	27	72	156	22
Horwich RMI	42	7	7	28	80	143	21
Droylsden	42	7	4	31	79	157	18

1939-45

The league did not operate any official competitions during the war. When it resumed in 1945, Bangor City, Clitheroe, Fleetwood, Great Harwood, Horwich RMI, Marine, New Brighton Reserves, Oldham Athletic Reserves, and Southport Reserves were not ready to compete. Droylsden and South Liverpool moved to the Cheshire League and Netherfield joined.

1945-46

Chorley	22	14	4	4	78	42	32
Netherfield	22	13	3	6	64	39	29
Barrow Reserves	22	12	4	6	62	43	28
Bacup Borough	22	12	3	7	49	41	27
Darwen	22	9	7	6	50	48	25
Rossendale United	22	9	4	9	53	47	22
Leyland Motors	22	9	3	10	50	56	21
Rochdale Reserves	22	9	2	11	52	53	20
Morecambe	22	6	6	10	54	68	18
Prescot Cables	22	6	5	11	57	81	17
Lancaster City	22	6	4	12	53	75	16
Accrington Stanley Reserves	22	3	4	15	38	67	10
	264	108	49	107			265

Bangor City, Clitheroe, Fleetwood, Great Harwood, Horwich RMI, Marine, New Brighton Reserves, Oldham Athletic Reserves and Southport Reserves rejoined the league. Nelson joined from the Nelson, Colne & District League.

1946-47

Bacup Borough	42	26	9	7	111	54	61
Marine	42	25	6	11	121	72	56
Netherfield	42	22	8	12	100	64	52
Morecambe	42	23	5	14	133	85	51
Rochdale Reserves	42	23	3	16	116	72	49
Prescot Cables	42	21	6	15	116	99	48
Lancaster City	42	22	3	17	104	66	47
Oldham Athletic Reserves	42	20	7	15	95	94	47
Clitheroe	42	19	7	16	107	105	45
Barrow Reserves	40	15	14	11	77	76	44
Nelson	42	18	7	17	100	85	43
Fleetwood	42	18	7	17	78	72	43
New Brighton Reserves	42	20	2	20	80	92	42
Horwich RMI	42	17	6	19	83	93	40
Bangor City	40	14	9	17	84	94	37
Southport Reserves	42	15	6	21	76	84	36
Chorley	42	13	9	20	84	92	35
Darwen	42	14	6	22	84	122	34
Leyland Motors	42	13	7	22	66	90	33
Rossendale United	42	11	10	21	76	113	32
Accrington Stanley Reserves	42	11	7	24	70	122	29
Great Harwood	42	6	4	32	63	178	16

Bangor City & Barrow Reserves did not meet due to travelling problems. Wigan Athletic joined from the Cheshire League.

A Division Two was formed, consisting of Great Harwood (relegated from Division One), plus Astley & Tyldesley Collieries, Bacup Borough Reserves, Barnoldswick & District, Belle Vue, Darwen Reserves, Horwich RMI Reserves, Nelson Reserves, Oldham Athletic "A", Rossendale United Reserves and Stubshaw Cross Rovers. The teams played each other 4 times.

1947-48

Relegated clubs are shown in italics.
Promoted clubs are shown in bold.

Division One

Wigan Athletic	42	25	9	8	72	37	59
Nelson	42	24	9	9	84	62	57
Barrow Reserves	42	24	7	11	88	55	55
Morecambe	42	24	6	12	98	59	54
Fleetwood	42	23	7	12	73	52	53
Marine	42	23	6	13	103	64	52
Netherfield	42	23	6	13	83	58	52
Lancaster City	42	21	7	14	80	69	49
Bacup Borough	42	20	6	16	96	67	46
Oldham Athletic Reserves	42	19	8	15	76	71	46
Chorley	42	19	7	16	89	74	45
Prescot Cables	42	19	6	17	87	80	44
Rochdale Reserves	42	14	8	20	79	76	36
Bangor City	42	14	8	20	62	77	36
Rossendale United	42	11	12	19	80	90	34
Darwen	42	12	9	21	60	91	33
Accrington Stanley Reserves	42	12	7	23	71	106	31
Clitheroe	42	13	5	24	70	110	31
New Brighton Reserves	42	11	8	23	56	85	30
Leyland Motors	42	11	7	24	73	115	29
Horwich RMI	*42*	*10*	*7*	*25*	*58*	*104*	*27*
Southport Reserves	42	9	7	26	57	93	25

Ashton United joined from the Cheshire League.

Division Two

Stubshaw Cross Rovers	32	23	4	5	88	43	50
Nelson Reserves	32	23	4	5	79	42	50
Astley & Tyldesley Collieries	32	18	3	11	88	76	39
Darwen Reserves	31	14	7	10	85	72	35
Great Harwood	32	9	10	13	61	69	28
Belle Vue	31	10	5	16	72	85	25
Bacup Borough Reserves	32	8	8	16	76	90	24
Barnoldswick and District	31	10	3	18	70	85	23
Oldham Athletic "A"	29	1	6	22	37	94	8

Rossendale United Reserves resigned during October and Horwich RMI Reserves resigned during February. Both of their records were deleted. Oldham Athletic "A" failed to complete their fixtures.

Astley & Tyldesley Collieries and Bacup Borough Reserves both left the league. Lytham joined from the West Lancashire League and Bootle joined as a newly formed club. ACI Horwich, Bolton Wanderers "B" and Lancaster City Reserves also joined.

1948-49

Division One

Netherfield	42	26	10	6	112	46	62
Chorley	42	23	12	7	72	55	58
Morecambe	42	22	6	14	80	60	50
Nelson	42	20	9	13	87	68	49
Darwen	42	21	7	14	81	65	49
Wigan Athletic	42	19	9	14	73	68	47
Bangor City	42	18	10	14	75	71	46
Prescot Cables	42	19	7	16	89	72	45
Lancaster City	42	15	14	13	58	50	44
Rochdale Reserves	42	17	10	15	75	71	44
Fleetwood	42	17	8	17	81	66	42
Rossendale United	42	17	8	17	85	78	42
Barrow Reserves	42	16	10	16	73	69	42
Oldham Athletic Reserves	42	13	15	14	80	71	41
Ashton United	42	14	13	15	73	79	41
Southport Reserves	42	17	7	18	60	69	41
Marine	42	14	10	18	73	83	38
Clitheroe	42	13	9	20	74	99	35
Accrington Stanley Reserves	42	14	6	22	69	86	34
New Brighton Reserves	42	9	13	20	53	82	31
Leyland Motors	*42*	*7*	*9*	*26*	*49*	*94*	*23*
Bacup Borough	*42*	*7*	*6*	*29*	*49*	*119*	*20*

Division Two

Bootle	**24**	**19**	**2**	**3**	**77**	**29**	**40**
Horwich RMI	**24**	**19**	**1**	**4**	**75**	**28**	**39**
Belle Vue	24	16	3	5	78	32	35
Stubshaw Cross Rovers	24	15	3	6	58	53	33
Lytham	24	15	2	7	61	42	32
Great Harwood	24	9	4	11	55	59	22
ACI Horwich	24	9	2	13	47	62	20
Nelson Reserves	24	7	5	12	44	53	19
Lancaster City Reserves	24	6	5	13	39	64	17
Darwen Reserves	24	5	4	15	33	55	14
Barnoldswick and District	24	4	6	14	29	55	14
Oldham Athletic "A"	24	6	2	16	47	90	14
Bolton Wanderers "B"	24	4	5	15	33	53	13
					676	*675*	

Oldham Athletic "A" left the league. Earlestown joined from the Liverpool County Combination and Blackpool "B", Chorley Reserves, De Havilland, Lomax, Padiham, St. Helens Town and Wigan Athletic Reserves all joined. Belle Vue changed their name to Droylsden United.

1949-50

Division One

Nelson	42	30	4	8	125	63	64
Wigan Athletic	42	24	8	10	79	47	56
Prescot Cables	42	22	12	8	102	64	56
Chorley	42	20	9	13	71	67	49
Ashton United	42	20	7	15	90	62	47
Rochdale Reserves	42	19	8	15	87	79	46
Bangor City	42	18	9	15	96	70	45
Fleetwood	42	18	9	15	76	67	45
Morecambe	42	17	11	14	62	55	45
Netherfield	42	20	5	17	88	83	45
Accrington Stanley Reserves	42	16	10	16	64	75	42
Southport Reserves	42	14	13	15	67	67	41
Oldham Athletic Reserves	42	15	10	17	77	72	40
Lancaster City	42	14	10	18	67	74	38
Barrow Reserves	42	14	10	18	63	81	38
Bootle	42	14	9	19	61	71	37
Darwen	42	13	11	18	55	66	37
Rossendale United	42	13	8	21	73	85	34
Clitheroe	42	13	8	21	66	90	34
New Brighton Reserves	42	13	6	23	63	102	32
Marine	42	11	9	22	74	104	31
Horwich RMI	*42*	*8*	*6*	*28*	*52*	*114*	*22*

Bangor City moved to the Cheshire League.

Division Two

Blackpool "B"	**38**	**29**	**3**	**6**	**139**	**38**	**61**
Earlestown	**38**	**29**	**2**	**7**	**149**	**60**	**60**
Leyland Motors	38	26	4	8	111	50	56
Bacup Borough	38	26	3	9	101	51	55
Stubshaw Cross Rovers	38	21	4	13	81	76	46
Droylesden United	38	20	5	13	103	80	45
St. Helens Town	38	16	11	11	84	77	43
Lytham	38	19	3	16	86	73	41
Nelson Reserves	38	20	1	17	100	89	41
Bolton Wanderers "B"	38	16	7	15	73	64	39
Chorley Reserves	38	16	5	17	96	88	37
Wigan Athletic Reserves	38	13	10	15	58	70	36
ACI Horwich	38	15	4	19	95	122	34
Lomax	38	13	6	19	84	107	32
Lancaster City Reserves	38	12	8	18	65	93	32
Padiham	38	12	4	22	91	106	28
Great Harwood	38	11	3	24	68	113	25
Barnoldswick and District	38	11	2	25	56	113	24
Darwen Reserves	38	7	5	26	64	117	19
De Havilland	38	2	2	34	43	160	6

De Havilland left the league and Atherton Collieries, Hindsford, Morecambe Reserves and Netherfield Reserves all joined.

1950-51

Division One

Wigan Athletic	42	27	7	8	98	43	61
Nelson	42	29	3	10	120	64	61
Netherfield	42	26	7	9	107	57	59
Fleetwood	42	21	10	11	100	70	52
Rochdale Reserves	42	20	10	12	87	69	50
Bootle	42	22	5	15	89	61	49
Southport Reserves	42	19	8	15	98	81	46
Chorley	42	17	10	15	91	93	44
Oldham Athletic Reserves	42	16	11	15	88	78	43
Barrow Reserves	42	17	9	16	68	63	43
Lancaster City	42	17	9	16	75	89	43
Ashton United	42	16	9	17	85	88	41
New Brighton Reserves	42	15	8	19	53	56	38
Darwen	42	12	12	18	62	79	36
Morecambe	42	12	12	18	56	73	36
Clitheroe	42	15	6	21	69	90	36
Earlestown	42	16	3	23	91	115	35
Blackpool "B"	42	13	8	21	69	87	34
Rossendale United	42	13	7	22	63	102	33
Marine	42	11	8	23	68	87	30
Prescot Cables	*42*	*10*	*10*	*22*	*57*	*89*	*30*
Accrington Stanley Reserves	*42*	*7*	*10*	*25*	*44*	*104*	*24*

Bootle changed their name to Bootle Athletic. New Brighton joined after failing to be re-elected to the Football League – Division Three (North) and replaced their reserves.

Division Two

St. Helens Town	42	29	6	7	132	49	64
Horwich RMI	42	30	4	8	154	60	64
Bacup Borough	42	26	4	12	109	65	56
Lytham	42	23	6	13	99	67	52
Nelson Reserves	42	22	8	12	84	60	52
Hindsford	42	23	6	13	87	83	52
Padiham	42	21	9	12	100	59	51
Bolton Wanderers "B"	42	22	6	14	117	72	50
Leyland Motors	42	18	8	16	93	78	44
Stubshaw Cross Rovers	42	18	8	16	85	83	44
Wigan Athletic Reserves	42	17	9	16	77	74	43
Netherfield Reserves	42	17	9	16	75	98	43
Droylsden United	42	18	5	19	95	97	41
ACI Horwich	42	18	5	19	88	91	41
Morecambe Reserves	42	13	10	19	75	106	36
Atherton Collieries	42	15	4	23	98	113	34
Lomax	42	13	7	22	105	125	33
Great Harwood	42	13	6	23	99	124	32
Chorley Reserves	42	12	7	23	77	126	31
Barnoldswick and District	42	10	6	26	65	130	26
Lancaster City Reserves	42	7	4	31	64	139	18
Darwen Reserves	42	6	5	31	63	142	17

Droylsden United changed their name to Droylsden. Lancaster City Reserves left the league and Astley Bridge joined.

Division Two

Prescot Cables	42	32	5	5	151	44	69
Nelson Reserves	42	30	6	6	123	49	66
Droylsden	42	28	7	7	172	78	63
Accrington Stanley Reserves	42	27	6	9	115	56	60
Leyland Motors	42	26	6	10	104	56	58
Bacup Borough	42	22	8	12	107	72	52
Lytham	42	20	7	15	100	68	47
Great Harwood	42	22	3	17	115	107	47
Barnoldswick and District	42	19	8	15	89	86	46
Bolton Wanderers "B"	42	18	6	18	107	75	42
Netherfield Reserves	42	15	11	16	79	87	41
Wigan Athletic Reserves	42	18	5	19	85	108	41
Astley Bridge	42	14	5	23	80	110	33
Hindsford	42	13	7	22	76	106	33
Stubshaw Cross Rovers	42	14	4	24	76	110	32
Padiham	42	12	7	23	81	112	31
Morecambe Reserves	42	13	4	25	68	139	30
Lomax	42	11	6	25	83	124	28
Chorley Reserves	42	11	5	26	72	120	27
ACI Horwich	42	11	5	26	76	137	27
Atherton Collieries	42	11	5	26	65	123	27
Darwen Reserves	42	10	4	28	64	121	24

Atherton Collieries moved to the Bolton Combination and ACI Horwich also left the league. South Liverpool joined from the Cheshire League and Crompton's Recreation also joined.

1951-52

Division One

Nelson	42	30	3	9	139	59	63
Lancaster City	42	24	7	11	89	69	55
Netherfield	42	22	10	10	108	63	54
Wigan Athletic	42	21	9	12	73	57	51
Morecambe	42	21	7	14	74	72	49
Ashton United	42	21	6	15	96	87	48
Rochdale Reserves	42	20	6	16	104	79	46
Barrow Reserves	42	19	8	15	73	66	46
Fleetwood	42	20	5	17	94	87	45
Bootle Athletic	42	17	8	17	73	73	42
Chorley	42	16	10	16	66	72	42
Horwich RMI	42	17	7	18	99	97	41
New Brighton	42	16	8	18	73	85	40
Blackpool "B"	42	18	4	20	72	88	40
Marine	42	13	12	17	77	85	38
Darwen	42	16	5	21	60	83	37
Oldham Athletic Reserves	42	13	9	20	87	91	35
Clitheroe	42	13	9	20	59	79	35
Southport Reserves	42	12	10	20	70	76	34
Rossendale United	42	13	5	24	77	95	31
St. Helens Town	*42*	*12*	*5*	*25*	*86*	*119*	*29*
Earlestown	*42*	*6*	*11*	*25*	*68*	*135*	*23*

1952-53

Division One

Wigan Athletic	42	27	13	2	124	45	67
Prescot Cables	42	25	5	12	83	46	55
Darwen	42	19	11	12	88	65	49
Marine	42	19	11	12	91	72	49
Nelson	42	20	8	14	86	72	48
Lancaster City	42	21	6	15	81	72	48
Horwich RMI	42	17	13	12	109	105	47
Ashton United	42	18	9	15	105	85	45
Netherfield	42	20	4	18	82	81	44
Southport Reserves	42	17	8	17	78	80	42
Morecambe	42	16	9	17	60	61	41
Bootle Athletic	42	16	8	18	64	64	40
Oldham Athletic Reserves	42	16	7	19	84	89	39
Rossendale United	42	16	7	19	84	92	39
Fleetwood	42	16	7	19	76	105	39
Chorley	42	16	5	21	81	87	37
New Brighton	42	14	9	19	61	70	37
Accrington Stanley Reserves	42	13	11	18	64	78	37
Rochdale Reserves	42	11	9	22	61	76	31
Barrow Reserves	42	10	11	21	57	80	31
Clitheroe	*42*	*11*	*9*	*22*	*69*	*115*	*31*
Blackpool "B"	*42*	*11*	*6*	*25*	*49*	*97*	*28*

Division Two

	P	W	D	L	F	A	Pts
Bolton Wanderers "B"	42	32	4	6	135	43	68
South Liverpool	42	32	2	8	164	61	66
Droylsden	42	28	6	8	145	66	62
St. Helens Town	42	26	5	11	137	75	57
Earlestown	42	23	6	13	110	69	52
Barnoldswick and District	42	23	6	13	125	108	52
Leyland Motors	42	21	9	12	84	67	51
Lytham	42	18	9	15	81	77	45
Crompton's Recreation	42	17	11	14	98	101	45
Astley Bridge	42	17	10	15	99	97	44
Bacup Borough	42	17	8	17	100	77	42
Lomax	42	17	6	19	82	103	40
Great Harwood	42	15	9	18	95	112	39
Padiham	42	15	8	19	87	101	38
Wigan Athletic Reserves	42	14	9	19	81	91	37
Chorley Reserves	42	14	9	19	94	112	37
Nelson Reserves	42	13	5	24	69	105	31
Netherfield Reserves	42	10	11	21	78	119	31
Stubshaw Cross Rovers	42	11	5	26	71	114	27
Darwen Reserves	42	6	10	26	52	105	22
Morecambe Reserves	42	7	8	27	68	141	22
Hindsford	42	5	6	31	70	181	16

Hindsford, Morecambe Reserves and Netherfield Reserves left the league. Burscough joined from the Liverpool County Combination while Burnley "A" and Prescot Cables Reserves also joined.

Division Two

	P	W	D	L	F	A	Pts
Burscough	42	33	4	5	155	38	70
Blackpool "B"	42	29	6	7	132	53	64
Burnley "A"	42	29	4	9	146	66	62
Earlestown	42	26	8	8	121	74	60
Droylsden	42	26	7	9	116	50	59
Nelson Reserves	42	25	4	13	101	85	54
Barnoldswick and District	42	21	8	13	120	95	50
Bacup Borough	42	20	8	14	99	86	48
Clitheroe	42	21	4	17	113	107	46
Leyland Motors	42	20	3	19	87	84	43
Lytham	42	17	9	16	66	78	43
Crompton's Recreation	42	19	3	20	88	111	41
Darwen Reserves	42	18	3	21	90	94	39
Prescot Cables Reserves	42	16	6	20	101	90	38
St. Helens Town	42	16	6	20	86	98	38
Chorley Reserves	42	12	8	22	81	111	32
Wigan Athletic Reserves	42	12	7	23	83	107	31
Padiham	42	12	3	27	60	118	27
Great Harwood	42	10	6	26	82	120	26
Lomax	42	12	1	29	73	139	25
Astley Bridge	42	7	4	31	65	160	18
Stubshaw Cross Rovers	42	4	2	36	51	152	10

Astley Bridge, Prescot Cables Reserves and Stubshaw Cross Rovers left the league. Blackburn Rovers "A" and Preston North End "A" both joined.

1953-54

Division One

	P	W	D	L	F	A	Pts
Wigan Athletic	40	31	4	5	110	48	66
Netherfield	40	20	11	9	104	73	51
Nelson	40	21	6	13	91	68	48
Horwich RMI	40	21	5	14	95	65	47
Darwen	40	18	9	13	80	49	45
Marine	40	17	6	17	70	77	40
South Liverpool	40	15	9	16	77	73	39
Oldham Athletic Reserves	40	17	5	18	77	81	39
Lancaster City	40	16	7	17	79	84	39
Southport Reserves	40	16	7	17	56	67	39
Accrington Stanley Reserves	40	17	3	20	91	88	37
Bolton Wanderers "B"	40	16	5	19	62	71	37
Rossendale United	40	14	8	18	87	89	36
Ashton United	40	17	2	21	74	85	36
Rochdale Reserves	40	14	8	18	61	80	36
Barrow Reserves	40	15	6	19	57	79	36
Fleetwood	40	14	7	19	78	88	35
Chorley	40	12	10	18	51	60	34
Morecambe	40	14	6	20	58	83	34
New Brighton	40	13	7	20	70	94	33
Prescot Cables	*40*	*13*	*7*	*20*	*63*	*89*	*33*

Bootle Athletic disbanded and their record was deleted.

1954-55

Division One

	P	W	D	L	F	A	Pts
Accrington Stanley Reserves	42	29	10	3	110	46	68
Rossendale United	42	24	6	12	123	84	54
Wigan Athletic	42	21	10	11	93	56	52
Burscough	42	22	8	12	75	49	52
Oldham Athletic Reserves	42	21	10	11	98	74	52
Blackpool "B"	42	22	5	15	101	59	49
Fleetwood	42	19	11	12	73	69	49
Horwich RMI	42	20	8	14	81	62	48
Morecambe	42	18	8	16	68	65	44
Marine	42	19	5	18	91	84	43
Netherfield	42	20	3	19	92	94	43
Darwen	42	15	13	14	64	79	43
Chorley	42	17	7	18	78	91	41
Lancaster City	42	16	9	17	68	84	41
Barrow Reserves	42	14	9	19	87	90	37
Nelson	42	14	8	20	82	84	36
Ashton United	42	13	9	20	75	107	35
Southport Reserves	42	12	9	21	74	79	33
Bolton Wanderers "B"	42	12	8	22	62	68	32
South Liverpool	42	12	8	22	67	105	32
Rochdale Reserves	42	8	9	25	58	92	25
New Brighton	42	6	3	33	48	147	15

Barrow Reserves, Blackpool "B", Bolton Wanderers "B", Oldham Athletic Reserves and Rochdale Reserves all left the league.

Division Two

Burnley "A"	38	33	1	4	137	39	67
Prescot Cables	**38**	**31**	**2**	**5**	**173**	**53**	**64**
Droylsden	38	29	3	6	128	54	61
Crompton's Recreation	38	23	6	9	119	71	52
Wigan Athletic Reserves	38	22	3	13	111	67	47
Bacup Borough	**38**	**22**	**3**	**13**	**105**	**75**	**47**
Clitheroe	38	19	4	15	86	75	42
Lytham	38	16	7	15	87	75	39
Leyland Motors	38	16	3	19	78	85	35
Blackburn Rovers "A"	38	15	5	18	84	93	35
Earlestown	38	14	7	17	81	93	35
Barnoldswick and District	38	14	6	18	78	89	34
Preston North End "A"	38	12	10	16	82	107	34
Nelson Reserves	38	10	8	20	56	87	28
Chorley Reserves	38	11	4	23	64	93	26
Great Harwood	38	11	4	23	67	114	26
Darwen Reserves	38	9	7	22	55	107	25
St. Helens Town	**38**	**10**	**5**	**23**	**48**	**115**	**25**
Lomax	38	9	3	26	63	117	21
Padiham	38	5	7	26	53	146	17

Barnoldswick & District, Blackburn Rovers Reserves, Burnley "A" and Preston North End "A" all left the league. Skelmersdale United joined from the Liverpool County Combination and Burscough Reserves, Prescot Cables Reserves, Rolls Royce and St. Annes Athletic also joined.

1955-56

Division One

Burscough	38	26	7	5	96	37	59
Horwich RMI	38	24	9	5	104	49	57
Accrington Stanley Reserves	38	20	10	8	87	56	50
Netherfield	38	21	7	10	95	55	49
Lancaster City	38	19	11	8	83	59	49
Wigan Athletic	38	18	10	10	80	56	46
New Brighton	38	18	8	12	78	57	44
Prescot Cables	38	19	6	13	104	92	44
Chorley	38	17	5	16	78	68	39
Marine	38	14	8	16	71	83	36
Southport Reserves	38	13	9	16	54	60	35
Ashton United	38	14	7	17	62	75	35
Darwen	38	13	8	17	66	85	34
Fleetwood	38	12	8	18	65	79	32
Nelson	38	12	8	18	60	89	32
Bacup Borough	38	10	9	19	58	76	29
Morecambe	38	12	5	21	62	94	29
South Liverpool	38	12	3	23	69	98	27
Rossendale United	*38*	*8*	*9*	*21*	*61*	*89*	*25*
St. Helens Town	*38*	*3*	*3*	*32*	*34*	*110*	*9*

Division Two

Skelmersdale United	**34**	**21**	**9**	**4**	**110**	**54**	**51**
Droylsden	**34**	**23**	**4**	**7**	**111**	**71**	**50**
Wigan Athletic Reserves	34	21	6	7	102	44	48
Burscough Reserves	34	23	1	10	91	49	47
Crompton's Recreation	34	20	7	7	94	55	47
Lytham	34	19	7	8	81	46	45
Clitheroe	34	19	4	11	82	69	42
Lomax	34	15	2	17	81	91	32
Chorley Reserves	34	11	6	17	59	76	28
Earlestown	34	10	6	18	60	77	26
Leyland Motors	34	10	6	18	65	87	26
Nelson Reserves	34	11	4	19	72	102	26
Prescot Cables Reserves	34	11	4	19	60	99	26
Great Harwood	34	9	7	18	65	74	25
St. Annes Athletic	34	10	5	19	63	97	25
Rolls Royce	34	10	4	20	77	109	24
Padiham	34	9	5	20	63	101	23
Darwen Reserves	34	6	9	19	43	78	21

1956-57

Division One

Prescot Cables	38	26	5	7	123	52	57
New Brighton	38	25	4	9	94	50	54
Morecambe	38	20	7	11	81	53	47
Horwich RMI	38	22	3	13	93	70	47
Burscough	38	19	7	12	86	58	45
Accrington Stanley Reserves	38	18	8	12	82	61	44
Ashton United	38	19	5	14	89	74	43
Chorley	38	15	8	15	74	74	38
Netherfield	38	15	8	15	73	73	38
Wigan Athletic	38	17	3	18	73	61	37
Lancaster City	38	14	8	16	71	91	36
Bacup Borough	38	12	11	15	80	88	35
Nelson	38	15	5	18	53	59	35
Skelmersdale United	38	14	6	18	67	82	34
South Liverpool	38	14	5	19	71	82	33
Fleetwood	38	13	7	18	56	70	33
Marine	38	12	8	18	62	84	32
Southport Reserves	38	12	7	19	62	88	31
Darwen	38	11	5	22	62	88	27
Droylsden	38	4	6	28	59	153	14

Division Two

Rossendale United	**34**	**25**	**3**	**6**	**111**	**34**	**53**
Crompton's Recreation	**34**	**19**	**7**	**8**	**72**	**45**	**45**
Clitheroe	34	17	10	7	90	56	44
Rolls Royce	34	20	4	10	100	74	44
Earlestown	34	20	1	13	95	86	41
St. Helens Town	34	15	9	10	87	67	39
Nelson Reserves	34	14	10	10	72	52	38
Lytham	34	15	8	11	73	59	38
Lomax	34	15	7	12	86	89	37
Prescot Cables Reserves	34	15	5	14	67	75	35
Burscough Reserves	34	14	4	16	72	75	32
Wigan Athletic Reserves	34	14	3	17	62	71	31
St. Annes Athletic	34	10	6	18	78	97	26
Darwen Reserves	34	10	5	19	48	101	25
Leyland Motors	34	10	3	21	57	81	23
Great Harwood	34	9	5	20	57	84	23
Chorley Reserves	34	9	4	21	52	95	22
Padiham	34	6	4	24	57	95	16

Burscough Reserves left. Glossop joined from the Manchester League and Northern Nomads joined from the Mid Cheshire League. Horwich RMI Reserves, Morecambe Reserves and Oldham Athletic Reserves also joined.

1957-58

Division One

Horwich RMI	42	28	7	7	109	47	63
Prescot Cables	42	26	9	7	117	49	61
New Brighton	42	23	8	11	85	61	54
Wigan Athletic	42	21	11	10	95	60	53
Accrington Stanley Reserves	42	23	6	13	92	71	52
Netherfield	42	20	9	13	87	70	49
Morecambe	42	18	12	12	66	50	48
Rossendale United	42	19	10	13	104	88	48
Chorley	42	20	7	15	123	85	47
Marine	42	17	7	18	74	103	41
Nelson	42	17	6	19	65	71	40
Ashton United	42	17	5	20	96	108	39
Lancaster City	42	15	7	20	74	93	37
Southport Reserves	42	16	5	21	69	102	37
Burscough	42	14	8	20	80	79	36
South Liverpool	42	15	6	21	94	102	36
Skelmersdale United	42	15	6	21	77	92	36
Darwen	42	14	6	22	71	104	34
Droylsden	42	13	7	22	75	99	33
Bacup Borough	42	12	8	22	88	115	32
Fleetwood	42	11	10	21	57	82	32
Crompton's Recreation	*42*	*5*	*6*	*31*	*51*	*118*	*16*

Accrington Stanley Reserves left the league.

Division Two

Oldham Athletic Reserves	38	28	4	6	135	45	60
Clitheroe	38	27	6	5	137	48	60
Earlestown	38	21	10	7	130	79	52
Padiham	38	20	9	9	84	64	49
Northern Nomads	38	21	6	11	88	58	48
Lytham	38	18	10	10	89	75	46
Chorley Reserves	38	19	7	12	103	64	45
Glossop	38	19	6	13	92	81	44
Wigan Athletic Reserves	38	18	7	13	101	64	43
St. Helens Town	38	17	7	14	87	67	41
Horwich RMI Reserves	38	17	6	15	80	87	40
Morecambe Reserves	38	13	8	17	68	86	34
Leyland Motors	38	14	4	20	81	98	32
Lomax	38	10	10	18	63	92	30
Rolls Royce	38	10	9	19	69	93	29
Prescot Cables Reserves	38	8	10	20	63	90	26
Nelson Reserves	38	6	11	21	65	134	23
St. Annes Athletic	38	7	8	23	68	117	22
Great Harwood	38	6	10	22	59	125	22
Darwen Reserves	38	6	2	30	36	131	14

Darwen Reserves and Prescot Cables Reserves left the league.
Netherfield Reserves and Rossendale United Reserves joined and St. Annes Athletic merged with Lytham.

1958-59

Division One

New Brighton	42	29	6	7	127	53	64
Prescot Cables	42	27	6	9	111	57	60
Horwich RMI	42	25	9	8	95	57	59
Skelmersdale United	42	22	10	10	107	69	54
Morecambe	42	22	9	11	77	44	53
Chorley	42	22	7	13	109	82	51
Netherfield	42	22	5	15	91	73	49
Bacup Borough	42	19	10	13	104	88	48
Nelson	42	19	9	14	82	74	47
Fleetwood	42	20	4	18	72	87	44
Marine	42	16	8	18	80	97	40
Burscough	42	15	9	18	60	69	39
South Liverpool	42	16	6	20	81	94	38
Darwen	42	16	6	20	75	93	38
Lancaster City	42	13	12	17	69	95	38
Rossendale United	42	16	5	21	88	89	37
Oldham Athletic Reserves	42	13	8	21	80	98	34
Wigan Athletic	42	12	7	23	60	84	31
Ashton United	42	12	6	24	69	103	30
Southport Reserves	42	10	8	24	70	104	28
Clitheroe	42	11	3	28	71	105	25
Droylsden	42	6	5	31	43	106	17

Division Two

Netherfield Reserves	34	23	7	4	110	46	53
Chorley Reserves	34	21	5	8	86	53	47
Earlestown	34	21	4	9	109	62	46
Lytham	34	18	8	8	89	72	44
Padiham	34	19	5	10	95	60	43
Northern Nomads	34	17	6	11	76	70	40
Leyland Motors	34	14	8	12	85	69	36
Crompton's Recreation	34	14	7	13	80	75	35
Glossop	34	14	6	14	75	64	34
St. Helens Town	34	15	3	16	73	62	33
Horwich RMI Reserves	34	13	4	17	71	73	30
Rossendale United Reserves	34	9	10	15	59	78	28
Lomax	34	12	4	18	71	105	28
Wigan Athletic Reserves	34	10	7	17	46	69	27
Great Harwood	34	10	6	18	62	100	26
Morecambe Reserves	34	10	5	19	56	86	25
Nelson Reserves	34	8	8	18	52	84	24
Rolls Royce	34	3	7	24	35	102	13

Rossendale United Reserves left the league and Lancaster City Reserves joined.

1959-60

Division One

Chorley	42	31	5	6	133	48	67
Wigan Athletic	42	27	6	9	101	51	60
New Brighton	42	28	4	10	103	54	60
Morecambe	42	28	2	12	103	54	58
Rossendale United	42	21	7	14	116	95	49
Burscough	42	20	8	14	94	73	48
Nelson	42	22	4	16	78	68	48
Netherfield	42	20	7	15	88	70	47
Marine	42	19	6	17	92	98	44
Horwich RMI	42	17	8	17	82	76	42
Prescot Cables	42	16	9	17	74	68	41
Oldham Athletic Reserves	42	16	7	19	64	66	39
Ashton United	42	13	12	17	61	86	38
Fleetwood	42	16	5	21	63	71	37
Bacup Borough	42	11	12	19	71	99	34
Earlestown	42	13	7	22	79	113	33
Lancaster City	42	12	9	21	73	107	33
Lytham	42	10	12	20	60	88	32
Skelmersdale United	42	13	6	23	59	97	32
Darwen	42	10	11	21	57	86	31
Southport Reserves	*42*	*9*	*10*	*23*	*57*	*92*	*28*
South Liverpool	*42*	*7*	*9*	*26*	*54*	*102*	*23*

Division Two

Clitheroe	34	26	3	5	81	28	55
Droylsden	34	25	3	6	106	55	53
Chorley Reserves	34	24	4	6	92	37	52
Glossop	34	19	3	12	75	57	41
St. Helens Town	34	17	7	10	63	52	41
Wigan Athletic Reserves	34	18	4	12	93	69	40
Morecambe Reserves	34	16	4	14	88	75	36
Crompton's Recreation	34	14	7	13	78	61	35
Padiham	34	16	3	15	74	65	35
Netherfield Reserves	34	13	8	13	77	74	34
Nelson Reserves	34	13	7	14	58	61	33
Horwich RMI Reserves	34	13	4	17	90	84	30
Rolls Royce	34	12	2	20	61	109	26
Leyland Motors	34	8	8	18	51	80	24
Lancaster City Reserves	34	9	4	21	48	88	22
Northern Nomads	34	8	3	23	52	91	19
Lomax	34	7	5	22	48	107	19
Great Harwood	34	7	3	24	44	86	17

Lomax left the league and Prescot Cables Reserves joined.

1960-61

Division One

Chorley	42	31	7	4	125	33	69
Nelson	42	29	7	6	106	47	65
Wigan Athletic	42	25	8	9	108	56	58
Burscough	42	25	8	9	76	49	58
Netherfield	42	24	8	10	123	71	56
Morecambe	42	23	5	14	96	76	51
Lancaster City	42	17	14	11	75	53	48
Prescot Cables	42	20	7	15	70	78	47
New Brighton	42	20	6	16	80	65	46
Marine	42	17	10	15	79	75	44
Clitheroe	42	17	7	18	84	88	41
Ashton United	42	18	5	19	78	88	41
Horwich RMI	42	14	7	21	75	94	35
Lytham	42	13	8	21	69	85	34
Skelmersdale United	42	12	9	21	71	85	33
Rossendale United	42	13	7	22	92	139	33
Oldham Athletic Reserves	42	13	6	23	71	84	32
Earlestown	42	12	8	22	74	103	32
Bacup Borough	42	11	9	22	76	96	31
Fleetwood	42	12	5	25	82	110	29
Droylsden	*42*	*10*	*5*	*27*	*73*	*132*	*25*
Darwen	42	7	2	33	45	121	16

Wigan Athletic moved to the Cheshire League.

Division Two

Chorley Reserves	34	24	6	4	120	56	54
Morecambe Reserves	34	21	8	5	92	46	50
Padiham	**34**	**21**	**6**	**7**	**94**	**55**	**48**
Wigan Athletic Reserves	34	22	3	9	105	47	47
Southport Reserves	**34**	**21**	**5**	**8**	**86**	**50**	**47**
South Liverpool	34	21	4	9	116	60	46
Northern Nomads	34	16	6	12	91	80	38
Netherfield Reserves	34	16	5	13	89	81	37
St. Helens Town	34	15	5	14	69	67	35
Glossop	34	13	5	16	64	86	31
Nelson Reserves	34	13	3	18	55	78	29
Leyland Motors	34	10	7	17	66	86	27
Crompton's Recreation	34	10	6	18	67	93	26
Horwich RMI Reserves	34	10	6	18	67	106	26
Prescot Cables Reserves	34	10	4	20	66	74	24
Great Harwood	34	8	5	21	56	104	21
Rolls Royce	34	6	1	27	50	117	13
Lancaster City Reserves	34	4	5	25	44	111	13

Wigan Athletic Reserves left the league. Wigan Rovers joined from the Cheshire League and Accrington Stanley Reserves, Barrow Reserves and Lucas Sports Club also joined.

1961-62

Division One

Morecambe	42	32	6	4	143	51	70
Netherfield	42	27	10	5	143	67	64
Horwich RMI	42	26	9	7	110	48	61
Burscough	42	26	8	8	122	68	60
Chorley	42	24	9	9	107	71	57
Rossendale United	42	22	6	14	114	89	50
Oldham Athletic Reserves	42	21	8	13	89	71	50
New Brighton	42	23	3	16	105	57	49
Lancaster City	42	18	12	12	75	63	48
Southport Reserves	42	18	9	15	102	77	45
Nelson	42	20	5	17	86	71	45
Clitheroe	42	18	9	15	85	83	45
Earlestown	42	17	6	19	89	102	40
Marine	42	15	7	20	94	99	37
Prescot Cables	42	14	9	19	66	83	37
Fleetwood	42	11	11	20	84	89	33
Skelmersdale United	42	12	7	23	62	103	31
Lytham	42	9	7	26	67	127	25
Darwen	42	8	9	25	56	119	25
Leyland Motors	42	6	8	28	67	126	20
Bacup Borough	42	6	4	32	52	149	16
Padiham	*42*	*4*	*8*	*30*	*51*	*154*	*16*

Oldham Athletic Reserves left the league.

Division Two

Ashton United	**36**	**29**	**4**	**3**	**124**	**32**	**62**
South Liverpool	**36**	**25**	**4**	**7**	**110**	**41**	**54**
Droylsden	36	25	3	8	126	46	53
Morecambe Reserves	36	24	3	9	91	63	51
Glossop	36	20	5	11	85	62	45
Barrow Reserves	36	20	4	12	81	46	44
Chorley Reserves	36	17	7	12	79	58	41
Netherfield Reserves	36	16	8	12	92	66	40
Nelson Reserves	36	16	6	14	87	62	38
St. Helens Town	36	13	8	15	67	62	34
Wigan Rovers	36	14	6	16	67	82	34
Lancaster City Reserves	36	14	2	20	77	80	30
Rolls Royce	36	12	6	18	100	108	30
Horwich RMI Reserves	36	13	3	20	77	85	29
Crompton's Recreation	36	12	3	21	73	109	27
Northern Nomads	36	10	6	20	68	94	26
Prescot Cables Reserves	36	10	4	22	63	107	24
Great Harwood	36	9	2	25	76	129	20
Lucas Sports Club	36	1	0	35	28	239	2

Accrington Stanley resigned from the Football League – Division Three (North) on 11th March 1962 and withdrew their reserves from Division Two of the Lancashire Combination at the same time. Their record was deleted. Their first team was subsequently accepted into Division Two of the Lancashire Combination for the 1962-63 season. Lucas Sports Club left the league and Blackpool Mechanics and Vulcan Institute joined.

1962-63

Division One

Morecambe	42	31	6	5	153	40	68
Chorley	42	31	6	5	137	59	68
Ashton United	42	25	8	9	101	57	58
Horwich RMI	42	25	5	12	107	59	55
Netherfield	42	23	7	12	125	69	53
Lancaster City	42	23	6	13	96	61	52
Marine	42	22	6	14	92	73	50
Nelson	42	22	4	16	95	81	48
Fleetwood	42	23	1	18	97	71	47
South Liverpool	42	20	3	19	76	65	43
New Brighton	42	18	5	19	83	76	41
Southport Reserves	42	17	7	18	80	76	41
Clitheroe	42	17	6	19	80	81	40
Rossendale United	42	17	6	19	103	138	40
Skelmersdale United	42	15	5	22	73	90	35
Burscough	42	15	5	22	68	93	35
Bacup Borough	42	14	6	22	81	110	34
Earlestown	42	14	3	25	88	132	31
Prescot Cables	42	13	5	24	71	108	31
Leyland Motors	42	9	7	26	54	106	25
Darwen	*42*	*5*	*6*	*31*	*41*	*117*	*16*
Lytham	*42*	*5*	*3*	*34*	*34*	*173*	*13*

Earlestown moved to the Liverpool County Combination.

Division Two

Crompton's Recreation	**38**	**29**	**5**	**4**	**138**	**52**	**63**
Droylsden	**38**	**27**	**6**	**5**	**124**	**31**	**60**
Morecambe Reserves	38	23	6	9	93	46	52
Barrow Reserves	**38**	**24**	**3**	**11**	**91**	**52**	**51**
Great Harwood	38	22	7	9	121	77	51
Horwich RMI Reserves	38	21	6	11	100	58	48
Chorley Reserves	38	21	5	12	94	63	47
Accrington Stanley	38	19	7	12	99	66	45
Glossop	38	15	9	14	75	73	39
St. Helens Town	38	16	6	16	59	58	38
Blackpool Mechanics	38	14	10	14	67	84	38
Rolls Royce	38	13	8	17	82	101	34
Netherfield Reserves	38	11	10	17	72	84	32
Wigan Rovers	38	10	10	18	73	98	30
Northern Nomads	38	10	8	20	64	93	28
Padiham	38	11	6	21	70	109	28
Lancaster City Reserves	38	9	6	23	67	111	24
Nelson Reserves	38	8	4	26	47	114	20
Vulcan Institute	38	9	1	28	74	137	19
Prescot Cables Reserves	38	5	3	30	40	143	13

Nelson Reserves, Prescot Cables Reserves and Rolls Royce left the league. Radcliffe Borough joined from the Manchester League and Kirkby Town also joined.

1963-64

Division One

Chorley	42	27	7	8	114	51	61
Netherfield	42	26	8	8	123	64	60
New Brighton	42	24	10	8	83	45	58
Horwich RMI	42	24	8	10	91	51	56
Ashton United	42	20	10	12	91	65	50
Lancaster City	42	21	8	13	90	69	50
Droylsden	42	21	7	14	80	58	49
Nelson	42	23	3	16	84	73	49
South Liverpool	42	19	9	14	88	62	47
Morecambe	42	19	8	15	93	71	46
Skelmersdale United	42	21	4	17	88	76	46
Southport Reserves	42	17	6	19	68	75	40
Bacup Borough	42	17	5	20	59	68	39
Marine	42	15	8	19	73	83	38
Burscough	42	11	11	20	80	84	33
Rossendale United	42	12	9	21	70	114	33
Fleetwood	42	10	13	19	54	88	33
Prescot Cables	42	11	9	22	66	98	31
Clitheroe	42	10	10	22	59	88	30
Leyland Motors	42	11	7	24	57	118	29
Barrow Reserves	42	8	9	25	56	109	25
Crompton's Recreation	42	8	5	29	58	115	21

Ashton United moved to the Midland League and Crompton's Recreation also left the league. Prescot Cables changed their name to Prescot Town.

Division Two

Accrington Stanley	**34**	**23**	**6**	**5**	**90**	**40**	**52**
Chorley Reserves	34	21	7	6	102	45	49
Great Harwood	**34**	**21**	**4**	**9**	**117**	**48**	**46**
St. Helens Town	34	21	3	10	95	52	45
Netherfield Reserves	34	20	4	10	73	48	44
Wigan Rovers	34	18	6	10	81	61	42
Horwich RMI Reserves	34	17	6	11	93	47	40
Glossop	34	17	5	12	73	61	39
Darwen	34	14	10	10	77	59	38
Northern Nomads	34	15	4	15	73	64	34
Morecambe Reserves	34	13	7	14	63	47	33
Radcliffe Borough	34	13	7	14	84	74	33
Lancaster City Reserves	34	11	4	19	57	80	26
Blackpool Mechanics	34	10	6	18	54	94	26
Lytham	34	8	7	19	48	108	23
Kirkby Town	34	9	2	23	59	110	20
Vulcan Institute	34	4	5	25	49	134	13
Padiham	34	4	1	29	38	154	9

Northern Nomads and Vulcan Institute left the league. Guinness Exports joined from the Liverpool County Combination and Accrington Stanley Reserves and Fleetwood Reserves also joined.

1964-65

Division One

Netherfield	42	30	6	6	143	53	66
Chorley	42	27	9	6	130	55	63
Morecambe	42	30	2	10	132	50	62
Horwich RMI	42	24	13	5	128	53	61
South Liverpool	42	27	5	10	97	67	59
Droylsden	42	23	6	13	81	67	52
New Brighton	42	21	9	12	82	48	51
Marine	42	21	6	15	90	69	48
Barrow Reserves	42	19	9	14	80	77	47
Great Harwood	42	19	7	16	85	83	45
Lancaster City	42	18	6	18	75	65	42
Fleetwood	42	14	12	16	68	93	40
Nelson	42	15	7	20	68	108	37
Skelmersdale United	42	15	6	21	83	84	36
Bacup Borough	42	16	2	24	61	94	34
Leyland Motors	42	13	7	22	74	105	33
Clitheroe	42	13	6	23	60	90	32
Rossendale United	42	13	6	23	75	114	32
Southport Reserves	42	11	5	26	51	99	27
Burscough	42	11	3	28	68	90	25
Accrington Stanley	*42*	*7*	*4*	*31*	*48*	*127*	*18*
Prescot Town	42	4	6	32	44	132	14

New Brighton moved to the Cheshire League.

Division Two

Netherfield Reserves	32	22	6	4	103	32	50
Chorley Reserves	32	22	3	7	90	36	47
St. Helens Town	**32**	**21**	**4**	**7**	**77**	**36**	**46**
Guinness Exports	**32**	**18**	**9**	**5**	**88**	**35**	**45**
Kirkby Town	32	17	9	6	90	45	43
Radcliffe Borough	32	17	6	9	77	44	40
Horwich RMI Reserves	32	17	4	11	101	58	38
Wigan Rovers	32	15	8	9	65	54	38
Blackpool Mechanics	32	16	3	13	62	47	35
Morecambe Reserves	32	13	9	10	68	62	35
Darwen	32	15	5	12	63	58	35
Lytham	32	14	4	14	58	52	32
Glossop	32	10	2	20	49	80	22
Fleetwood Reserves	32	5	2	25	42	121	12
Lancaster City Reserves	32	5	2	25	33	102	12
Padiham	32	3	2	27	30	122	8
Accrington Stanley Reserves	32	2	2	28	30	142	6

Accrington Stanley Reserves left the league.

1965-66

Division One

South Liverpool	42	29	6	7	128	56	64
Chorley	42	24	12	6	121	56	60
Skelmersdale United	42	28	4	10	120	62	60
Marine	42	27	4	11	129	66	58
Horwich RMI	42	26	3	13	100	58	55
Netherfield	42	20	13	9	104	70	53
Morecambe	42	19	12	11	105	65	50
Lancaster City	42	19	10	13	77	59	48
Clitheroe	42	20	8	14	77	73	48
Great Harwood	42	18	10	14	81	73	46
Barrow Reserves	42	19	8	15	88	85	46
Droylsden	42	15	12	15	80	78	42
Fleetwood	42	18	5	19	95	101	41
Guinness Exports	42	14	5	23	74	103	33
Leyland Motors	42	14	5	23	52	99	33
Burscough	42	13	6	23	76	89	32
St. Helens Town	42	11	5	26	65	125	27
Rossendale United	42	9	9	24	48	97	27
Bacup Borough	42	11	5	26	57	126	27
Southport Reserves	42	9	7	26	65	98	25
Nelson	*42*	*10*	*5*	*27*	*56*	*121*	*25*
Prescot Town	*42*	*8*	*8*	*26*	*66*	*104*	*24*

Division Two

Wigan Rovers	26	20	5	1	91	22	45
Chorley Reserves	26	17	4	5	60	31	38
Darwen	26	15	2	9	52	33	32
Glossop	26	12	5	9	42	40	29
Radcliffe Borough	26	11	7	8	54	54	29
Netherfield Reserves	26	10	6	10	51	45	26
Kirkby Town	26	8	10	8	36	35	26
Horwich RMI Reserves	26	11	2	13	53	53	24
Morecambe Reserves	26	9	5	12	52	54	23
Fleetwood Reserves	26	8	6	12	53	65	22
Blackpool Mechanics	26	6	8	12	33	48	20
Lytham	26	7	6	13	35	54	20
Lancaster City Reserves	26	5	6	15	42	70	16
Padiham	26	5	4	17	34	84	14

Accrington Stanley disbanded and their record was deleted. Glossop moved to the Manchester League. Ashton United joined from the Midland League while Dukinfield Town and Oldham Athletic Reserves also joined.

1966-67

Division One

Morecambe	41	30	9	2	90	24	69
Horwich RMI	42	27	9	6	88	37	63
Netherfield	42	27	8	7	122	54	62
Chorley	42	23	9	10	97	59	55
Fleetwood	42	22	10	10	103	62	54
South Liverpool	42	24	6	12	94	61	54
Marine	42	20	9	13	84	69	49
Wigan Rovers	42	16	15	11	78	64	47
Skelmersdale United	41	20	5	16	99	77	45
Lancaster City	42	18	6	18	66	72	42
Southport Reserves	42	16	8	18	72	77	40
Bacup Borough	42	15	9	18	53	57	39
Droylsden	42	14	9	19	59	68	37
Burscough	42	16	5	21	55	85	37
St. Helens Town	42	13	9	20	66	76	35
Guinness Exports	42	12	11	19	62	87	35
Barrow Reserves	42	13	8	21	80	84	34
Rossendale United	42	12	8	22	64	90	32
Clitheroe	42	10	10	22	56	93	30
Great Harwood	42	11	5	26	56	101	27
Darwen	42	6	12	24	56	102	24
Leyland Motors	42	4	4	34	28	129	12

Skelmersdale United suffered from fixture congestion after reaching the F.A. Amateur Cup Final and were not able to fulfil their final fixture against Morecambe.

Division Two

Kirkby Town	30	22	7	1	84	26	51
Prescot Town	30	20	4	6	67	35	44
Ashton United	30	17	4	9	74	61	38
Netherfield Reserves	30	15	7	8	74	55	37
Radcliffe Borough	30	14	8	8	77	65	36
Morecambe Reserves	30	16	2	12	56	48	34
Oldham Athletic Reserves	30	12	8	10	68	40	32
Horwich RMI Reserves	30	13	5	12	52	52	31
Chorley Reserves	30	11	6	13	52	55	28
Blackpool Mechanics	30	11	4	15	42	61	26
Dukinfield Town	30	10	5	15	56	69	25
Lancaster City Reserves	30	6	10	14	48	73	22
Nelson	30	8	5	17	44	73	21
Lytham	30	8	3	19	36	58	19
Fleetwood Reserves	30	8	3	19	38	66	19
Padiham	30	6	5	19	52	83	17

Wigan Athletic Reserves joined the league.

1967-68

Division One

Morecambe	42	28	9	5	112	41	65
Guinness Exports	42	29	6	7	85	37	64
Skelmersdale United	42	23	10	9	94	49	56
Fleetwood	42	22	10	10	72	43	54
Marine	42	21	10	11	78	60	52
Great Harwood	42	20	11	11	71	50	51
South Liverpool	42	21	7	14	76	53	49
Netherfield	42	20	9	13	103	88	49
Horwich RMI	42	19	9	14	79	52	47
Lancaster City	42	18	11	13	72	67	47
Chorley	42	17	9	16	72	65	43
St. Helens Town	42	16	8	18	68	65	40
Kirkby Town	42	13	13	16	54	60	39
Burscough	42	13	10	19	53	64	36
Droylsden	42	13	10	19	52	84	36
Wigan Rovers	42	14	6	22	56	69	34
Clitheroe	42	14	6	22	58	86	34
Southport Reserves	42	12	9	21	59	66	33
Barrow Reserves	42	13	4	25	55	78	30
Prescot Town	42	12	1	29	53	109	25
Bacup Borough	42	8	6	28	34	105	22
Rossendale United	42	6	6	30	50	115	18

Chorley, Fleetwood, Morecambe, Netherfield and South Liverpool all left to become founder members of the Northern Premier League and Droylsden, Guinness Exports, Horwich RMI and Skelmersdale United all moved to the Cheshire League. Southport Reserves also left. Formby joined from the Liverpool County Combination and Prestwich Heys joined from the Manchester League.

Division Two

Oldham Athletic Reserves	32	23	7	2	102	21	53
Darwen	32	21	6	5	72	35	48
Morecambe Reserves	32	17	7	8	77	50	41
Ashton United	32	17	5	10	67	52	39
Radcliffe Borough	32	17	4	11	62	52	38
Leyland Motors	32	15	5	12	55	66	35
Dukinfield Town	32	14	5	13	69	54	33
Chorley Reserves	32	13	7	12	68	55	33
Fleetwood Reserves	32	13	7	12	71	71	33
Blackpool Mechanics	32	11	8	13	62	58	30
Wigan Athletic Reserves	32	13	3	16	67	66	29
Nelson	32	12	5	15	63	67	29
Netherfield Reserves	32	8	6	18	63	92	22
Lancaster City Reserves	32	8	6	18	45	85	22
Lytham	32	7	7	18	42	82	21
Horwich RMI Reserves	32	5	9	18	50	82	19
Padiham	32	7	5	20	43	90	19

Ashton United moved to the Cheshire League while Chorley Reserves, Fleetwood Reserves, Horwich RMI Reserves, Lancaster City Reserves, Morecambe Reserves, Netherfield Reserves, Oldham Athletic Reserves and Padiham also left the league.

The remaining 8 clubs were promoted to Division One and Division Two closed down so that the Lancashire Combination continued with a single division.

1968-69

Great Harwood	42	33	6	3	115	35	72
Kirkby Town	42	27	11	4	126	36	65
Lancaster City	42	28	3	11	120	58	59
Burscough	42	23	11	8	110	51	57
Prestwich Heys	42	24	7	11	109	58	55
St. Helens Town	42	22	10	10	84	44	54
Marine	42	22	9	11	95	48	53
Darwen	42	17	9	16	59	64	43
Blackpool Mechanics	42	16	10	16	76	68	42
Formby	42	17	7	18	82	72	41
Wigan Rovers	42	17	7	18	68	82	41
Radcliffe Borough	42	16	8	18	86	72	40
Rossendale United	42	16	8	18	68	83	40
Clitheroe	42	15	8	19	68	74	38
Wigan Athletic Reserves	42	13	9	20	73	80	35
Prescot Town	42	12	11	19	49	80	35
Barrow Reserves	42	11	10	21	51	82	32
Nelson	42	12	8	22	66	110	32
Dukinfield Town	42	9	11	22	63	98	29
Leyland Motors	42	9	11	22	44	90	29
Bacup Borough	42	9	3	30	33	109	21
Lytham	42	3	5	34	23	174	11

Great Harwood were promoted to the Northern Premier League and Marine moved to the Cheshire League. Barrow Reserves also left. Chorley joined, having been relegated from the Northern Premier League.

1969-70

Burscough	38	30	4	4	116	35	64
Prestwich Heys	38	28	5	5	127	46	61
Chorley	38	27	6	5	112	35	60
Kirkby Town	38	25	9	4	98	38	59
Radcliffe Borough	38	22	7	9	84	45	51
Lancaster City	38	22	6	10	84	43	50
Rossendale United	38	22	4	12	96	50	48
St. Helens Town	38	21	4	13	69	42	46
Blackpool Mechanics	38	20	4	14	78	56	44
Darwen	38	15	11	12	78	67	41
Bacup Borough	38	18	5	15	78	72	41
Formby	38	13	7	18	48	71	33
Wigan Athletic Reserves	38	10	9	19	44	61	29
Prescot Town	38	10	6	22	58	85	26
Dukinfield Town	38	6	11	21	49	96	23
Nelson	38	8	5	25	60	106	21
Clitheroe	38	6	7	25	40	107	19
Leyland Motors	38	5	8	25	37	96	18
Lytham	38	6	4	28	29	109	16
Wigan Rovers	38	1	8	29	22	147	10

Chorley, Kirkby Town and Lancaster City were promoted to the Northern Premier League. Burscough and Rossendale United moved to the Cheshire League. Accrington Stanley (1968) joined as a newly formed club.

1970-71

Prestwich Heys	30	23	3	4	85	35	49
Dukinfield Town	30	19	7	4	65	36	45
Radcliffe Borough	30	16	9	5	64	35	41
Wigan Athletic Reserves	30	18	3	9	68	35	39
Formby	30	15	7	8	47	35	37
Accrington Stanley (1968)	30	15	5	10	65	52	35
Blackpool Mechanics	30	14	6	10	49	38	34
Clitheroe	30	11	8	11	52	63	30
Prescot Town	30	11	6	13	37	40	28
Nelson	30	9	8	13	55	59	26
Darwen	30	10	6	14	44	57	26
St. Helens Town	30	8	9	13	36	42	25
Bacup Borough	30	9	4	17	48	66	22
Leyland Motors	30	8	5	17	39	69	21
Lytham	30	5	5	20	38	78	15
Wigan Rovers	30	2	3	25	26	78	7

Formby, Prestwich Heys and Radcliffe Borough all moved to the Cheshire League and Lytham moved to the West Lancashire League. Wigan Athletic Reserves also left. Ashton Town joined from the Warrington League, Atherton Collieries joined from the Bolton Combination while Corinthians and Kirkby Town Reserves also joined.

1971-72

St. Helens Town	28	20	7	1	56	16	47
Accrington Stanley (1968)	28	18	5	5	81	40	41
Blackpool Mechanics	28	17	4	7	63	31	38
Clitheroe	28	16	5	7	52	45	37
Ashton Town	28	15	4	9	59	45	34
Dukinfield Town	28	12	9	7	57	41	33
Nelson	28	13	5	10	69	49	31
Prescot Town	28	9	9	10	39	35	27
Darwen	28	10	6	12	48	57	26
Atherton Collieries	28	9	7	12	45	51	25
Leyland Motors	28	8	5	15	54	66	21
Bacup Borough	28	9	1	18	55	74	19
Kirkby Town Reserves	28	6	6	16	32	59	18
Wigan Rovers	28	6	3	19	34	65	15
Corinthians	28	3	2	23	24	94	8

Kirkby Town were relegated from the Northern Premier League, replacing their reserves in the Lancashire Combination. Corinthians left the league. Ford Motors, Great Harwood Reserves, Lomond, Maghull, Skelmersdale United Reserves and Wren Rovers all joined.

1972-73

Darwen	38	30	4	4	105	39	64
Bacup Borough	38	27	5	6	101	36	59
Accrington Stanley (1968)	38	26	7	5	96	36	59
St. Helens Town	38	22	9	7	55	29	53
Skelmersdale United Reserves	38	24	5	9	76	46	53
Wren Rovers	38	18	10	10	62	46	46
Blackpool Mechanics	38	15	14	9	62	45	44
Dukinfield Town	38	19	3	16	63	65	41
Ashton Town	38	16	5	17	60	60	37
Clitheroe	38	14	8	16	73	79	36
Leyland Motors	38	13	8	17	41	56	34
Nelson	38	12	7	19	60	76	31
Prescot Town	38	10	9	19	46	72	29
Kirkby Town	38	11	7	20	43	68	29
Maghull	38	9	9	20	49	64	27
Ford Motors	38	11	5	22	49	83	27
Atherton Collieries	38	10	7	21	46	84	27
Lomond	38	6	12	20	28	73	24
Great Harwood Reserves	38	7	7	24	55	77	21
Wigan Rovers	38	5	9	24	41	78	19
					1211	1212	

Wigan Rovers left the league and Ellesmere Port Town joined after being relegated from the Northern Premier League.

1973-74

Accrington Stanley (1968)	38	29	5	4	80	26	63
Darwen	38	24	10	4	89	38	58
Bacup Borough	38	24	10	4	76	35	58
Skelmersdale United Reserves	38	22	6	10	76	34	50
St. Helens Town	38	24	2	12	73	34	50
Wren Rovers	38	17	11	10	68	47	45
Maghull	38	18	8	12	59	42	44
Blackpool Mechanics	38	18	7	13	52	47	43
Dukinfield Town	38	14	12	12	59	56	40
Leyland Motors	38	14	11	13	60	55	39
Clitheroe	38	16	6	16	73	53	38
Atherton Collieries	38	14	10	14	68	63	38
Great Harwood Reserves	38	12	8	18	54	68	32
Kirkby Town	38	10	9	19	54	70	29
Ashton Town	38	10	9	19	46	64	29
Ellesmere Port Town	38	10	9	19	40	67	29
Lomond	38	6	9	23	25	72	21
Prescot Town	38	6	6	26	34	89	18
Ford Motors	38	5	8	25	30	81	18
Nelson	38	6	6	26	36	111	18

Lomond left the league and Bootle joined from the Liverpool County Combination.

1974-75

Darwen	38	26	8	4	97	36	60
Blackpool Mechanics	38	25	9	4	70	21	59
Bootle	38	19	14	5	75	30	52
Bacup Borough	38	20	12	6	69	31	52
St. Helens Town	38	22	5	11	69	40	49
Nelson	38	19	8	11	77	50	46
Kirkby Town	38	17	10	11	65	49	44
Leyland Motors	38	19	5	14	76	51	43
Clitheroe	38	17	8	13	70	51	42
Accrington Stanley (1968)	38	17	7	14	75	55	41
Maghull	38	16	8	14	60	58	40
Wren Rovers	38	13	8	17	47	72	34
Great Harwood Reserves	38	14	5	19	58	75	33
Ford Motors	38	10	12	16	49	71	32
Skelmersdale United Reserves	38	10	7	21	52	77	27
Atherton Collieries	38	8	10	20	46	80	26
Dukinfield Town	38	10	5	23	49	86	25
Ellesmere Port Town	38	8	9	21	27	57	25
Prescot Town	38	7	6	25	53	107	20
Ashton Town	38	3	4	31	38	125	10

Darwen and St. Helens Town moved to the Cheshire League, Dukinfield Town moved to the Manchester League, Prescot Town moved to th Mid Cheshire League and Ellesmere Port Town disbanded while Great Harwood Reserves also left. Colne Dynamoes and Lytham joined from the West Lancashire League while Morecambe Reserves and Wigan Athletic Reserves also joined.

1975-76

Bootle	34	28	3	3	82	29	59
Accrington Stanley (1968)	34	25	5	4	104	36	55
Kirkby Town	34	18	9	7	69	38	45
Blackpool Mechanics	34	18	9	7	48	32	45
Nelson	34	18	5	11	59	35	41
Colne Dynamoes	34	13	10	11	59	55	36
Maghull	34	14	6	14	54	62	34
Lytham	34	11	9	14	53	54	31
Clitheroe	34	11	9	14	51	54	31
Bacup Borough	34	9	12	13	44	59	30
Ford Motors	34	10	10	14	37	50	30
Wren Rovers	34	10	10	14	37	51	30
Skelmersdale United Reserves	34	11	8	15	35	56	30
Morecambe Reserves	34	12	3	19	50	57	27
Leyland Motors	34	9	9	16	46	54	27
Wigan Athletic Reserves	34	11	3	20	37	57	25
Atherton Collieries	34	6	8	20	48	72	20
Ashton Town	34	6	4	24	33	95	16

Skelmersdale United were relegated from the Northern Premier League and replaced their reserves in the Lancashire Combination.

1976-77

Bootle	34	30	2	2	100	21	62
Kirkby Town	34	28	3	3	89	18	59
Accrington Stanley (1968)	34	25	7	2	86	20	57
Wren Rovers	34	17	11	6	49	33	45
Lytham	34	17	7	10	58	42	41
Maghull	34	13	11	10	55	50	37
Colne Dynamoes	34	14	6	14	54	53	34
Nelson	34	15	3	16	48	46	33
Blackpool Mechanics	34	13	6	15	53	49	32
Skelmersdale United	34	11	8	15	43	49	30
Bacup Borough	34	9	8	17	46	65	26
Atherton Collieries	34	9	8	17	50	79	26
Wigan Athletic Reserves	34	9	7	18	43	53	25
Clitheroe	34	10	5	19	43	63	25
Ford Motors	34	7	9	18	34	68	23
Ashton Town	34	9	2	23	37	91	20
Morecambe Reserves	34	7	5	22	46	87	19
Leyland Motors	34	7	4	23	43	90	18

Wigan Athletic Reserves left the league and Padiham joined.

1977-78

Accrington Stanley (1968)	34	25	7	2	99	32	57
Wren Rovers	34	22	8	4	64	27	52
Bootle	34	19	9	6	74	32	47
Kirkby Town	34	19	6	9	72	38	44
Colne Dynamoes	34	18	5	11	80	42	41
Maghull	34	15	11	8	57	41	41
Leyland Motors	34	15	10	9	63	47	40
Skelmersdale United	34	14	10	10	53	41	38
Atherton Collieries	34	14	8	12	63	52	36
Lytham	34	13	8	13	54	66	34
Ford Motors	34	11	8	15	57	64	30
Padiham	34	12	6	16	51	60	30
Bacup Borough	34	12	5	17	43	63	29
Blackpool Mechanics	34	10	6	18	38	65	26
Morecambe Reserves	34	6	9	19	36	69	21
Clitheroe	34	7	6	21	41	87	20
Ashton Town	34	4	5	25	32	89	13
Nelson	34	4	5	25	33	94	13
					1010	1009	

Accrington Stanley (1968), Ashton Town, Atherton Collieries, Bootle, Ford Motors, Kirkby Town, Maghull, and Skelmersdale United all moved to the Cheshire League while Morecambe Reserves also left. Ashton Athletic joined from the Warrington League, Daisy Hill joined from the Bolton Combination, Whitworth Valley joined from the South-East Lancashire League and Wigan Rovers joined from the West Lancashire League. Barrow Reserves and Chorley Reserves also joined.

1978-79

Wren Rovers	28	21	5	2	51	10	47
Leyland Motors	28	18	6	4	63	26	42
Whitworth Valley	28	15	8	5	49	35	38
Colne Dynamoes	28	13	8	7	50	32	34
Bacup Borough	28	14	6	8	48	36	34
Padiham	28	14	5	9	40	35	33
Lytham	28	11	8	9	41	34	30
Nelson	28	7	10	11	31	33	24
Blackpool Mechanics	28	7	10	11	21	33	24
Chorley Reserves	28	6	11	11	34	37	23
Wigan Rovers	28	6	9	13	25	40	21
Barrow Reserves	28	6	8	14	25	39	20
Daisy Hill	28	5	10	13	26	45	20
Clitheroe	28	7	5	16	31	46	19
Ashton Athletic	28	3	5	20	17	67	11
					552	548	

Great Harwood Town joined from the West Lancashire League and Vulcan Newton joined from the Warrington League.

1979-80

Clitheroe	32	17	12	3	55	25	46
Colne Dynamoes	32	18	8	6	54	35	44
Barrow Reserves	32	16	9	7	56	30	41
Great Harwood Town	32	15	11	6	53	29	41
Vulcan Newton	32	14	12	6	60	34	40
Bacup Borough	32	16	8	8	63	41	40
Padiham	32	15	8	9	49	34	38
Chorley Reserves	32	11	13	8	42	38	35
Whitworth Valley	32	13	9	10	52	53	35
Leyland Motors	32	10	14	8	50	36	34
Lytham	32	10	9	13	42	63	29
Daisy Hill	32	11	6	15	35	40	28
Wren Rovers	32	9	8	15	38	48	26
Nelson	32	7	8	17	46	67	22
Blackpool Mechanics	32	5	9	18	27	56	19
Ashton Athletic	32	7	3	22	25	68	17
Wigan Rovers	32	2	5	25	29	79	9

Leyland Motors moved to the Cheshire League and Barrow Reserves also left the league. Caernarfon Town joined from the Welsh League (North), Chadderton joined from the Manchester League and Manchester Polytechnic also joined.

1981-82

Caernarfon Town	34	23	8	3	71	27	54
Colne Dynamoes	34	24	4	6	72	33	52
Nelson	34	19	7	8	66	44	45
Wren Rovers	34	18	7	9	67	47	43
Clitheroe	34	13	16	5	67	40	42
Great Harwood Town	34	16	8	10	61	47	40
Chadderton	34	17	5	12	62	43	39
Blackpool Mechanics	34	14	9	11	47	34	37
Vulcan Newton	34	13	8	13	61	56	34
Padiham	34	14	6	14	47	47	34
Lytham	34	11	11	12	74	66	33
Oldham Dew	34	12	6	16	48	61	30
Wigan Rovers	34	11	7	16	44	53	29
Bacup Borough	34	9	8	17	47	77	26
Whitworth Valley	34	5	12	17	42	68	22
Daisy Hill	34	5	9	20	31	64	19
Bolton ST	34	7	4	23	40	86	18
Ashton Athletic	34	4	7	23	22	76	15

At the end of the season, the Lancashire Combination merged with the Cheshire County League to form the North West Counties League and all of its members joined this new league.

1980-81

Wren Rovers	34	24	7	3	75	25	55
Colne Dynamoes	34	21	5	8	57	30	47
Great Harwood Town	34	18	7	9	68	42	43
Padiham	34	16	11	7	57	40	41
Chorley Reserves	34	15	11	8	53	42	41
Caernarfon Town	34	15	7	12	55	37	37
Vulcan Newton	34	15	6	13	53	44	36
Lytham	34	14	8	12	51	45	36
Clitheroe	34	14	7	13	42	36	35
Chadderton	34	14	7	13	58	64	35
Whitworth Valley	34	13	8	13	50	54	34
Wigan Rovers	34	13	8	13	50	60	34
Daisy Hill	34	12	9	13	52	48	33
Bacup Borough	34	9	11	14	47	57	29
Ashton Athletic	34	9	6	19	47	73	24
Blackpool Mechanics	34	6	11	17	32	57	23
Nelson	34	7	3	24	29	60	17
Manchester Polytechnic	34	2	6	26	24	86	10

Padiham had 2 points deducted

Chorley Reserves and Manchester Polytechnic left the league. Bolton ST joined from the Bolton Combination and Oldham Dew joined from the Manchester Amateur League where they had been known as G. Dew & Co..

CENTRAL LEAGUE 1911-1921

The Central League was formed in 1911, at the instigation of a number of Football League clubs whose reserve sides who were playing in the Lancashire Combination and wished to start their own competition. However, in order to provide a full set of fixtures, they also included a number of leading non-League clubs, all of whom later joined the Football League.

The non-League clubs who played in the Central League in its early years were:

Crewe Alexandra, Lincoln City, Nelson, Port Vale, Rochdale, Southport, Stalybridge Celtic and Tranmere Rovers.

In 1921, the Football League introduced the new Third Division (North), and all first teams remaining in the Central League moved to the new division. Since then, the Central League has continued exclusively for Football League reserve sides and therefore falls outside the scope of our "Non-League Tables" books.

The Central League began in 1911 with the reserve sides of 13 Football League clubs, all of which had been playing in the Lancashire Combination: Blackburn Rovers, Blackpool, Bolton Wanderers, Burnley, Bury, Everton, Glossop, Liverpool, Manchester City, Manchester United, Oldham Athletic, Preston North End and Stockport County.

There were also 4 clubs who fielded their first teams in the new league: Southport Central, who had also been playing in the Lancashire Combination; Lincoln City, who had failed to be re-elected to the Football League; Crewe Alexandra, who joined from the Birmingham League; and Port Vale, who joined from the North Staffordshire League.

Throughout the notes and tables below, first teams are shown in Bold Type to clearly distinguish them from the clubs playing their reserves in the league.

1911-12

Lincoln City	32	18	12	2	81	30	48
Port Vale	32	15	12	5	48	23	42
Crewe Alexandra	32	14	9	9	65	63	37
Everton Reserves	32	14	8	10	66	51	36
Liverpool Reserves	32	13	8	11	68	57	34
Bolton Wanderers Reserves	32	9	15	8	46	45	33
Manchester City Reserves	32	14	5	13	56	60	33
Manchester United Reserves	32	13	6	13	56	60	32
Blackpool Reserves	32	12	8	12	43	52	32
Burnley Reserves	32	13	5	14	66	62	31
Preston North End Reserves	32	10	11	11	50	40	31
Blackburn Rovers Reserves	32	12	6	14	60	54	30
Oldham Athletic Reserves	32	12	6	14	60	59	30
Bury Reserves	32	10	8	14	57	69	28
Glossop Reserves	32	7	10	15	29	58	24
Southport Central	32	8	6	18	48	79	22
Stockport County Reserves	32	6	9	17	27	64	21

Lincoln City left to join the Football League – Division Two. Rochdale and Stalybridge Celtic joined from the Lancashire Combination, Bradford City Reserves joined from the Yorkshire Combination and Barnsley Reserves joined from the Midland League.

1912-13

Manchester United Reserves	38	22	11	5	79	30	55
Bradford City Reserves	38	22	6	10	96	50	50
Burnley Reserves	38	22	4	12	87	46	48
Port Vale	38	19	7	12	55	38	45
Stalybridge Celtic	38	16	13	9	65	48	45
Oldham Athletic Reserves	38	18	9	11	58	50	45
Rochdale	38	17	10	11	67	51	44
Barnsley Reserves	38	19	6	13	57	49	44
Liverpool Reserves	38	18	7	13	56	45	43
Everton Reserves	38	18	5	15	80	68	41
Blackburn Rovers Reserves	38	15	10	13	68	62	40
Manchester City Reserves	38	12	12	14	46	54	36
Crewe Alexandra	38	13	5	20	64	68	31
Bolton Wanderers Reserves	38	9	13	16	43	50	31
Southport Central	38	12	6	20	45	75	30
Blackpool Reserves	38	9	12	17	41	63	30
Stockport County Reserves	38	11	7	20	43	75	29
Preston North End Reserves	38	9	8	21	47	77	26
Bury Reserves	38	8	8	22	46	95	24
Glossop Reserves	38	7	9	22	40	89	23

Glossop Reserves left the league. It is believed that they played only friendlies in 1913-14. Huddersfield Town Reserves joined from the Yorkshire Combination.

1913-14

Team	P	W	D	L	F	A	Pts
Everton Reserves	38	20	9	9	83	57	49
Crewe Alexandra	38	20	8	10	57	49	48
Stalybridge Celtic	38	20	7	11	72	43	47
Port Vale	38	17	11	10	78	62	45
Blackburn Rovers Reserves	38	18	7	13	93	72	43
Manchester United Reserves	38	19	4	15	49	43	42
Liverpool Reserves	38	17	8	13	57	54	42
Bradford City Reserves	38	18	4	16	68	56	40
Manchester City Reserves	38	16	8	14	57	51	40
Rochdale	38	15	9	14	60	51	39
Burnley Reserves	38	16	6	16	57	72	38
Blackpool Reserves	38	13	11	14	48	52	37
Oldham Athletic Reserves	38	14	8	16	51	49	36
Huddersfield Town Reserves	38	11	11	16	46	49	33
Bury Reserves	38	14	5	19	59	86	33
Preston North End Reserves	38	11	9	18	62	81	31
Southport Central	38	10	10	18	43	58	30
Barnsley Reserves	38	12	6	20	46	63	30
Stockport County Reserves	38	11	7	20	44	71	29
Bolton Wanderers Reserves	38	10	8	20	48	59	28

There were no changes in Central League membership for 1914-15.

1914-15

Team	P	W	D	L	F	A	Pts
Huddersfield Town Reserves	38	27	5	6	90	39	59
Manchester City Reserves	38	26	4	8	76	50	56
Port Vale	38	25	3	10	84	42	53
Burnley Reserves	38	21	5	12	80	41	47
Stockport County Reserves	38	18	8	12	66	57	44
Liverpool Reserves	38	18	7	13	64	47	43
Bradford City Reserves	38	18	7	13	66	55	43
Manchester United Reserves	38	14	10	14	59	47	38
Rochdale	38	12	13	13	63	50	37
Bolton Wanderers Reserves	38	16	5	17	70	76	37
Bury Reserves	38	13	9	16	59	66	35
Everton Reserves	38	14	6	18	71	77	34
Preston North End Reserves	38	11	11	16	49	56	33
Barnsley Reserves	38	13	7	18	48	70	33
Crewe Alexandra	38	14	5	19	54	83	33
Oldham Athletic Reserves	38	12	8	18	50	52	32
Blackburn Rovers Reserves	38	14	4	20	71	87	32
Stalybridge Celtic	38	9	9	20	42	77	27
Southport Central	38	10	6	22	42	68	26
Blackpool Reserves	38	7	4	27	35	99	18

1915-19

The Central League closed down in 1915 due to the onset of war and did not resume operations until 1919.

When Southport Central restarted after the war ended in 1918, they at first assumed the title of Southport Vulcan before changing their name once again in 1919, since when they have been known just as Southport.

Barnsley Reserves did not resume in the Central League after the war, joining the Midland League instead. There were three new members:

Nelson, who joined from the Lancashire Combination, Aston Villa Reserves, who joined from the Birmingham League and Leeds City Reserves, who joined from the Midland League.

1919-20

Team	P	W	D	L	F	A	Pts
Blackpool Reserves	42	28	2	12	94	51	58
Aston Villa Reserves	42	26	4	12	104	57	56
Crewe Alexandra	42	23	8	11	86	56	54
Tranmere Rovers	42	23	5	14	103	61	51
Preston North End Reserves	42	21	9	12	104	65	51
Stalybridge Celtic	42	21	9	12	72	51	51
Manchester United Reserves	42	21	5	16	86	79	47
Everton Reserves	42	19	8	15	83	66	46
Blackburn Rovers Reserves	42	18	6	18	79	82	42
Liverpool Reserves	42	15	11	16	65	64	41
Bradford City Reserves	42	17	7	18	78	77	41
Huddersfield Town Reserves	42	16	8	18	69	73	40
Nelson	42	16	8	18	63	71	40
Port Vale (Reserves)	42	16	7	19	67	69	39
Manchester City Reserves	42	17	5	20	65	77	39
Southport	42	15	6	21	71	76	36
Oldham Athletic Reserves	42	15	6	21	67	92	36
Burnley Reserves	42	15	5	22	66	71	35
Rochdale	42	12	10	20	59	88	34
Bolton Wanderers Reserves	42	13	8	21	61	106	34
Bury Reserves	42	11	10	21	53	83	32
Stockport County Reserves	42	8	5	29	43	123	21

In 1919, the Football League and the F.A. set up a joint commission to investigate allegations that Leeds City had made illegal payments to players during the war. The commission ordered Leeds City to produce their books covering the period in question but the club did not do so and, on 19th October, the club was ordered to disband immediately.

Leeds City's first team were playing in the Second Division of the Football League at the time and their Reserves were playing in the Central League. Port Vale had begun the season in the Central League but they moved up to Division Two of the Football League and took over Leeds City's first team fixtures. Port Vale Reserves completed their club's Central League fixtures. Leeds City Reserves' place in the Central League was taken over by Tranmere Rovers, who had begun the season in the Lancashire Combination. Leeds City Reserves had played 7 Central League games, (Won 2, Drew 2, Lost 3, For 15, Against 14, Points 6) before their remaining 35 fixtures were fulfilled by Tranmere Rovers.

1920-21

Team	P	W	D	L	F	A	Pts
Manchester United Reserves	42	26	5	11	102	57	57
Crewe Alexandra	42	23	7	12	92	57	53
Bolton Wanderers Reserves	42	22	8	12	71	58	52
Aston Villa Reserves	42	22	7	13	102	52	51
Preston North End Reserves	42	21	8	13	76	55	50
Oldham Athletic Reserves	42	21	8	13	56	54	50
Tranmere Rovers	42	21	7	14	87	63	49
Everton Reserves	42	21	6	15	85	74	48
Burnley Reserves	42	18	7	17	84	73	43
Rochdale	42	19	5	18	63	73	43
Manchester City Reserves	42	12	18	12	62	57	42
Blackburn Rovers Reserves	42	14	14	14	74	71	42
Stalybridge Celtic	42	16	9	17	73	74	41
Huddersfield Town Reserves	42	17	7	18	57	59	41
Liverpool Reserves	42	16	8	18	72	65	40
Blackpool Reserves	42	15	9	18	59	62	39
Nelson	42	14	9	19	71	70	37
Southport	42	13	6	23	68	99	32
Port Vale Reserves	42	10	11	21	41	73	31
Bradford City Reserves	42	12	7	23	49	89	31
Stockport County Reserves	42	10	10	22	45	118	30
Bury Reserves	42	5	12	25	46	82	22

Crewe Alexandra, Stalybridge Celtic, Southport, Nelson, Tranmere Rovers and Rochdale all left to become founder members of the Football League – Third Division (North). Stockport County Reserves left to join the Lancashire Combination.

Seven more reserve sides joined the Central League. These were:

Birmingham, Stoke, West Bromwich Albion and Wolverhampton Wanderers who all moved from the Birmingham League, Leeds United and Sheffield United who moved from the Midland League and Derby County who moved from the Central Alliance.

The Central League then consisted solely of Reserve sides, a position that has not since changed up to the present time. Since 1921, the Central League has therefore fallen outside the scope of our "Non-League Tables" books.

CHESHIRE COUNTY LEAGUE 1919-1982

Following the closure of The Combination in 1911 and the Manchester League a year later, senior non-League clubs in Cheshire found that there was no suitable league covering the county and so they had little alternative other than to join the more northerly based Lancashire Combination. However after the intervention of the war there was a new opportunity to organise themselves and so the Cheshire County League (more commonly known as just the 'Cheshire League') was founded on 23rd April, 1919 at a meeting held at the Moseley Hotel, Manchester.

The 13 founder members of the league were: Altrincham, Chester, Crewe Alexandra Reserves, Crichton's Athletic, Macclesfield, Monk's Hall, Mossley, Nantwich Town, Northwich Victoria, Runcorn, Tranmere Rovers Reserves, Winsford United and Witton Albion.

Dukinfield were one of eight clubs who had attended the initial meeting but were unable to take up their place due to lack of a suitable ground.

Before the war, seven of the 13 founder members – Altrincham, Chester, Crewe Alexandra Reserves, Macclesfield, Nantwich Town, Northwich Victoria and Witton Albion – had played in the Lancashire Combination and Tranmere Rovers Reserves had played in the West Cheshire League. Mossley had played in the Ashton and District League before the war and joined the Manchester Section of the Lancashire Combination in the unofficial 1918-19 season. Monk's Hall also played in the Lancashire Combination's Manchester Section in 1918-19 but their immediate pre-war league and those of Crichton's Athletic and Winsford United have not been found. Runcorn were a recently formed club who had taken part in the Lancashire Combination's Liverpool Section during the 1918-19 season.

1919-1920

Runcorn	22	17	2	3	57	19	36
Mossley	22	11	3	8	41	43	25
Witton Albion	22	10	4	8	41	38	24
Crewe Alexandra Reserves	22	10	3	9	45	45	23
Crichton's Athletic	22	9	4	9	48	38	22
Chester	22	9	4	9	55	55	22
Winsford United	22	10	1	11	45	34	21
Altrincham	22	7	6	9	38	47	20
Macclesfield	22	8	4	10	36	54	20
Monk's Hall	22	8	2	12	47	54	18
Nantwich	22	8	2	12	39	54	18
Northwich Victoria	22	5	5	12	33	44	15

Tranmere Rovers Reserves left during the season and replaced their first team in the Lancashire Combination. This allowed their first team to move to the Central League where they replaced Port Vale, who themselves had moved into the Football League to replace Leeds City who had been disbanded by order of the Football Association.
Tranmere Rovers Reserves' record in the Cheshire League was expunged.

At the end of the season, the league was increased to 18 clubs by the election of 6 new members. The 6 were (previous league shown in brackets where known): Ashton National, Congleton Town (North Staffordshire & District League), Connah's Quay & Shotton (a newly formed club), Sandbach Ramblers (North Staffordshire & District League), Stalybridge Celtic Reserves (Lancashire Combination) and Tranmere Rovers Reserves (Lancashire Combination).

Subsidiary Competition – Section A

Mossley	10	6	2	2	24	14	14
Altrincham	10	3	5	2	15	13	11
Northwich Victoria	10	3	5	2	14	13	11
Witton Albion	10	3	2	5	15	15	8
Winsford United	10	2	4	4	15	16	8
Macclesfield	10	2	4	4	11	23	8

Subsidiary Competition – Section B

Crewe Alexandra Reserves	10	7	1	2	33	13	15
Runcorn	10	5	4	1	20	15	14
Monk's Hall	10	5	1	4	26	19	11
Crichton's Athletic	10	5	0	5	15	21	10
Chester	10	2	1	7	23	37	5
Nantwich Town	10	2	1	7	14	26	5

Subsidiary Competition – Final

Mossley vs Crewe Alexandra Reserves   2-1, 0-4

Crewe Alexandra Reserves won 5-2 on aggregate.

1920-21

Winsford United	34	19	6	9	67	48	44
Congleton Town	34	17	8	9	68	56	42
Runcorn	34	17	7	10	64	42	41
Monk's Hall	34	16	9	9	58	40	41
Crewe Alexandra Reserves	34	15	9	10	80	51	39
Macclesfield	34	16	7	11	67	50	39
Crichton's Athletic	34	16	6	12	72	62	38
Mossley	34	14	8	12	49	48	36
Altrincham	34	14	8	12	59	70	36
Chester	34	15	5	14	72	74	35
Nantwich Town	34	14	6	14	82	72	34
Ashton National	34	14	5	15	69	64	33
Northwich Victoria	34	12	5	17	53	60	29
Tranmere Rovers Reserves	34	13	3	18	52	69	29
Stalybridge Celtic Reserves	34	11	5	18	61	74	27
Sandbach Ramblers	34	8	9	17	42	68	25
Witton Albion	34	10	3	21	48	77	23
Connah's Quay & Shotton	34	6	9	19	44	82	21

The league was increased to 20 clubs by the election of Ellesmere Port Cement from the West Cheshire League and Whitchurch. Crichton's Athletic changed their name to Saltney Athletic.

1921-22

Chester	38	25	3	10	78	50	53
Congleton Town	38	22	6	10	82	49	50
Ashton National	38	23	2	13	78	63	48
Witton Albion	38	20	7	11	77	54	47
Stalybridge Celtic Reserves	38	18	8	12	71	59	44
Nantwich Town	38	15	13	10	71	57	43
Northwich Victoria	38	15	10	13	62	40	40
Macclesfield	38	13	13	12	60	64	39
Connah's Quay & Shotton	38	13	12	13	51	52	38
Whitchurch	38	16	6	16	65	71	38
Winsford United	38	13	12	13	53	64	38
Altrincham	38	13	9	16	75	70	35
Sandbach Ramblers	38	13	9	16	51	54	35
Ellesmere Port Cement	38	14	6	18	61	63	34
Crewe Alexandra Reserves	38	13	8	17	61	70	34
Saltney Athletic	38	9	15	14	65	75	33
Mossley	38	11	7	20	54	84	29
Stockport County "A"	38	11	6	21	57	102	28
Tranmere Rovers Reserves	38	10	7	21	59	66	27
Runcorn	38	10	7	21	56	80	27

Monk's Hall resigned and disbanded and their fixtures were completed by Stockport County "A".
At the end of the season, Stockport County Reserves moved from the Lancashire Combination and replaced their "A" team. Connah's Quay & Shotton moved to the Welsh National League (North). Middlewich also joined the league.

1922-23

Crewe Alexandra Reserves	38	27	6	5	102	42	60
Stockport County Reserves	38	20	8	10	89	58	48
Altrincham	38	19	10	9	86	60	48
Macclesfield	38	18	10	10	84	52	46
Ellesmere Port Cement	38	18	7	13	69	48	43
Saltney Athletic	38	20	3	15	75	83	43
Winsford United	38	17	7	14	51	52	41
Tranmere Rovers Reserves	38	16	9	13	69	71	41
Mossley	38	15	10	13	76	62	40
Stalybridge Celtic Reserves	38	15	9	14	56	49	39
Ashton National	38	14	10	14	75	57	38
Whitchurch	38	14	9	15	66	78	37
Congleton Town	38	14	8	16	64	71	36
Nantwich Town	38	15	5	18	61	84	35
Chester	38	13	8	17	59	60	34
Sandbach Ramblers	38	10	10	18	53	81	30
Runcorn	38	11	5	22	56	85	27
Northwich Victoria	38	8	10	20	47	75	26
Witton Albion	38	9	7	22	43	83	25
Middlewich	38	8	7	23	40	70	23

Saltney Athletic left nthe league.
Hurst joined from the Lancashire Combination, Port Vale Reserves joined from the Central League and Wallasey United joined as a new club, having been formed following a split between members of New Brighton FC. Stalybridge Celtic also joined, replacing their reserves, after resigning from the Football League Division Three (North).

1923-24

Crewe Alexandra Reserves	42	28	5	9	96	62	61
Port Vale Reserves	42	24	10	8	109	60	58
Whitchurch	42	24	8	10	81	52	56
Stalybridge Celtic	42	24	6	12	93	50	54
Stockport County Reserves	42	21	12	9	92	56	54
Northwich Victoria	42	18	10	14	85	77	46
Congleton Town	42	18	9	15	86	59	45
Hurst	42	19	7	16	78	76	45
Macclesfield	42	18	6	18	82	67	42
Altrincham	42	19	4	19	69	75	42
Ashton National	42	15	11	16	59	60	41
Ellesmere Port Cement	42	14	12	16	66	64	40
Mossley	42	16	8	18	77	90	40
Winsford United	42	17	5	20	56	77	39
Wallasey United	42	13	12	17	50	71	38
Chester	42	11	15	16	59	66	37
Witton Albion	42	14	9	19	55	67	37
Tranmere Rovers Reserves	42	13	9	20	78	90	35
Runcorn	42	13	9	20	54	68	35
Middlewich	42	12	8	22	56	101	32
Nantwich Town	42	9	6	27	53	101	24
Sandbach Ramblers	42	7	9	26	41	85	23

Wallasey United disbanded and Stockport County Reserves left the league.
Manchester North End joined from the Lancashire Combination and Ellesmere Port Town joined from the Liverpool County Combination.

1924-25

Port Vale Reserves	42	25	10	7	112	43	60
Northwich Victoria	42	25	6	11	94	58	56
Stalybridge Celtic	42	24	7	11	92	52	55
Ashton National	42	24	6	12	94	50	54
Hurst	42	22	10	10	101	61	54
Macclesfield	42	21	6	15	79	77	48
Tranmere Rovers Reserves	42	21	5	16	106	79	47
Crewe Alexandra Reserves	42	20	5	17	91	68	45
Mossley	42	17	8	17	85	83	42
Winsford United	42	18	6	18	83	87	42
Middlewich	42	18	6	18	67	71	42
Altrincham	42	16	7	19	70	93	39
Manchester North End	42	15	7	20	96	95	37
Congleton Town	42	14	8	20	77	93	36
Whitchurch	42	12	12	18	55	86	36
Sandbach Ramblers	42	12	11	19	57	81	35
Chester	42	14	7	21	59	103	35
Witton Albion	42	13	7	22	59	82	33
Nantwich Town	42	12	9	21	72	102	33
Runcorn	42	14	5	23	62	94	33
Ellesmere Port Cement	42	13	6	23	67	84	32
Ellesmere Port Town	42	12	6	24	56	88	30

Ellesmere Port Cement moved to the West Cheshire League.
Eccles United joined from the Lancashire Combination.

1925-26

Chester	42	29	5	8	110	57	63
Port Vale Reserves	42	26	6	10	115	58	58
Congleton Town	42	25	6	11	125	74	56
Stalybridge Celtic	42	24	4	14	133	77	52
Witton Albion	42	21	8	13	121	85	50
Ashton National	42	20	8	14	98	84	48
Winsford United	42	22	3	17	96	87	47
Nantwich Town	42	19	9	14	90	90	47
Tranmere Rovers Reserves	42	17	11	14	104	97	45
Manchester North End	42	18	7	17	92	111	43
Crewe Alexandra Reserves	42	18	6	18	96	75	42
Runcorn	42	19	4	19	79	92	42
Hurst	42	16	9	17	114	95	41
Mossley	42	14	8	20	80	106	36
Ellesmere Port Town	42	16	4	22	73	107	36
Altrincham	42	15	4	23	85	94	34
Sandbach Ramblers	42	14	6	22	81	92	34
Northwich Victoria	42	14	5	23	75	101	33
Whitchurch	42	14	4	24	85	124	32
Macclesfield	42	12	8	22	88	142	32
Middlewich	42	13	4	25	76	120	30
Eccles United	42	9	5	28	84	132	23

1927-28

Port Vale Reserves	42	31	5	6	147	48	67
Stockport County Reserves	42	26	9	7	158	81	61
Ashton National	42	28	5	9	145	78	61
Congleton Town	42	26	7	9	105	60	59
Chester	42	23	6	13	120	73	52
Winsford United	42	21	9	12	122	101	51
Stalybridge Celtic	42	21	6	15	120	93	48
Runcorn	42	19	10	13	86	81	48
Manchester North End	42	20	7	15	133	101	47
Hurst	42	19	7	16	105	101	45
Tranmere Rovers Reserves	42	21	3	18	104	101	45
Crewe Alexandra Reserves	42	17	9	16	112	98	43
Witton Albion	42	18	7	17	89	98	43
Middlewich	42	15	8	19	87	102	38
Sandbach Ramblers	42	13	8	21	89	101	34
Nantwich Town	42	15	3	24	103	133	33
Macclesfield	42	13	5	24	75	117	31
Northwich Victoria	42	10	9	23	88	136	29
Mossley	42	12	5	25	86	138	29
Altrincham	42	10	4	28	77	146	24
Whitchurch	42	8	2	32	77	166	18
Eccles United	42	7	4	31	64	153	18

Stockport County Reserves moved to the Central League and Eccles United moved to the Manchester League.

1926-27

Chester	42	31	3	8	147	67	65
Ashton National	42	29	4	9	119	63	62
Tranmere Rovers Reserves	42	28	4	10	163	72	60
Congleton Town	42	27	5	10	125	59	59
Stalybridge Celtic	42	26	6	10	136	79	58
Crewe Alexandra Reserves	42	26	6	10	118	81	58
Port Vale Reserves	42	24	5	13	119	74	53
Manchester North End	42	24	3	15	156	90	51
Altrincham	42	20	7	15	129	108	47
Runcorn	42	19	7	16	94	101	45
Macclesfield	42	19	5	18	113	112	43
Nantwich Town	42	16	10	16	95	86	42
Winsford United	42	18	5	19	120	97	41
Middlewich	42	15	6	21	99	132	36
Witton Albion	42	13	6	23	79	108	32
Eccles United	42	10	9	23	84	127	29
Mossley	42	11	7	24	88	146	29
Northwich Victoria	42	11	4	27	70	141	26
Whitchurch	42	10	6	26	62	134	26
Hurst	42	8	6	28	65	119	22
Sandbach Ramblers	42	7	7	28	59	124	21
Ellesmere Port Town	42	8	3	31	77	196	19

Ellesmere Port Town resigned and disbanded.
Stockport County Reserves joined the league.

1928-29

Port Vale Reserves	38	24	6	8	121	64	54
Ashton National	38	23	5	10	115	70	51
Winsford United	38	22	7	9	109	74	51
Congleton Town	38	21	7	10	97	76	49
Manchester North End	38	20	8	10	122	81	48
Tranmere Rovers Reserves	38	18	8	12	128	88	44
Stalybridge Celtic	38	19	6	13	92	75	44
Chester	38	19	5	14	99	75	43
Crewe Alexandra Reserves	38	18	5	15	92	84	41
Macclesfield	38	17	3	18	94	93	37
Runcorn	38	13	11	14	86	94	37
Hurst	38	14	8	16	126	119	36
Mossley	38	14	8	16	89	93	36
Northwich Victoria	38	13	7	18	85	90	33
Sandbach Ramblers	38	14	2	22	101	116	30
Whitchurch	38	13	4	21	96	115	30
Witton Albion	38	9	12	17	62	82	30
Middlewich	38	11	4	23	51	125	26
Altrincham	38	8	7	23	74	128	23
Nantwich Town	38	8	1	29	62	159	17

Connah's Quay & Shotton joined from the Welsh National League (North) and Manchester Central Reserves joined from the Manchester League.

1929-30

Port Vale Reserves	42	29	6	7	146	49	64
Connah's Quay & Shotton	42	30	3	9	148	59	63
Tranmere Rovers Reserves	42	26	6	10	154	90	58
Macclesfield	42	24	7	11	139	109	55
Ashton National	42	24	4	14	118	70	52
Stalybridge Celtic	42	25	2	15	136	109	52
Runcorn	42	23	5	14	123	98	51
Sandbach Ramblers	42	21	5	16	112	108	47
Chester	42	18	5	19	120	109	41
Mossley	42	18	5	19	99	126	41
Crewe Alexandra Reserves	42	15	10	17	99	115	40
Northwich Victoria	42	19	2	21	95	111	40
Witton Albion	42	15	8	19	105	120	38
Winsford United	42	16	5	21	105	128	37
Manchester Central Reserves	42	15	4	23	92	125	34
Manchester North End	42	14	4	24	115	130	32
Congleton Town	42	11	10	21	69	92	32
Whitchurch	42	14	4	24	86	122	32
Hurst	42	14	2	26	96	130	30
Nantwich Town	42	12	5	25	69	112	29
Middlewich	42	12	5	25	70	125	29
Altrincham	42	12	3	27	81	140	27

Middlewich left the league and Hyde United joined from the Manchester League.

1930-31

Port Vale Reserves	42	33	5	4	163	48	71
Chester	42	31	6	5	170	59	68
Hyde United	42	25	6	11	133	84	56
Altrincham	42	22	8	12	123	96	52
Runcorn	42	20	9	13	129	83	49
Stalybridge Celtic	42	21	6	15	122	114	48
Crewe Alexandra Reserves	42	19	8	15	132	104	46
Ashton National	42	18	8	16	114	90	44
Macclesfield	42	20	4	18	112	101	44
Sandbach Ramblers	42	19	4	19	123	124	42
Witton Albion	42	18	6	18	97	103	42
Tranmere Rovers Reserves	42	18	6	18	105	120	42
Manchester North End	42	19	4	19	97	119	42
Hurst	42	18	5	19	132	115	41
Congleton Town	42	14	8	20	68	112	36
Mossley	42	12	10	20	104	124	34
Northwich Victoria	42	15	3	24	105	135	33
Connah's Quay & Shotton	42	15	2	25	96	122	32
Winsford United	42	13	4	25	98	151	30
Whitchurch	42	10	7	25	79	160	27
Nantwich Town	42	9	8	25	83	132	26
Manchester Central Reserves	42	7	5	30	51	140	19

Chester were elected to the Football League Division Three (North) and were replaced in the Cheshire League by their reserves. Manchester Central joined from the Lancashire Combination and their reserves moved to the Manchester League.

1931-32

Macclesfield	40	25	8	7	119	65	58
Port Vale Reserves	40	25	5	10	110	50	55
Stalybridge Celtic	40	25	5	10	124	71	55
Altrincham	40	25	5	10	94	69	55
Manchester Central	40	23	7	10	108	68	53
Hyde United	40	22	7	11	98	66	51
Tranmere Rovers Reserves	40	22	4	14	116	80	48
Congleton Town	40	20	6	14	105	81	46
Chester Reserves	40	17	10	13	82	73	44
Crewe Alexandra Reserves	40	19	6	15	89	107	44
Runcorn	40	18	5	17	104	97	41
Manchester North End	40	18	4	18	106	103	40
Hurst	40	16	6	18	98	108	38
Ashton National	40	16	3	21	110	92	35
Mossley	40	13	7	20	71	104	33
Winsford United	40	12	4	24	70	99	28
Whitchurch	40	10	8	22	74	109	28
Witton Albion	40	10	7	23	73	116	27
Northwich Victoria	40	10	7	23	76	122	27
Sandbach Ramblers	40	8	5	27	68	120	21
Nantwich Town	40	1	11	28	60	155	13

Connah's Quay & Shotton resigned and disbanded in November 1931 after suffering from financial difficulties. Their record was deleted.
Manchester Central resigned and disbanded. Buxton joined from the Manchester League and Wigan Athletic joined as a new club, formed as a replacement for the former Football League club Wigan Borough who had disbanded during the 1931-32 season.

1932-33

Macclesfield	42	29	5	8	121	64	63
Port Vale Reserves	42	26	5	11	112	57	57
Manchester North End	42	24	7	11	124	78	55
Hurst	42	25	4	13	129	98	54
Wigan Athletic	42	21	11	10	121	54	53
Ashton National	42	23	7	12	130	83	53
Congleton Town	42	22	6	14	105	103	50
Hyde United	42	22	5	15	105	93	49
Crewe Alexandra Reserves	42	19	8	15	110	77	46
Stalybridge Celtic	42	19	8	15	132	100	46
Chester Reserves	42	21	2	19	118	109	44
Altrincham	42	17	9	16	108	95	43
Mossley	42	19	4	19	96	101	42
Tranmere Rovers Reserves	42	18	5	19	108	118	41
Northwich Victoria	42	17	6	19	100	123	40
Buxton	42	16	5	21	81	92	37
Runcorn	42	15	6	21	88	109	36
Nantwich Town	42	12	7	23	84	133	31
Witton Albion	42	9	7	26	71	119	25
Winsford United	42	8	6	28	65	143	22
Sandbach Ramblers	42	6	7	29	63	146	19
Whitchurch	42	6	6	30	70	146	18

Port Vale Reserves moved to the Birmingham League and Whitchurch also left the league. Prescot Cables joined from the Lancashire Combination and Stockport County Reserves joined from the Central League.

1933-34

Wigan Athletic	42	30	6	6	111	46	66
Macclesfield	42	29	3	10	142	71	61
Witton Albion	42	21	9	12	85	75	51
Stockport County Reserves	42	23	3	16	104	77	49
Prescot Cables	42	21	7	14	93	78	49
Altrincham	42	19	9	14	99	72	47
Tranmere Rovers Reserves	42	22	3	17	110	98	47
Manchester North End	42	21	4	17	132	105	46
Stalybridge Celtic	42	18	9	15	100	84	45
Ashton National	42	21	3	18	89	85	45
Hyde United	42	19	6	17	99	84	44
Mossley	42	15	12	15	91	87	42
Runcorn	42	19	2	21	91	104	40
Chester Reserves	42	16	7	19	84	97	39
Buxton	42	14	11	17	81	95	39
Hurst	42	17	3	22	103	111	37
Nantwich Town	42	15	4	23	77	112	34
Crewe Alexandra Reserves	42	16	2	24	71	111	34
Congleton Town	42	11	8	23	84	97	30
Northwich Victoria	42	14	2	26	63	87	30
Winsford United	42	11	6	25	70	118	28
Sandbach Ramblers	42	8	5	29	57	142	21

Sandbach Ramblers left the league.
Port Vale Reserves joined from the Birmingham League.

1935-36

Wigan Athletic	42	31	6	5	136	46	68
Altrincham	42	22	11	9	88	51	55
Stockport County Reserves	42	23	8	11	103	57	54
Chester Reserves	42	22	9	11	104	85	53
Stalybridge Celtic	42	23	6	13	112	64	52
Runcorn	42	21	8	13	129	88	50
Northwich Victoria	42	20	10	12	98	74	50
Crewe Alexandra Reserves	42	21	6	15	113	84	48
Macclesfield	42	21	4	17	105	106	46
Port Vale Reserves	42	17	10	15	69	72	44
Buxton	42	18	7	17	95	90	43
Hurst	42	16	10	16	89	106	42
Tranmere Rovers Reserves	42	16	9	17	113	120	41
Manchester North End	42	17	6	19	94	107	40
Hyde United	42	17	5	20	107	108	39
Mossley	42	16	4	22	90	113	36
Congleton Town	42	15	4	23	95	114	34
Prescot Cables	42	15	4	23	59	94	34
Nantwich Town	42	13	7	22	74	115	33
Witton Albion	42	11	5	26	58	96	27
Ashton National	42	7	8	27	64	114	22
Winsford United	42	4	5	33	44	135	13

Prescot Cables moved to the Lancashire Combination and Rhyl joined from the Birmingham League.

1934-35

Wigan Athletic	42	27	9	6	153	59	63
Altrincham	42	26	11	5	118	57	63
Stalybridge Celtic	42	28	7	7	136	74	63
Port Vale Reserves	42	23	6	13	113	69	52
Hyde United	42	21	6	15	89	73	48
Stockport County Reserves	42	21	5	16	94	88	47
Chester Reserves	42	22	2	18	116	98	46
Macclesfield	42	19	7	16	137	83	45
Buxton	42	19	5	18	95	95	43
Manchester North End	42	15	9	18	112	110	39
Congleton Town	42	17	5	20	93	113	39
Mossley	42	17	5	20	97	119	39
Ashton National	42	15	7	20	68	86	37
Witton Albion	42	16	5	21	60	106	37
Hurst	42	13	10	19	82	101	36
Northwich Victoria	42	14	7	21	83	95	35
Prescot Cables	42	13	9	20	79	100	35
Winsford United	42	12	9	21	68	104	33
Tranmere Rovers Reserves	42	14	4	24	82	110	32
Runcorn	42	14	3	25	95	147	31
Nantwich Town	42	11	9	22	71	121	31
Crewe Alexandra Reserves	42	12	6	24	72	105	30

1936-37

Runcorn	42	30	6	6	156	60	66
Stockport County Reserves	42	23	11	8	105	55	57
Northwich Victoria	42	27	3	12	92	52	57
Witton Albion	42	24	8	10	107	56	56
Port Vale Reserves	42	22	8	12	97	91	52
Buxton	42	22	6	14	107	89	50
Ashton National	42	18	9	15	97	96	45
Wigan Athletic	42	19	6	17	94	73	44
Stalybridge Celtic	42	19	6	17	96	81	44
Rhyl	42	17	9	16	75	71	43
Crewe Alexandra Reserves	42	18	5	19	77	88	41
Chester Reserves	42	14	9	19	79	93	37
Altrincham	42	14	8	20	91	94	36
Congleton Town	42	15	6	21	83	104	36
Winsford United	42	14	8	20	75	94	36
Tranmere Rovers Reserves	42	15	6	21	74	100	36
Mossley	42	11	13	18	84	108	35
Manchester North End	42	15	5	22	85	113	35
Macclesfield	42	14	6	22	74	96	34
Hyde United	42	13	7	22	97	114	33
Nantwich Town	42	11	6	25	78	146	28
Hurst	42	9	5	28	76	125	23

1937-38

Tranmere Rovers Reserves	42	30	6	6	148	45	66
Runcorn	42	30	3	9	123	54	63
Stockport County Reserves	42	29	4	9	104	48	62
Hyde United	42	24	8	10	105	67	56
Crewe Alexandra Reserves	42	21	11	10	99	61	53
Witton Albion	42	20	7	15	104	68	47
Mossley	42	19	9	14	86	76	47
Northwich Victoria	42	19	6	17	86	79	44
Altrincham	42	17	10	15	77	80	44
Stalybridge Celtic	42	18	6	18	96	86	42
Wigan Athletic	42	19	4	19	95	89	42
Port Vale Reserves	42	16	7	19	77	76	39
Chester Reserves	42	17	4	21	84	92	38
Manchester North End	42	18	2	22	112	131	38
Macclesfield	42	14	10	18	96	115	38
Congleton Town	42	16	6	20	74	122	38
Ashton National	42	16	5	21	78	92	37
Buxton	42	14	5	23	87	108	33
Winsford United	42	12	6	24	71	98	30
Rhyl	42	11	7	24	74	117	29
Nantwich Town	42	8	4	30	59	149	20
Hurst	42	7	4	31	63	145	18

Nantwich Town left the league.
Wellington Town joined from the Birmingham League.

1938-39

Runcorn	42	28	6	8	134	60	62
Tranmere Rovers Reserves	42	29	2	11	136	63	60
Ashton National	42	25	7	10	131	90	57
Crewe Alexandra Reserves	42	26	4	12	132	74	56
Wellington Town	42	23	8	11	108	68	54
Chester Reserves	42	22	8	12	111	74	52
Wigan Athletic	42	21	5	16	104	84	47
Northwich Victoria	42	20	7	15	88	87	47
Witton Albion	42	17	9	16	94	78	43
Hyde United	42	20	3	19	84	91	43
Congleton Town	42	16	10	16	80	89	42
Mossley	42	14	12	16	77	78	40
Port Vale Reserves	42	18	4	20	84	86	40
Hurst	42	15	10	17	86	113	40
Stockport County Reserves	42	18	3	21	86	90	39
Buxton	42	12	11	19	71	93	35
Macclesfield	42	14	7	21	55	90	35
Stalybridge Celtic	42	13	8	21	87	108	34
Rhyl	42	12	9	21	94	117	33
Altrincham	42	9	7	26	72	119	25
Winsford United	42	8	6	28	57	134	22
Manchester North End	42	7	4	31	57	142	18

Manchester North End resigned and disbanded due to financial difficulties.
Wrexham Reserves joined from the Midland Mid-Week League.

1939-40

The planned 1939-40 season started on 26th August 1939 but was suspended when war was declared on 3rd September. It is believed that all 22 clubs played their opening two games but not all results have been traced.

Instead of the planned peace-time competition, the Cheshire League organised a scaled down competition of 16 clubs playing in two geographically based sections, East and West. There were two competitions in each section, the first ran from the end of September 1939 until the end of December, and the second ran from January until May, 1940. The clubs who finished top of the table in the two east competitions then met in a play-off and the overall championship was decided by another play-off between the east section play-off winners and Runcorn, who had won both west section competitions.

Seven of the 22 members of the league did not compete, probably due to war-time difficulties such as travel. These seven were: Congleton Town, Crewe Alexandra Reserves, Port Vale Reserves, Rhyl, Tranmere Rovers Reserves, Wellington Town and Wrexham Reserves. The number of clubs competing was made up to 16 by the inclusion of Droylsden who had started the 1939-40 peace-time season in the Lancashire Combination. Stockport County Reserves only played 11 of their planned 14 games in the 1939 East section and withdrew from the 1940 series of games. Buxton also withdrew from the 1940 East section series but this was made up to 7 clubs by the transfer of Macclesfield from the West section. The 1940 West section series was maintained at 8 clubs by the replacement of Macclesfield with South Liverpool who, like Droylsden, had started the 1939-40 peace-time season in the Lancashire Combination.

1939-40 – Unofficial war-time competition

East section – 1939 series

Droylsden	14	9	2	3	52	31	20
Ashton National	13	7	3	3	47	35	17
Hyde United	14	7	3	4	27	24	17
Hurst	13	7	1	5	29	32	15
Buxton	14	5	4	5	29	31	14
Stalybridge Celtic	14	5	1	8	34	38	11
Mossley	13	2	3	8	26	35	7
Stockport County Reserves	11	2	1	8	22	40	5

Three games were not played.

West section – 1939 series

Runcorn	14	7	6	1	46	28	20
Altrincham	14	7	3	4	45	29	17
Witton Albion	14	5	5	4	32	28	15
Winsford United	14	6	3	5	25	25	15
Northwich Victoria	13	6	3	4	23	26	15
Chester Reserves	13	5	1	7	32	40	11
Wigan Athletic	14	3	3	8	37	46	9
Macclesfield	14	3	2	9	28	46	8

One game was not played.

East section – 1940 series

Hyde United	12	8	2	2	40	21	18
Droylsden	12	7	1	4	35	25	15
Ashton National	12	6	1	5	36	31	13
Mossley	12	5	3	4	24	27	13
Hurst	12	4	3	5	29	33	11
Macclesfield	12	4	0	8	23	42	8
Stalybridge Celtic	12	1	4	7	26	36	6

West section – 1940 series

Runcorn	14	9	4	1	49	21	22
Witton Albion	14	8	2	4	31	24	18
Altrincham	14	8	1	5	35	31	17
Chester Reserves	14	6	2	6	31	33	14
South Liverpool	14	4	4	6	34	36	12
Northwich Victoria	14	5	1	8	20	33	11
Wigan Athletic	14	4	3	7	32	46	11
Winsford United	14	2	3	9	16	24	7

East Section Play-off

Droylsden vs Hyde United		6-5, 1-0

Droylsden won 7-5 on aggregate.

West Section

Runcorn won both competitions.

Championship Play-off

Runcorn vs Droylsden		4-1, 1-2

Runcorn won 5-3 on aggregate.

1940-45

The Cheshire League did not operate between 1940 and 1945 but restarted after the war for the 1945-46 season. Of the 22 members who had started the 1939-40 peace-time season, 17 rejoined the league but 5 did not.

These 5 clubs were: Altrincham, Ashton National, Congleton Town, Macclesfield and Winsford United.

Of these 5, Ashton National joined the Manchester League instead while Altrincham, Congleton Town and Macclesfield rejoined the league for the 1946-47 season and Winsford United rejoined for the 1947-48 season.

The membership for 1945-46 season was made up to 20 by the addition of Droylsden and South Liverpool, who had both played in the Lancashire Combination before the war but had joined the Cheshire League's unofficial war-time competition in 1939, and Oldham Athletic Reserves who had also played in the Lancashire Combination before the war.

1945-46

Wellington Town	38	29	1	8	150	53	59
Droylsden	38	24	3	11	126	65	51
Buxton	38	21	8	9	131	72	50
Witton Albion	38	21	4	13	98	69	46
Chester Reserves	38	20	4	14	118	86	44
Stalybridge Celtic	38	19	6	13	102	99	44
South Liverpool	38	19	5	14	99	94	43
Hyde United	38	17	8	13	83	66	42
Runcorn	38	17	6	15	97	98	40
Hurst	38	17	6	15	95	108	40
Northwich Victoria	38	16	4	18	79	102	36
Stockport County Reserves	38	15	4	19	79	107	34
Oldham Athletic Reserves	38	13	6	19	87	116	32
Crewe Alexandra Reserves	38	11	9	18	74	104	31
Rhyl	38	11	8	19	96	116	30
Wigan Athletic	38	12	6	20	88	117	30
Wrexham Reserves	38	12	6	20	54	76	30
Port Vale Reserves	38	11	5	22	73	91	27
Tranmere Rovers Reserves	38	12	2	24	76	115	26
Mossley	38	11	3	24	85	136	25

Oldham Athletic Reserves moved to the Lancashire Combination. Altrincham, Congleton Town and Macclesfield rejoined, Macclesfield having changed their name to Macclesfield Town. Winsford United also applied to rejoin but were refused as it was considered that their ground needed further renewal work.

1946-47

Wellington Town	42	25	7	10	113	69	57
Buxton	42	24	8	10	117	79	56
South Liverpool	42	23	9	10	92	62	55
Port Vale Reserves	42	24	6	12	100	58	54
Northwich Victoria	42	21	11	10	95	69	53
Stalybridge Celtic	42	24	5	13	108	89	53
Witton Albion	42	20	7	15	96	84	47
Droylsden	42	22	1	19	108	101	45
Mossley	42	17	10	15	94	90	44
Altrincham	42	17	8	17	85	83	42
Hyde United	42	19	3	20	108	100	41
Runcorn	42	13	13	16	80	89	39
Wrexham Reserves	42	17	4	21	81	80	38
Rhyl	42	16	6	20	96	106	38
Macclesfield Town	42	16	6	20	77	89	38
Chester Reserves	42	16	4	22	70	91	36
Congleton Town	42	15	5	22	83	100	35
Tranmere Rovers Reserves	42	14	7	21	70	89	35
Stockport County Reserves	42	14	7	21	79	104	35
Crewe Alexandra Reserves	42	13	6	23	90	120	32
Hurst	42	8	10	24	65	107	26
Wigan Athletic	42	9	7	26	66	114	25

Hurst changed their name to Ashton United on 1st February 1947. Wigan Athletic moved to the Lancashire Combination and Winsford United rejoined following ground improvements.

1947-48

Rhyl	42	30	8	4	121	54	68
Northwich Victoria	42	24	9	9	109	58	57
Witton Albion	42	24	8	10	104	59	56
Wellington Town	42	23	8	11	111	65	54
Stalybridge Celtic	42	18	11	13	85	87	47
Tranmere Rovers Reserves	42	18	9	15	76	62	45
Winsford United	42	22	1	19	90	83	45
Crewe Alexandra Reserves	42	19	7	16	80	80	45
South Liverpool	42	18	7	17	81	81	43
Chester Reserves	42	18	6	18	83	92	42
Stockport County Reserves	42	16	9	17	87	84	41
Hyde United	42	18	4	20	88	83	40
Wrexham Reserves	42	17	5	20	85	71	39
Runcorn	42	15	9	18	79	88	39
Altrincham	42	17	5	20	100	115	39
Port Vale Reserves	42	16	7	19	53	69	39
Droylsden	42	13	11	18	80	82	37
Macclesfield Town	42	13	11	18	78	83	37
Buxton	42	13	6	23	89	113	32
Mossley	42	14	4	24	66	99	32
Ashton United	42	11	3	28	74	143	25
Congleton Town	42	9	4	29	50	118	22

Ashton United moved to the Lancashire Combination.
Ellesmere Port Town joined from the Liverpool County Combination.

1948-49

Witton Albion	42	29	6	7	106	39	64
Rhyl	42	27	7	8	110	53	61
Northwich Victoria	42	26	9	7	118	67	61
Winsford United	42	25	8	9	95	59	58
Mossley	42	21	9	12	97	74	51
Wellington Town	42	20	10	12	91	68	50
South Liverpool	42	18	9	15	94	91	45
Wrexham Reserves	42	17	10	15	81	77	44
Stalybridge Celtic	42	18	7	17	79	90	43
Altrincham	42	18	6	18	91	95	42
Macclesfield Town	42	16	9	17	82	80	41
Runcorn	42	17	7	18	76	79	41
Chester Reserves	42	17	4	21	78	88	38
Hyde United	42	14	9	19	80	87	37
Ellesmere Port Town	42	14	8	20	80	96	36
Port Vale Reserves	42	13	10	19	65	79	36
Buxton	42	15	6	21	77	104	36
Crewe Alexandra Reserves	42	13	7	22	74	88	33
Stockport County Reserves	42	10	12	20	65	81	32
Congleton Town	42	11	7	24	78	113	29
Tranmere Rovers Reserves	42	11	4	27	57	101	26
Droylsden	42	7	6	29	59	124	20

1949-50

	P	W	D	L	F	A	Pts
Witton Albion	42	25	13	4	101	42	63
Rhyl	42	28	6	8	116	42	62
Stockport County Reserves	42	21	14	7	78	46	56
Northwich Victoria	42	22	7	13	101	61	51
Winsford United	42	16	18	8	78	56	50
Altrincham	42	20	10	12	79	64	50
Runcorn	42	18	11	13	70	52	47
Macclesfield Town	42	21	5	16	88	76	47
Wellington Town	42	17	13	12	70	67	47
Crewe Alexandra Reserves	42	16	10	16	86	78	42
Hyde United	42	16	10	16	81	83	42
Ellesmere Port Town	42	16	10	16	69	79	42
Buxton	42	11	16	15	78	88	38
Tranmere Rovers Reserves	42	15	8	19	62	80	38
Congleton Town	42	15	5	22	65	99	35
Chester Reserves	42	12	11	19	56	89	35
South Liverpool	42	12	9	21	65	78	33
Port Vale Reserves	42	9	15	18	51	62	33
Mossley	42	8	16	18	53	92	32
Stalybridge Celtic	42	9	11	22	57	85	29
Droylsden	42	9	9	24	69	114	27
Wrexham Reserves	42	9	7	26	54	94	25

Droylsden moved to the Manchester League.
Bangor City joined from the Lancashire Combination.

1951-52

	P	W	D	L	F	A	Pts
Wellington Town	42	26	9	7	85	44	61
Rhyl	42	25	8	9	101	58	58
Port Vale Reserves	42	21	11	10	77	41	53
Witton Albion	42	22	7	13	77	46	51
Tranmere Rovers Reserves	42	20	9	13	79	57	49
Northwich Victoria	42	21	6	15	78	70	48
Mossley	42	22	4	16	90	89	48
Altrincham	42	19	9	14	78	72	47
Crewe Alexandra Reserves	42	19	8	15	114	83	46
Stockport County Reserves	42	16	12	14	66	61	44
Bangor City	42	17	9	16	79	68	43
Wrexham Reserves	42	16	10	16	88	83	42
Runcorn	42	16	10	16	75	76	42
Macclesfield Town	42	15	12	15	62	69	42
Winsford United	42	17	6	19	72	84	40
Congleton Town	42	17	5	20	66	93	39
Chester Reserves	42	15	7	20	65	79	37
Stalybridge Celtic	42	13	7	22	56	83	33
Buxton	42	10	11	21	73	84	31
Ellesmere Port Town	42	11	4	27	70	104	26
South Liverpool	42	7	10	25	45	98	24
Hyde United	42	7	6	29	66	120	20

South Liverpool moved to the Lancashire Combination.
Stafford Rangers joined from the Birmingham Combination.

1950-51

	P	W	D	L	F	A	Pts
Rhyl	42	31	6	5	99	36	68
Witton Albion	42	28	4	10	116	56	60
Northwich Victoria	42	27	5	10	116	58	59
Tranmere Rovers Reserves	42	23	5	14	73	52	51
Macclesfield Town	42	20	11	11	90	67	51
Wellington Town	42	20	9	13	80	55	49
Bangor City	42	20	8	14	85	70	48
Port Vale Reserves	42	19	10	13	71	66	48
Winsford United	42	19	9	14	84	67	47
Altrincham	42	19	8	15	77	63	46
Wrexham Reserves	42	19	6	17	88	68	44
Ellesmere Port Town	42	17	6	19	73	78	40
Stockport County Reserves	42	15	9	18	52	50	39
Runcorn	42	15	8	19	81	89	38
Buxton	42	14	9	19	55	69	37
Crewe Alexandra Reserves	42	15	6	21	88	102	36
South Liverpool	42	13	6	23	65	101	32
Hyde United	42	11	6	25	51	90	28
Stalybridge Celtic	42	12	4	26	55	125	28
Mossley	42	11	5	26	51	91	27
Congleton Town	42	9	9	24	54	102	27
Chester Reserves	42	6	9	27	65	114	21

1952-53

	P	W	D	L	F	A	Pts
Macclesfield Town	42	27	8	7	103	63	62
Wellington Town	42	25	9	8	89	44	59
Stockport County Reserves	42	24	9	9	85	52	57
Rhyl	42	20	14	8	104	76	54
Bangor City	42	23	7	12	87	68	53
Tranmere Rovers Reserves	42	18	14	10	95	71	50
Port Vale Reserves	42	17	14	11	77	65	48
Witton Albion	42	18	9	15	107	100	45
Buxton	42	17	10	15	76	81	44
Crewe Alexandra Reserves	42	18	5	19	72	75	41
Stalybridge Celtic	42	16	9	17	84	88	41
Runcorn	42	18	3	21	83	97	39
Chester Reserves	42	12	13	17	78	78	37
Wrexham Reserves	42	15	7	20	69	78	37
Ellesmere Port Town	42	16	5	21	70	81	37
Northwich Victoria	42	13	8	21	61	82	34
Winsford United	42	13	7	22	70	82	33
Mossley	42	13	6	23	57	86	32
Hyde United	42	11	10	21	71	108	32
Stafford Rangers	42	11	9	22	67	73	31
Congleton Town	42	11	8	23	64	91	30
Altrincham	42	8	12	22	54	84	28

1953-54

Witton Albion	42	27	7	8	117	62	61
Bangor City	42	23	7	12	104	63	53
Stockport County Reserves	42	22	7	13	93	75	51
Hyde United	42	19	12	11	86	73	50
Macclesfield Town	42	20	9	13	97	78	49
Altrincham	42	21	7	14	75	67	49
Crewe Alexandra Reserves	42	19	10	13	87	65	48
Tranmere Rovers Reserves	42	18	11	13	79	62	47
Wrexham Reserves	42	21	5	16	85	69	47
Wellington Town	42	21	5	16	80	66	47
Rhyl	42	19	9	14	70	61	47
Chester Reserves	42	16	8	18	67	70	40
Port Vale Reserves	42	17	6	19	69	75	40
Winsford United	42	15	8	19	70	76	38
Ellesmere Port Town	42	13	9	20	54	75	35
Stalybridge Celtic	42	14	7	21	62	88	35
Mossley	42	11	12	19	66	89	34
Runcorn	42	13	8	21	63	86	34
Northwich Victoria	42	13	7	22	72	97	33
Stafford Rangers	42	11	10	21	73	89	32
Congleton Town	42	11	5	26	66	109	27
Buxton	42	10	7	25	58	98	27

1954-55

Hyde United	42	25	10	7	125	64	60
Wellington Town	42	24	7	11	91	59	55
Stafford Rangers	42	19	14	9	74	50	52
Wrexham Reserves	42	20	11	11	105	68	51
Stockport County Reserves	42	22	6	14	96	65	50
Stalybridge Celtic	42	21	8	13	73	68	50
Macclesfield Town	42	20	7	15	103	82	47
Ellesmere Port Town	42	18	9	15	62	63	45
Runcorn	42	20	4	18	86	74	44
Tranmere Rovers Reserves	42	19	5	18	82	85	43
Port Vale Reserves	42	17	8	17	71	71	42
Altrincham	42	15	11	16	71	77	41
Witton Albion	42	17	5	20	98	95	39
Chester Reserves	42	13	13	16	76	86	39
Bangor City	42	16	7	19	78	96	39
Rhyl	42	14	9	19	66	75	37
Winsford United	42	16	5	21	68	78	37
Mossley	42	11	13	18	65	75	35
Crewe Alexandra Reserves	42	11	12	19	75	97	34
Congleton Town	42	12	8	22	65	88	32
Northwich Victoria	42	11	6	25	68	117	28
Buxton	42	7	10	25	59	124	24

1955-56

Hyde United	42	27	7	8	138	78	61
Rhyl	42	22	12	8	93	68	56
Wellington Town	42	22	10	10	112	59	54
Northwich Victoria	42	22	10	10	99	70	54
Ellesmere Port Town	42	20	13	9	81	51	53
Port Vale Reserves	42	21	8	13	94	80	50
Witton Albion	42	16	16	10	91	80	48
Wrexham Reserves	42	19	8	15	109	88	46
Chester Reserves	42	16	13	13	90	74	45
Runcorn	42	20	5	17	93	88	45
Buxton	42	19	6	17	94	78	44
Winsford United	42	16	11	15	73	76	43
Stockport County Reserves	42	17	8	17	82	76	42
Altrincham	42	15	8	19	74	78	38
Tranmere Rovers Reserves	42	13	12	17	59	74	38
Stalybridge Celtic	42	13	10	19	64	82	36
Bangor City	42	13	7	22	71	107	33
Stafford Rangers	42	12	9	21	52	80	33
Mossley	42	10	13	19	68	114	33
Congleton Town	42	10	6	26	68	104	26
Macclesfield Town	42	10	6	26	70	115	26
Crewe Alexandra Reserves	42	8	4	30	55	110	20

1956-57

Northwich Victoria	42	25	7	10	139	72	57
Hyde United	42	25	5	12	129	102	55
Wellington Town	42	22	10	10	92	58	54
Witton Albion	42	22	9	11	84	66	53
Rhyl	42	22	6	14	111	71	50
Stockport County Reserves	42	19	12	11	105	73	50
Chester Reserves	42	20	8	14	86	87	48
Winsford United	42	20	6	16	92	77	46
Buxton	42	19	7	16	79	86	45
Macclesfield Town	42	17	10	15	102	73	44
Ellesmere Port Town	42	17	10	15	86	77	44
Wrexham Reserves	42	15	10	17	98	101	40
Stalybridge Celtic	42	15	9	18	86	111	39
Runcorn	42	13	13	16	67	88	39
Tranmere Rovers Reserves	42	16	6	20	99	95	38
Altrincham	42	14	7	21	94	102	35
Port Vale Reserves	42	13	9	20	78	96	35
Mossley	42	10	15	17	62	96	35
Congleton Town	42	12	10	20	79	111	34
Stafford Rangers	42	12	9	21	57	74	33
Bangor City	42	10	8	24	73	115	28
Crewe Alexandra Reserves	42	9	4	29	72	139	22

1957-58

Ellesmere Port Town	42	24	10	8	91	53	58
Hyde United	42	26	6	10	106	68	58
Northwich Victoria	42	22	10	10	91	66	54
Port Vale Reserves	42	22	8	12	80	51	52
Chester Reserves	42	22	7	13	91	63	51
Tranmere Rovers Reserves	42	21	7	14	103	72	49
Buxton	42	20	9	13	86	66	49
Bangor City	42	19	11	12	81	68	49
Rhyl	42	22	4	16	94	76	48
Witton Albion	42	19	8	15	91	84	46
Wrexham Reserves	42	19	8	15	71	67	46
Wellington Town	42	19	8	15	89	88	46
Winsford United	42	17	8	17	87	83	42
Runcorn	42	15	10	17	71	74	40
Altrincham	42	14	10	18	70	78	38
Stafford Rangers	42	14	8	20	68	104	36
Crewe Alexandra Reserves	42	12	11	19	86	95	35
Congleton Town	42	13	8	21	52	76	34
Stockport County Reserves	42	11	10	21	67	84	32
Stalybridge Celtic	42	7	7	28	57	96	21
Macclesfield Town	42	6	9	27	71	136	21
Mossley	42	7	5	30	57	112	19

Wellington Town moved to the Southern League and Stockport County Reserves moved to become a founder member of the North Regional League.

1958-59

	P	W	D	L	F	A	Pts
Ellesmere Port Town	38	25	7	6	106	41	57
Bangor City	38	22	5	11	85	61	49
Tranmere Rovers Reserves	38	21	5	12	90	55	47
Port Vale Reserves	38	20	6	12	90	51	46
Chester Reserves	38	20	6	12	73	63	46
Wrexham Reserves	38	20	3	15	85	75	43
Rhyl	38	15	12	11	72	76	42
Hyde United	38	19	3	16	73	69	41
Buxton	38	16	8	14	87	71	40
Northwich Victoria	38	16	7	15	96	74	39
Winsford United	38	15	9	14	80	69	39
Runcorn	38	13	11	14	67	57	37
Altrincham	38	14	6	18	57	64	34
Crewe Alexandra Reserves	38	13	8	17	73	94	34
Mossley	38	13	5	20	78	97	31
Witton Albion	38	12	6	20	71	90	30
Stafford Rangers	38	11	8	19	60	98	30
Macclesfield Town	38	11	5	22	67	99	27
Congleton Town	38	12	3	23	60	104	27
Stalybridge Celtic	38	8	5	25	60	122	21

Crewe Alexandra Reserves and Port Vale Reserves both moved to the North Regional League. Oswestry Town joined from the Birmingham League and Wigan Rovers joined as a newly formed club.

1960-61

	P	W	D	L	F	A	Pts
Macclesfield Town	42	26	9	7	133	69	61
Ellesmere Port Town	42	25	6	11	111	61	56
Frickley Colliery	42	24	8	10	103	65	56
Mossley	42	23	7	12	93	66	53
Oswestry Town	42	23	7	12	113	84	53
Bangor City	42	22	8	12	103	65	52
Wrexham Reserves	42	22	6	14	109	83	50
Buxton	42	21	7	14	96	76	49
Hyde United	42	19	10	13	91	60	48
Runcorn	42	18	10	14	89	77	46
Witton Albion	42	16	14	12	89	78	46
Northwich Victoria	42	20	6	16	93	84	46
Tranmere Rovers Reserves	42	19	5	18	93	90	43
Winsford United	42	14	9	19	76	101	37
Chester Reserves	42	14	8	20	67	85	36
Sankeys (Wellington)	42	13	10	19	77	98	36
Congleton Town	42	14	7	21	67	91	35
Rhyl	42	11	7	24	65	85	29
Stalybridge Celtic	42	11	5	26	85	123	27
Stafford Rangers	42	8	10	24	54	84	26
Altrincham	42	8	6	28	68	125	22
Wigan Rovers	42	7	3	32	44	169	17

Wigan Rovers moved to the Lancashire Combination and Wigan Athletic joined from the Lancashire Combination.

1959-60

	P	W	D	L	F	A	Pts
Ellesmere Port Town	38	25	6	7	80	46	56
Hyde United	38	22	8	8	100	56	52
Winsford United	38	19	11	8	85	48	49
Buxton	38	21	7	10	85	56	49
Runcorn	38	21	5	12	87	70	47
Northwich Victoria	38	17	11	10	70	44	45
Bangor City	38	18	6	14	86	58	42
Mossley	38	18	6	14	77	70	42
Altrincham	38	14	11	13	65	73	39
Oswestry Town	38	15	8	15	82	84	38
Tranmere Rovers Reserves	38	16	5	17	72	73	37
Rhyl	38	15	7	16	50	58	37
Macclesfield Town	38	15	6	17	83	81	36
Wrexham Reserves	38	14	7	17	70	83	35
Stalybridge Celtic	38	13	6	19	65	86	32
Witton Albion	38	13	4	21	86	96	30
Chester Reserves	38	12	6	20	57	83	30
Congleton Town	38	9	8	21	59	87	26
Stafford Rangers	38	11	4	23	54	83	26
Wigan Rovers	38	4	4	30	41	119	12

Frickley Colliery joined from the Midland League and Sankeys (Wellington) joined from the Shropshire County League.

1961-62

	P	W	D	L	F	A	Pts
Ellesmere Port Town	42	25	13	4	103	52	63
Macclesfield Town	42	25	10	7	109	61	60
Runcorn	42	27	3	12	108	60	57
Northwich Victoria	42	25	5	12	103	56	55
Wigan Athletic	42	24	7	11	86	51	55
Hyde United	42	24	4	14	81	65	52
Buxton	42	21	6	15	98	79	48
Mossley	42	20	7	15	87	78	47
Stalybridge Celtic	42	17	7	18	79	74	41
Bangor City	42	15	11	16	86	86	41
Altrincham	42	15	10	17	58	64	40
Sankeys (Wellington)	42	16	7	19	76	74	39
Stafford Rangers	42	12	13	17	72	84	37
Rhyl	42	12	11	19	52	63	35
Congleton Town	42	12	11	19	57	78	35
Wrexham Reserves	42	12	11	19	53	79	35
Oswestry Town	42	13	8	21	76	103	34
Winsford United	42	12	8	22	73	100	32
Chester Reserves	42	11	10	21	66	106	32
Tranmere Rovers Reserves	42	10	9	23	73	111	29
Frickley Colliery	42	10	9	23	65	108	29
Witton Albion	42	11	6	25	70	99	28

1962-63

Team	P	W	D	L	F	A	Pts
Runcorn	42	26	13	3	95	43	65
Buxton	42	24	7	11	104	71	55
Tranmere Rovers Reserves	42	19	15	8	88	57	53
Stalybridge Celtic	42	22	9	11	98	71	53
Macclesfield Town	42	20	12	10	87	59	52
Ellesmere Port Town	42	19	14	9	78	57	52
Wigan Athletic	42	22	6	14	70	54	50
Altrincham	42	19	8	15	90	68	46
Northwich Victoria	42	15	15	12	77	68	45
Winsford United	42	16	11	15	69	73	43
Frickley Colliery	42	16	11	15	66	79	43
Hyde United	42	14	14	14	81	74	42
Bangor City	42	13	16	13	71	68	42
Witton Albion	42	16	10	16	84	86	42
Wrexham Reserves	42	18	4	20	72	86	40
Congleton Town	42	16	7	19	73	80	39
Rhyl	42	12	10	20	64	86	34
Sankeys (Wellington)	42	10	13	19	64	76	33
Mossley	42	10	9	23	55	81	29
Stafford Rangers	42	9	10	23	50	90	28
Chester Reserves	42	7	7	28	62	105	21
Oswestry Town	42	6	5	31	53	119	17

1963-64

Team	P	W	D	L	F	A	Pts
Macclesfield Town	42	30	9	3	112	38	69
Sankeys (Wellington)	42	23	10	9	98	57	56
Altrincham	42	22	8	12	94	68	52
Bangor City	42	21	9	12	75	55	51
Witton Albion	42	22	7	13	67	64	51
Tranmere Rovers Reserves	42	19	10	13	108	71	48
Runcorn	42	19	10	13	81	71	48
Ellesmere Port Town	42	20	8	14	77	76	48
Buxton	42	18	11	13	92	77	47
Hyde United	42	18	11	13	64	60	47
Frickley Colliery	42	18	9	15	65	57	45
Wigan Athletic	42	18	7	17	94	82	43
Mossley	42	16	7	19	66	77	39
Rhyl	42	13	12	17	73	88	38
Oswestry Town	42	13	10	19	85	94	36
Stafford Rangers	42	15	6	21	66	89	36
Chester Reserves	42	15	5	22	70	82	35
Stalybridge Celtic	42	14	6	22	66	80	34
Northwich Victoria	42	13	6	23	64	87	32
Winsford United	42	9	11	22	61	98	29
Congleton Town	42	4	13	25	43	95	21
Wrexham Reserves	42	7	5	30	58	113	19

1964-65

Team	P	W	D	L	F	A	Pts
Wigan Athletic	42	32	3	7	121	46	67
Macclesfield Town	42	28	6	8	115	45	62
Runcorn	42	27	5	10	121	60	59
Bangor City	42	25	4	13	94	58	54
Tranmere Rovers Reserves	42	22	6	14	93	70	50
Hyde United	42	22	6	14	96	76	50
Frickley Colliery	42	21	8	13	79	74	50
Altrincham	42	18	12	12	74	55	48
Stalybridge Celtic	42	17	11	14	78	74	45
Ellesmere Port Town	42	19	6	17	79	60	44
Northwich Victoria	42	18	6	18	100	87	42
Rhyl	42	17	6	19	69	79	40
Oswestry Town	42	17	5	20	100	100	39
Mossley	42	13	12	17	57	62	38
Buxton	42	15	7	20	77	99	37
Witton Albion	42	14	8	20	79	90	36
Winsford United	42	15	5	22	66	96	35
Wrexham Reserves	42	13	9	20	58	99	35
Sankeys (Wellington)	42	10	13	19	70	87	33
Chester Reserves	42	11	8	23	65	99	30
Stafford Rangers	42	6	5	31	44	120	17
Congleton Town	42	3	7	32	46	145	13

Congleton Town moved to the Manchester League and Sankeys
(Wellington) moved to the Shropshire County League.
New Brighton joined from the Lancashire Combination and Stockport
County Reserves also joined.

1965-66

Team	P	W	D	L	F	A	Pts
Altrincham	42	33	7	2	132	49	73
Wigan Athletic	42	32	8	2	133	40	72
Macclesfield Town	42	26	8	8	102	48	60
Bangor City	42	24	6	12	91	67	54
Runcorn	42	22	7	13	105	77	51
Stalybridge Celtic	42	21	8	13	98	84	50
Northwich Victoria	42	20	6	16	93	77	46
Hyde United	42	16	11	15	74	72	43
Ellesmere Port Town	42	16	10	16	97	80	42
Stockport County Reserves	42	14	13	15	61	65	41
New Brighton	42	17	6	19	76	86	40
Buxton	42	15	8	19	74	82	38
Tranmere Rovers Reserves	42	13	11	18	85	88	37
Frickley Colliery	42	13	11	18	76	102	37
Mossley	42	13	10	19	66	72	36
Oswestry Town	42	15	6	21	78	102	36
Witton Albion	42	14	7	21	93	107	35
Wrexham Reserves	42	15	5	22	92	107	35
Stafford Rangers	42	9	10	23	60	109	28
Rhyl	42	8	10	24	57	104	26
Chester Reserves	42	9	7	26	52	116	25
Winsford United	42	6	7	29	55	127	19

1966-67

Altrincham	42	31	5	6	123	45	67
Wigan Athletic	42	26	8	8	101	61	60
Northwich Victoria	42	22	13	7	91	55	57
Hyde United	42	24	8	10	101	56	56
Macclesfield Town	42	24	8	10	78	47	56
Witton Albion	42	21	9	12	74	56	51
Bangor City	42	20	8	14	90	77	48
Frickley Colliery	42	18	10	14	71	69	46
Runcorn	42	16	11	15	75	75	43
New Brighton	42	16	7	19	69	73	39
Mossley	42	15	9	18	66	71	39
Chester Reserves	42	13	12	17	72	71	38
Oswestry Town	42	15	8	19	64	89	38
Ellesmere Port Town	42	11	15	16	61	70	37
Stafford Rangers	42	12	12	18	59	66	36
Buxton	42	13	10	19	69	78	36
Tranmere Rovers Reserves	42	14	8	20	66	84	36
Stockport County Reserves	42	12	9	21	58	76	33
Rhyl	42	11	9	22	59	86	31
Stalybridge Celtic	42	11	8	23	52	85	30
Wrexham Reserves	42	11	3	28	66	114	25
Winsford United	42	8	6	28	46	107	22

1968-69

Skelmersdale United	38	29	6	3	103	34	64
Stafford Rangers	38	26	6	6	98	46	58
Mossley	38	26	5	7	90	45	57
Guinness Exports	38	19	9	10	75	46	47
Stalybridge Celtic	38	19	6	13	88	66	44
Tranmere Rovers Reserves	38	17	8	13	63	46	42
New Brighton	38	18	5	15	51	48	41
Buxton	38	16	8	14	71	53	40
Witton Albion	38	15	9	14	62	60	39
Horwich RMI	38	13	13	12	54	63	39
Frickley Colliery	38	12	12	14	64	65	36
Nantwich Town	38	13	9	16	74	79	35
Droylsden	38	14	7	17	64	89	35
Ellesmere Port Town	38	12	9	17	57	66	33
Oswestry Town	38	12	9	17	67	90	33
Winsford United	38	12	6	20	49	70	30
Rhyl	38	11	6	21	58	78	28
Sandbach Ramblers	38	9	4	25	54	91	22
Chester Reserves	38	8	5	25	47	99	21
Ashton United	38	5	6	27	44	99	16

Stafford Rangers moved to the Northern Premier League and Chester Reserves also left. Marine joined from the Lancashire Combination and Port Vale Reserves also joined.

1967-68

Macclesfield Town	42	28	10	4	96	39	66
Altrincham	42	28	7	7	108	64	63
Bangor City	42	24	9	9	99	61	57
Witton Albion	42	21	12	9	90	65	54
Mossley	42	20	13	9	90	62	53
Tranmere Rovers Reserves	42	22	6	14	71	50	50
Northwich Victoria	42	22	6	14	82	64	50
Wigan Athletic	42	18	12	12	62	48	48
Stafford Rangers	42	18	11	13	88	58	47
Hyde United	42	17	12	13	97	74	46
New Brighton	42	16	10	16	60	69	42
Ellesmere Port Town	42	15	11	16	68	67	41
Runcorn	42	16	8	18	99	95	40
Wrexham Reserves	42	16	8	18	72	77	40
Buxton	42	14	8	20	71	86	36
Rhyl	42	12	10	20	63	78	34
Winsford United	42	13	7	22	50	82	33
Oswestry Town	42	13	6	23	63	106	32
Frickley Colliery	42	10	10	22	61	83	30
Stockport County Reserves	42	10	7	25	55	92	27
Stalybridge Celtic	42	6	14	22	54	93	26
Chester Reserves	42	2	5	35	48	134	9

Altrincham, Bangor City, Hyde United, Macclesfield Town, Northwich Victoria, Runcorn and Wigan Athletic all left to become founder members of the new Northern Premier League. Stockport County Reserves and Wrexham Reserves also left. Ashton United, Droylsden, Guinness Exports, Horwich RMI and Skelmersdale United all joined from the Lancashire Combination while Nantwich Town joined from the Manchester League and Sandbach Ramblers joined from the Mid Cheshire League.

1969-70

Skelmersdale United	38	30	6	2	104	18	66
Mossley	38	23	6	9	101	47	52
Stalybridge Celtic	38	20	9	9	81	54	49
Horwich RMI	38	21	6	11	93	59	48
Buxton	38	19	8	11	64	59	46
Guinness Exports	38	20	5	13	76	64	45
Tranmere Rovers Reserves	38	18	7	13	68	52	43
Rhyl	38	16	11	11	70	55	43
Ellesmere Port Town	38	18	6	14	54	49	42
Marine	38	15	8	15	69	68	38
Droylsden	38	16	5	17	72	68	37
Oswestry Town	38	16	5	17	63	66	37
Witton Albion	38	15	6	17	71	80	36
Frickley Colliery	38	15	5	18	60	71	35
Sandbach Ramblers	38	14	6	18	57	80	34
Nantwich Town	38	11	4	23	53	78	26
Winsford United	38	10	5	23	43	79	25
Ashton United	38	10	3	25	56	98	23
Port Vale Reserves	38	7	4	27	46	100	18
New Brighton	38	4	9	25	31	87	17

Frickley Colliery moved to the Midland League and Tranmere Rovers Reserves also left the league. Burscough and Rossendale United both joined from the Lancashire Combination, Hyde United joined from the Northern Premier League and Oldham Athletic Reserves also joined. Guinness Exports changed their name to Ormskirk.

1970-71

Rossendale United	42	28	11	3	84	39	67
Burscough	42	24	12	6	106	61	60
Skelmersdale United	42	22	12	8	87	48	56
Mossley	42	24	6	12	81	51	54
Ellesmere Port Town	42	16	17	9	56	38	49
Stalybridge Celtic	42	20	7	15	74	59	47
Horwich RMI	42	16	12	14	67	55	44
Buxton	42	18	8	16	69	72	44
Marine	42	16	11	15	66	59	43
Ormskirk	42	17	8	17	62	64	42
Oswestry Town	42	15	12	15	75	81	42
Witton Albion	42	12	17	13	68	68	41
Ashton United	42	15	9	18	65	72	39
Rhyl	42	13	13	16	49	56	39
Sandbach Ramblers	42	14	10	18	54	67	38
Hyde United	42	12	13	17	69	80	37
Oldham Athletic Reserves	42	13	9	20	64	74	35
Nantwich Town	42	11	13	18	56	70	35
Droylsden	42	9	16	17	59	72	34
Winsford United	42	10	14	18	55	80	34
Port Vale Reserves	42	7	10	25	38	88	24
New Brighton	42	7	6	29	35	85	20

Skelmersdale United and Ellesmere Port Town both moved to the Northern Premier League and Port Vale Reserves also left. Formby, Prestwich Heys and Radcliffe Borough all joined from the Lancashire Combination.

1971-72

Rhyl	42	31	4	7	95	33	66
Rossendale United	42	26	5	11	90	65	57
Marine	42	23	9	10	72	48	55
Buxton	42	21	12	9	81	47	54
Oswestry Town	42	21	7	14	84	66	49
Mossley	42	20	7	15	74	55	47
Burscough	42	19	9	14	71	56	47
Hyde United	42	17	10	15	79	72	44
Droylsden	42	16	11	15	77	70	43
Oldham Athletic Reserves	42	16	9	17	66	63	41
Stalybridge Celtic	42	16	9	17	68	65	41
Prestwich Heys	42	13	14	15	74	94	40
Horwich RMI	42	16	6	20	61	82	38
Witton Albion	42	17	3	22	75	82	37
Winsford United	42	16	5	21	57	82	37
Ormskirk	42	12	11	19	54	54	35
Sandbach Ramblers	42	11	13	18	51	68	35
Ashton United	42	14	7	21	57	79	35
Radcliffe Borough	42	11	10	21	65	82	32
Formby	42	11	10	21	61	92	32
New Brighton	42	11	8	23	58	86	30
Nantwich Town	42	12	5	25	59	88	29

Mossley moved to the Northern Premier League and Chorley joined from the Northern Premier League.

1972-73

Buxton	42	28	8	6	89	32	64
Marine	42	27	7	8	73	36	61
Hyde United	42	22	9	11	75	49	53
Stalybridge Celtic	42	17	19	6	83	57	53
Rossendale United	42	21	9	12	62	40	51
Sandbach Ramblers	42	19	10	13	66	55	48
Burscough	42	17	13	12	63	53	47
Formby	42	17	12	13	60	64	46
Chorley	42	18	9	15	69	50	45
Witton Albion	42	16	11	15	63	51	43
Oldham Athletic Reserves	42	16	8	18	60	52	40
New Brighton	42	16	8	18	47	64	40
Oswestry Town	42	12	15	15	75	73	39
Ormskirk	42	12	14	16	53	60	38
Winsford United	42	13	12	17	57	72	38
Rhyl	42	9	16	17	52	73	34
Droylsden	42	11	11	20	62	75	33
Radcliffe Borough	42	11	11	20	60	88	33
Nantwich Town	42	10	12	20	44	69	32
Ashton United	42	12	6	24	61	86	30
Horwich RMI	42	6	16	20	57	83	28
Prestwich Heys	42	9	10	23	47	96	28

Buxton moved to the Northern Premier League and Leek Town joined from the Manchester League.

1973-74

Marine	42	28	8	6	79	26	64
Rossendale United	42	29	6	7	87	39	64
Chorley	42	23	11	8	68	39	57
Leek Town	42	23	11	8	75	49	57
Sandbach Ramblers	42	19	16	7	66	40	54
Burscough	42	19	10	13	70	54	48
Formby	42	17	12	13	62	53	46
Stalybridge Celtic	42	17	12	13	65	63	46
Witton Albion	42	14	17	11	57	48	45
Oldham Athletic Reserves	42	15	11	16	53	49	41
Winsford United	42	12	16	14	51	51	40
Radcliffe Borough	42	12	15	15	57	67	39
Droylsden	42	13	12	17	57	68	38
New Brighton	42	16	6	20	52	63	38
Rhyl	42	14	10	18	67	82	38
Hyde United	42	14	8	20	65	67	36
Oswestry Town	42	12	12	18	61	78	36
Nantwich Town	42	8	13	21	57	82	29
Ashton United	42	11	7	24	59	97	29
Horwich RMI	42	10	7	25	52	74	27
Ormskirk	42	9	9	24	51	88	27
Prestwich Heys	42	7	11	24	54	88	25

Ormskirk disbanded. New Mills joined from the Manchester League.

1974-75

Leek Town	42	27	9	6	92	49	63
Winsford United	42	26	9	7	108	58	61
Sandbach Ramblers	42	21	15	6	80	56	57
Oldham Athletic Reserves	42	24	8	10	85	43	56
Marine	42	24	7	11	73	40	55
Chorley	42	19	11	12	86	68	49
Burscough	42	19	10	13	70	49	48
Rossendale United	42	17	13	12	77	64	47
Formby	42	16	13	13	55	55	45
Oswestry Town	42	16	10	16	56	52	42
Horwich RMI	42	17	7	18	60	59	41
New Mills	42	14	11	17	68	82	39
Stalybridge Celtic	42	14	10	18	66	69	38
Rhyl	42	14	10	18	72	78	38
New Brighton	42	12	14	16	53	60	38
Witton Albion	42	10	17	15	59	69	37
Droylsden	42	14	8	20	53	78	36
Nantwich Town	42	9	14	19	63	87	32
Ashton United	42	11	7	24	43	86	29
Hyde United	42	9	8	25	62	80	26
Radcliffe Borough	42	6	12	24	50	97	24
Prestwich Heys	42	8	7	27	48	100	23

Oswestry Town moved to the Southern League and Oldham Athletic Reserves and Sandbach Ramblers also left. Darwen and St. Helens Town both joined from the Lancashire Combination and Middlewich Athletic joined from the Mid Cheshire League.

1975-76

Marine	42	28	8	6	94	34	64
Chorley	42	29	5	8	88	33	63
Leek Town	42	27	7	8	74	33	61
Winsford United	42	24	10	8	83	44	58
Witton Albion	42	20	14	8	71	37	54
Nantwich Town	42	23	8	11	88	54	54
Middlewich Athletic	42	20	8	14	61	51	48
Stalybridge Celtic	42	20	6	16	67	47	46
Droylsden	42	17	11	14	66	55	45
New Brighton	42	19	7	16	59	57	45
Rossendale United	42	17	9	16	69	62	43
Burscough	42	16	10	16	68	73	42
Hyde United	42	15	11	16	73	75	41
St. Helens Town	42	14	11	17	54	57	39
Formby	42	10	15	17	44	59	35
Ashton United	42	13	8	21	50	63	34
Radcliffe Borough	42	13	5	24	56	94	31
Horwich RMI	42	8	13	21	42	90	29
Rhyl	42	8	10	24	46	83	26
Darwen	42	9	7	26	49	89	25
New Mills	42	8	6	28	47	95	22
Prestwich Heys	42	6	7	29	39	103	19

1976-77

Winsford United	42	31	8	3	98	41	70
Chorley	42	28	6	8	80	35	62
Witton Albion	42	27	6	9	91	32	60
Leek Town	42	24	10	8	91	37	58
Stalybridge Celtic	42	23	10	9	66	44	56
Nantwich Town	42	22	7	13	72	59	51
Marine	42	18	14	10	62	40	50
Horwich RMI	42	18	10	14	72	58	46
Formby	42	17	9	16	59	56	43
St. Helens Town	42	16	10	16	51	58	42
New Brighton	42	13	14	15	64	60	40
Ashton United	42	15	10	17	65	72	40
Prestwich Heys	42	16	8	18	56	63	40
Burscough	42	12	15	15	60	65	39
Rhyl	42	13	9	20	54	69	35
Droylsden	42	13	8	21	60	78	34
Hyde United	42	12	9	21	57	74	33
New Mills	42	10	10	22	47	67	30
Darwen	42	10	8	24	50	81	28
Rossendale United	42	9	10	23	48	85	28
Middlewich Athletic	42	9	4	29	48	108	22
Radcliffe Borough	42	4	9	29	44	113	17

1977-78

Marine	42	26	10	6	101	48	62
Stalybridge Celtic	42	23	12	7	75	47	58
Witton Albion	42	21	14	7	98	54	56
Hyde United	42	21	13	8	68	37	55
Winsford United	42	24	7	11	80	51	55
Ashton United	42	20	13	9	88	56	53
Horwich RMI	42	19	14	9	62	50	52
Leek Town	42	20	10	12	62	45	50
Chorley	42	19	11	12	69	48	49
Formby	42	18	11	13	71	57	47
Middlewich Athletic	42	15	15	12	67	66	45
St. Helens Town	42	15	15	12	53	55	45
Droylsden	42	15	10	17	54	56	40
Burscough	42	13	12	17	56	63	38
Darwen	42	14	6	22	50	68	34
Nantwich Town	42	9	13	20	56	69	31
Rhyl	42	10	10	22	44	67	30
New Brighton	42	10	10	22	35	69	30
New Mills	42	9	9	24	42	72	27
Rossendale United	42	11	4	27	51	110	26
Prestwich Heys	42	6	9	27	42	88	21
Radcliffe Borough	42	7	6	29	46	94	20

A new Second Division of the league was formed.

All existing members were placed in the new Division One with the exception of Prestwich Heys who were placed in Division Two. Fleetwood Town were elected to Division One as a newly formed club that replaced the former Northern Premier League club Fleetwood, who had disbanded in 1976.

Division Two was formed with 18 clubs. In addition to Prestwich Heys (who were in effect relegated from Division One), the other 17 clubs were: Accrington Stanley, Ashton Town, Atherton Collieries, Bootle, Ford Motors, Kirkby Town, Maghull and Skelmersdale United who all joined from the Lancashire Combination; Congleton Town, Prescot Town and Warrington Town joined from the Mid Cheshire League; Anson Villa, Curzon Ashton, Glossop and Irlam Town joined from the Manchester League; Eastwood Hanley joined from the West Midlands League and Prescot BI joined from the Liverpool County Combination.

Goal difference was used instead of goal average to determine the position of teams level on points from the next season onwards.

1978-79

Relegated clubs are shown in *italics*.   Promoted clubs are shown in **bold**.

Division One

Horwich RMI	42	35	2	5	89	45	72
Witton Albion	42	30	4	8	114	38	64
Marine	42	29	5	8	104	38	63
Stalybridge Celtic	42	25	5	12	93	47	55
Burscough	42	19	15	8	59	31	53
Winsford United	42	21	11	10	74	49	53
Chorley	42	21	8	13	66	43	50
Formby	42	20	9	13	73	57	49
Leek Town	42	19	10	13	62	43	48
Droylsden	42	18	9	15	62	61	45
Nantwich Town	42	18	8	16	76	72	44
Fleetwood Town	42	17	10	15	70	68	44
Hyde United	42	15	12	15	59	57	42
St. Helens Town	42	16	9	17	59	57	41
Darwen	42	15	9	18	52	53	39
Rhyl	42	15	8	19	53	60	38
Ashton United	42	13	5	24	63	94	31
New Mills	42	9	11	22	58	82	29
Rossendale United	42	11	6	25	51	108	28
Radcliffe Borough	42	4	7	31	37	115	15
New Brighton	42	3	5	34	36	115	11
Middlewich Athletic	42	3	4	35	43	120	10

Marine and Witton Albion both moved to the Northern Premier League.

Division Two

Bootle	34	19	9	6	61	35	47
Curzon Ashton	34	18	9	7	57	32	45
Prescot Town	34	20	5	9	68	37	43
Kirkby Town	34	18	6	10	66	42	42
Accrington Stanley	34	18	6	10	65	43	42
Irlam Town	34	16	10	8	47	33	42
Congleton Town	34	14	13	7	52	31	41
Prescot BI	34	15	11	8	55	42	41
Eastwood Hanley	34	15	9	10	60	47	39
Prestwich Heys	34	17	5	12	53	41	37
Maghull	34	11	7	16	41	50	29
Ford Motors	34	9	10	15	38	52	28
Anson Villa	34	10	7	17	39	60	27
Warrington Town	34	11	5	18	45	69	27
Atherton Collieries	34	8	9	17	43	56	25
Skelmersdale United	34	9	6	19	36	53	24
Glossop	34	6	6	22	42	83	18
Ashton Town	34	3	5	26	22	84	11

Prescot Town and Prestwich Heys each had 2 points deducted.

1979-80

Division One

Stalybridge Celtic	38	26	7	5	94	46	59
Winsford United	38	23	6	9	72	41	52
Chorley	38	20	11	7	60	35	51
Ashton United	38	15	15	8	71	65	45
Burscough	38	16	11	11	67	54	43
Hyde United	38	16	10	12	60	48	42
Droylsden	38	15	10	13	63	45	40
Horwich RMI	38	13	12	13	53	52	38
Curzon Ashton	38	11	14	13	48	55	36
Darwen	38	12	12	14	41	52	36
Rossendale United	38	12	12	14	48	73	36
St. Helens Town	38	10	15	13	59	55	35
Bootle	38	14	7	17	50	53	35
Nantwich Town	38	14	7	17	53	62	35
New Mills	38	11	13	14	44	57	35
Formby	38	13	7	18	50	58	33
Fleetwood Town	38	10	11	17	51	63	31
Leek Town	38	10	9	19	45	66	29
Rhyl	38	10	7	21	54	66	27
Radcliffe Borough	38	6	10	22	45	82	22

Division Two

Prescot Town	34	22	7	5	89	25	51
Accrington Stanley	34	20	9	5	67	33	49
Kirkby Town	34	23	3	8	70	40	49
Prescot BI	34	19	7	8	77	54	45
Congleton Town	34	18	8	8	61	42	44
Eastwood Hanley	34	15	10	9	65	44	40
Glossop	34	14	7	13	53	45	35
Maghull	34	12	10	12	49	49	34
Ford Motors	34	13	6	15	48	44	32
New Brighton	34	13	6	15	59	63	32
Atherton Collieries	34	9	14	11	44	48	32
Irlam Town	34	12	7	15	48	49	31
Middlewich Athletic	34	12	6	16	55	64	30
Skelmersdale United	34	9	10	15	46	69	28
Warrington Town	34	9	6	19	48	80	24
Prestwich Heys	34	8	6	20	36	71	22
Ashton Town	34	3	12	19	35	83	18
Anson Villa	34	5	6	23	29	76	16

Prescot Town changed their name to Prescot Cables.
Anson Villa left the league. Leyland Motors joined from the Lancashire Combination, Atherton Laburnum Rovers joined from the Bolton Combination and Salford joined from the Manchester League.

1980-81

Division One

Nantwich Town	38	26	6	6	87	34	58
Hyde United	38	23	9	6	75	27	55
Winsford United	38	20	10	8	75	38	50
Formby	38	21	7	10	65	39	49
Stalybridge Celtic	38	16	15	7	62	50	47
Chorley	38	17	11	10	65	48	45
Bootle	38	18	7	13	68	53	43
Prescot Cables	38	16	9	13	60	46	41
Horwich RMI	38	15	9	14	53	49	39
Leek Town	38	15	9	14	50	47	39
Ashton United	38	12	12	14	70	73	36
Curzon Ashton	38	14	8	16	48	63	36
St. Helens Town	38	14	7	17	63	82	35
Fleetwood Town	38	9	13	16	53	53	31
Rossendale United	38	9	12	17	49	69	30
Burscough	38	11	6	21	52	62	28
Darwen	38	8	10	20	46	74	26
Droylsden	38	9	8	21	49	82	26
Kirkby Town	38	6	11	21	30	65	23
New Mills	38	8	7	23	34	80	23

Division Two

Accrington Stanley	38	26	3	9	73	20	55
Glossop	38	23	9	6	76	38	55
Leyland Motors	38	20	10	8	68	42	50
Middlewich Athletic	38	20	10	8	56	32	50
Atherton Laburnum Rovers	38	19	11	8	61	39	49
Prescot BI	38	20	5	13	59	40	45
Rhyl	38	20	5	13	69	57	45
Maghull	38	15	12	11	55	41	42
Ford Motors	38	16	9	13	49	52	41
Congleton Town	38	16	8	14	67	55	40
Radcliffe Borough	38	15	10	13	58	48	40
Irlam Town	38	15	6	17	49	51	36
Warrington Town	38	15	5	18	59	78	35
Prestwich Heys	38	15	4	19	66	68	34
Salford	38	9	13	16	50	70	31
Eastwood Hanley	38	12	6	20	47	55	30
Skelmersdale United	38	9	10	19	51	68	28
Atherton Collieries	38	8	5	25	39	83	21
Ashton Town	38	6	5	27	40	93	17
New Brighton	38	6	4	28	31	93	16

New Brighton moved to the South Wirral League.
Ellesmere Port & Neston joined from the Clwyd League.

1981-82

Division One

Hyde United	38	27	8	3	91	34	62
Chorley	38	23	9	6	70	34	55
Burscough	38	21	10	7	70	39	52
Winsford United	38	21	9	8	68	43	51
Rossendale United	38	18	10	10	62	44	46
Glossop	38	13	19	6	52	30	45
Darwen	38	16	10	12	63	62	40
Curzon Ashton	38	12	15	11	57	50	39
Prescot Cables	38	16	8	14	51	45	38
Stalybridge Celtic	38	14	9	15	71	66	37
Fleetwood Town	38	12	13	13	42	55	37
Formby	38	12	11	15	42	55	35
Accrington Stanley	38	11	11	16	40	57	33
Nantwich Town	38	10	13	15	48	49	31
Leek Town	38	10	11	17	39	45	31
Horwich RMI	38	12	7	19	58	72	31
Bootle	38	11	12	15	49	47	30
St. Helens Town	38	7	11	20	34	71	25
Ashton United	38	8	6	24	38	77	22
Droylsden	38	3	4	31	26	96	10

Darwen, Prescot Cables and Nantwich Town each had 2 points deducted and Bootle had 4 points deducted.

Division Two

Congleton Town	38	25	9	4	67	20	59
Rhyl	38	24	10	4	84	29	58
Irlam Town	38	23	10	5	67	27	56
Leyland Motors	38	19	14	5	79	45	52
Maghull	38	20	7	11	64	48	47
Radcliffe Borough	38	18	7	13	64	39	43
Kirkby Town	38	17	9	12	53	42	43
Warrington Town	38	17	8	13	52	35	42
Eastwood Hanley	38	16	9	13	62	51	39
Middlewich Athletic	38	15	11	12	42	34	39
Atherton Laburnum Rovers	38	14	11	13	46	46	39
Ford Motors	38	13	10	15	48	59	36
Prescot BI	38	14	7	17	64	70	35
Ellesmere Port & Neston	38	13	6	19	43	55	32
Skelmersdale United	38	13	5	20	32	49	29
Salford	38	9	6	23	34	65	24
Atherton Collieries	38	8	7	23	41	85	23
Ashton Town	38	6	9	23	40	76	21
New Mills	38	6	8	24	31	93	20
Prestwich Heys	38	5	7	26	30	75	15

Eastwood Hanley, Middlewich Athletic, Prestwich Heys and Skelmersdale United each had 2 points deducted for fielding ineligible players.

At the end of the season, the Cheshire League merged with the Lancashire Combination to form the North West Counties League and 37 of the 40 Cheshire League clubs took their place in the new league. The 3 exceptions were Chorley and Hyde United who moved to the Northern Premier League, and Middlewich Athletic who initially applied to join the new league but then withdrew their application and rejoined the Mid Cheshire League instead.

All other Division One clubs moved to Division One of the North West Counties League with the exceptions of Droylsden, Fleetwood Town and Rossendale United who moved to Division Two. All other Cheshire League Division Two clubs moved into Division Two of the North West Counties League with the exceptions of Congleton Town, Leyland Motors and Rhyl who moved into Division One and Ashton Town, Atherton Collieries, Maghull, Prestwich Heys and Warrington Town who moved into Division Three.

The Cheshire League then closed down.

MID CHESHIRE LEAGUE 1948-2016

(renamed CHESHIRE LEAGUE in 2007)

The Mid Cheshire League was formed at a special meeting of the Northwich & District F.A. held at the Cock Hotel, Northwich on 6th May 1948.

Football was experiencing unprecedented levels of support throughout the country in the immediate aftermath of war but there was a wide gap in standards in the central Cheshire area. The Cheshire County League was an extremely strong competition, sitting just one level below the Football League itself, but for other clubs in that area, the next level down was the Northwich & District League. Any move up to the Cheshire County League would be a huge step for clubs who wanted to progress from this level. Additionally, the Northwich & District League had insufficient members to continue to operate and so a number of the more senior clubs from central Cheshire were playing in other leagues outside the area. The formation of the Mid Cheshire League was intended to bring these clubs together.

There were 14 founder members: Altrincham Reserves and Northwich Victoria Reserves who both came from the Manchester League; there were 5 clubs from the Crewe & District League – Barnton, I.C.I. (Salt) who were based in Winsford, Nantwich, Sandbach and Seddons Ramblers; Congleton Town Reserves from the North Staffordshire League; Goostrey from the Macclesfield Senior League; Knutsford from the Altrincham & District League; Lostock Gralam from the Manchester Amateur League; Runcorn Athletic from the Liverpool County Combination; Whitchurch Alport from the Shrewsbury & District League and Moulton who had only just re-formed after the war.

1948-49

Altrincham Reserves	26	19	3	4	72	33	41
Runcorn Athletic	26	17	2	7	69	42	36
Congleton Town Reserves	26	16	3	7	63	47	35
Barnton	26	12	5	9	74	51	29
Northwich Victoria Reserves	26	12	5	9	55	49	29
Lostock Gralam	26	11	6	9	57	33	28
Nantwich	26	10	8	8	64	48	28
Whitchurch Alport	26	11	6	9	48	44	28
Seddons Ramblers	26	11	2	13	77	58	24
Sandbach Town	26	8	6	12	48	75	22
ICI (Salt)	26	7	4	15	54	68	18
Knutsford	26	6	6	14	48	71	18
Goostrey	26	7	2	17	42	84	16
Moulton	26	3	6	17	40	92	12

Moulton disbanded. Linotype joined as a newly re-formed club and Fodens Recreation, Crewe Alexandra "A", Winsford United Reserves and Parkside (Macclesfield) also joined.

1949-50

Altrincham Reserves	34	23	7	4	114	45	53
Whitchurch Alport	34	21	6	7	93	52	48
Seddons Ramblers	34	18	10	6	88	47	46
Knutsford	34	20	4	10	92	61	44
Nantwich	34	20	3	11	96	51	43
Barnton	34	16	9	9	87	54	41
Fodens Recreation	34	16	8	10	82	70	40
Lostock Gralam	34	15	8	11	74	48	38
Runcorn Athletic	34	14	8	12	91	94	36
Linotype	34	12	8	14	79	97	32
Congleton Town Reserves	34	13	5	16	67	67	31
Crewe Alexandra "A"	34	11	6	17	70	84	28
Parkside (Macclesfield)	34	13	2	19	67	94	28
Sandbach Town	34	13	2	19	65	94	28
Northwich Victoria Reserves	34	10	6	18	71	87	26
Winsford United Reserves	34	10	5	19	65	73	25
ICI (Salt)	34	6	2	26	56	123	14
Goostrey	34	4	3	27	49	125	11

ICI (Salt) resigned before the start of the season as they were unable to find a ground. ICI Alkali and Mirrlees (from Stockport) joined the league.

1950-51

Lostock Gralam	36	30	3	3	131	49	63
Nantwich	36	21	8	7	90	42	50
ICI Alkali	36	21	4	11	109	58	46
Runcorn Athletic	36	20	4	12	92	65	44
Altrincham Reserves	36	19	6	11	93	68	44
Northwich Victoria Reserves	36	20	2	14	96	84	42
Whitchurch Alport	36	18	4	14	88	72	40
Knutsford	36	15	10	11	64	57	40
Seddons Ramblers	36	17	5	14	51	69	39
Mirrlees	36	16	2	18	85	82	34
Linotype	36	13	7	16	69	82	33
Congleton Town Reserves	36	14	4	18	76	83	32
Winsford United Reserves	36	12	6	18	85	75	30
Barnton	36	13	4	19	60	72	30
Goostrey	36	13	2	21	84	97	28
Crewe Alexandra "A"	36	12	3	21	87	94	27
Sandbach Town	36	11	5	20	53	93	27
Parkside (Macclesfield)	36	10	2	24	77	128	22
Fodens Recreation	36	5	3	28	50	144	13

Seddons Ramblers disbanded and Sandbach Town changed their name to Sandbach Ramblers. Fodens Recreation and Parkside (Macclesfield) left the league and Wilmslow Albion joined from the South-East Lancashire League. Witton Albion Reserves also joined.

1951-52

Lostock Gralam	34	24	5	5	116	43	53
Barnton	34	22	5	7	96	46	49
Knutsford	34	20	6	8	97	50	46
Nantwich	34	19	7	8	93	60	45
ICI Alkali	34	20	4	10	88	58	44
Northwich Victoria Reserves	34	19	5	10	82	53	43
Altrincham Reserves	34	17	5	12	88	66	39
Whitchurch Alport	34	17	4	13	80	57	38
Mirrlees	34	13	9	12	72	90	35
Wilmslow Albion	34	15	4	15	69	80	34
Crewe Alexandra "A"	34	15	2	17	85	74	32
Winsford United Reserves	34	13	3	18	55	83	29
Linotype	34	11	4	19	58	82	26
Goostrey	34	9	7	18	73	102	25
Congleton Town Reserves	34	10	3	21	46	87	23
Runcorn Athletic	34	8	6	20	53	111	22
Witton Albion Reserves	34	8	2	24	67	104	18
Sandbach Ramblers	34	5	1	28	47	126	11

Northwich Victoria and Witton Albion both disbanded their reserve sides and Mirrlees also left the league. Leek Town joined from the Manchester League and Middlewich Athletic joined as a newly formed club. Crewe Alexandra "A" changed their name to Crewe LMR.

1952-53

Lostock Gralam	32	28	2	2	128	23	58
ICI Alkali	32	24	2	6	134	46	50
Knutsford	32	20	7	5	113	43	47
Barnton	32	19	3	10	115	70	41
Linotype	32	17	7	8	86	65	41
Whitchurch Alport	32	17	1	14	76	65	35
Middlewich Athletic	32	13	6	13	87	74	32
Winsford United Reserves	32	15	2	15	73	81	32
Nantwich	32	13	5	14	72	72	31
Wilmslow Albion	32	13	5	14	86	85	31
Congleton Town Reserves	32	12	5	15	67	71	29
Altrincham Reserves	32	9	8	15	53	76	26
Goostrey	32	10	4	18	66	82	24
Crewe LMR	32	8	8	16	58	99	24
Runcorn Athletic	32	9	4	19	53	133	22
Leek Town	32	7	3	22	59	107	17
Sandbach Ramblers	32	1	2	29	32	137	4

Leek Town moved to the Manchester League and Winsford United disbanded their reserve side. Northwich Victoria Reserves joined after

being re-formed and Stockton Heath joined from the Warrington & District League. Crewe LMR changed their name back to Crewe Alexandra "A".

1953-54

ICI Alkali	32	24	5	3	102	38	53
Lostock Gralam	32	24	4	4	93	27	52
Stockton Heath	32	22	5	5	111	57	49
Whitchurch Alport	32	18	3	11	86	57	39
Linotype	32	15	6	11	76	57	36
Wilmslow Albion	32	14	8	10	87	70	36
Knutsford	32	15	6	11	83	67	36
Northwich Victoria Reserves	32	14	5	13	54	51	33
Runcorn Athletic	32	13	6	13	75	69	32
Middlewich Athletic	32	13	4	15	84	92	30
Altrincham Reserves	32	12	3	17	65	79	27
Nantwich	32	10	7	15	59	73	27
Barnton	32	12	3	17	73	92	27
Sandbach Ramblers	32	10	4	18	57	86	24
Crewe Alexandra "A"	32	6	6	20	47	107	18
Congleton Town Reserves	32	7	3	22	58	93	17
Goostrey	32	3	2	27	39	127	8

Altrincham disbanded their reserve side while Winsford United Reserves joined after being re-formed. Wallasey Borough also joined the league.

1954-55

ICI Alkali	34	25	4	5	120	42	54
Whitchurch Alport	34	20	4	10	107	67	44
Barnton	34	18	7	9	79	50	43
Lostock Gralam	34	19	4	11	104	61	42
Runcorn Athletic	34	20	2	12	103	75	42
Congleton Town Reserves	34	18	6	10	80	60	42
Linotype	34	19	3	12	125	67	41
Stockton Heath	34	19	1	14	121	76	39
Sandbach Ramblers	34	18	3	13	88	74	39
Wilmslow Albion	34	16	4	14	98	92	36
Northwich Victoria Reserves	34	16	4	14	84	91	36
Wallasey Borough	34	12	7	15	83	101	31
Knutsford	34	11	5	18	75	107	27
Crewe Alexandra "A"	34	9	6	19	59	102	24
Middlewich Athletic	34	8	6	20	55	111	22
Nantwich	34	8	4	22	56	96	20
Goostrey	34	5	7	22	35	103	17
Winsford United Reserves	34	5	3	26	39	136	13

1955-56

Runcorn Athletic	34	25	6	3	134	56	56
Middlewich Athletic	34	25	5	4	165	56	55
Stockton Heath	34	26	3	5	148	54	55
Linotype	34	21	6	7	102	58	48
Whitchurch Alport	34	22	4	8	90	69	48
ICI Alkali	34	19	4	11	105	64	42
Lostock Gralam	34	18	4	12	79	78	40
Northwich Victoria Reserves	34	15	8	11	95	58	38
Sandbach Ramblers	34	12	8	14	84	87	32
Nantwich	34	11	9	14	65	75	31
Knutsford	34	11	7	16	85	75	29
Winsford United Reserves	34	10	8	16	64	96	28
Congleton Town Reserves	34	11	5	18	76	100	27
Crewe Alexandra "A"	34	10	7	17	54	89	27
Wilmslow Albion	34	6	5	23	54	134	17
Barnton	34	5	4	25	46	93	14
Wallasey Borough	34	5	4	25	44	129	14
Goostrey	34	4	3	27	48	168	11

Northwich Victoria Reserves and Wallasey Borough both left the league. Altrincham Reserves joined after being re-formed and Northern Nomads joined, having played only cup ties previously. They shared Stalybridge Celtic's Bower Fold ground.

1956-57

Northern Nomads	34	27	3	4	125	45	57
Runcorn Athletic	34	27	3	4	106	43	57
Linotype	34	22	5	7	109	56	49
Lostock Gralam	34	22	5	7	99	57	49
Stockton Heath	34	18	7	9	110	61	43
Middlewich Athletic	34	20	1	13	103	67	41
Altrincham Reserves	34	17	6	11	93	73	40
Whitchurch Alport	34	14	7	13	77	56	35
Nantwich	34	12	8	14	74	88	32
Winsford United Reserves	34	13	5	16	70	75	31
Knutsford	34	13	5	16	100	105	31
ICI Alkali	34	10	9	15	70	92	29
Sandbach Ramblers	34	10	6	18	67	94	26
Congleton Town Reserves	34	11	3	20	71	92	25
Goostrey	34	8	6	20	70	113	22
Barnton	34	6	9	19	52	81	21
Crewe Alexandra "A"	34	5	3	26	48	148	13
Wilmslow Albion	34	3	5	26	44	141	11

Northern Nomads moved to the Lancashire Combination and Goostrey disbanded.

1957-58

Runcorn Athletic	30	23	6	1	109	37	52
Stockton Heath	30	20	6	4	107	41	46
Lostock Gralam	30	19	5	6	123	58	43
Middlewich Athletic	30	16	4	10	76	55	36
Knutsford	30	15	6	9	91	62	36
Whitchurch Alport	30	16	3	11	68	62	35
ICI Alkali	30	12	7	11	79	76	31
Linotype	30	12	6	12	75	61	30
Winsford United Reserves	30	10	7	13	55	64	27
Altrincham Reserves	30	9	9	12	58	65	27
Barnton	30	8	11	11	70	78	27
Congleton Town Reserves	30	9	5	16	57	107	23
Sandbach Ramblers	30	8	5	17	60	86	21
Nantwich	30	4	8	18	54	91	16
Crewe Alexandra "A"	30	6	3	21	61	107	15
Wilmslow Albion	30	6	3	21	47	141	15

Altrincham Reserves and Winsford United Reserves both left the league. Norley United joined from the Chester & District League.

1958-59

Runcorn Athletic	28	21	4	3	89	41	46
Knutsford	28	16	5	7	66	37	37
Linotype	28	16	4	8	82	50	36
ICI Alkali	28	16	3	9	85	55	35
Lostock Gralam	28	15	4	9	68	40	34
Sandbach Ramblers	28	14	4	10	78	52	32
Middlewich Athletic	28	15	2	11	74	71	32
Stockton Heath	28	13	5	10	62	53	31
Wilmslow Albion	28	10	8	10	60	57	28
Whitchurch Alport	28	10	4	14	50	62	24
Norley United	28	8	7	13	60	65	23
Nantwich	28	10	3	15	53	75	23
Barnton	28	8	3	17	48	71	19
Crewe Alexandra "A"	28	5	5	18	48	108	15
Congleton Town Reserves	28	2	1	25	29	116	5

Northwich Victoria Reserves and Witton Albion Reserves both joined the league.

1959-60

Linotype	32	24	2	6	85	36	50
Wilmslow Albion	32	22	5	5	77	37	49
Middlewich Athletic	32	18	6	8	73	47	42
Lostock Gralam	32	18	5	9	63	35	41
Knutsford	32	17	6	9	82	49	40
Stockton Heath	32	15	9	8	66	37	39
Norley United	32	16	5	11	71	43	37
Sandbach Ramblers	32	16	3	13	69	51	35
ICI Alkali	32	14	6	12	72	59	34
Whitchurch Alport	32	13	7	12	79	65	33
Northwich Victoria Reserves	32	14	5	13	76	66	33
Runcorn Athletic	32	14	5	13	61	56	33
Barnton	32	8	4	20	36	84	20
Congleton Town Reserves	32	6	6	20	47	92	18
Nantwich	32	6	5	21	32	70	17
Witton Albion Reserves	32	5	4	23	50	109	14
Crewe Alexandra "A"	32	3	3	26	46	129	9

Crewe Rolls Royce joined the league.

1960-61

Stockton Heath	34	21	7	6	92	43	49
Norley United	34	23	3	8	88	53	49
Linotype	34	18	7	9	80	46	43
Wilmslow Albion	34	19	5	10	70	42	43
Knutsford	34	18	4	12	86	55	40
Nantwich	34	18	3	13	79	63	39
Runcorn Athletic	34	17	5	12	74	64	39
ICI Alkali	34	16	6	12	63	53	38
Northwich Victoria Reserves	34	17	4	13	95	66	38
Middlewich Athletic	34	14	7	13	75	65	35
Sandbach Ramblers	34	16	3	15	73	72	35
Lostock Gralam	34	15	5	14	72	74	35
Witton Albion Reserves	34	12	3	19	77	82	27
Barnton	34	12	3	19	67	91	27
Congleton Town Reserves	34	10	5	19	59	81	25
Whitchurch Alport	34	9	5	20	67	93	23
Crewe Rolls Royce	34	5	5	24	43	102	15
Crewe Alexandra "A"	34	4	4	26	50	120	12

Northwich Victoria Reserves and Witton Albion Reserves left the league. Hartford and Moulton Youth Club both joined from the Northwich Senior League. Stockton Heath changed their name to Warrington Town.

1961-62

Middlewich Athletic	34	28	3	3	116	38	59
Nantwich	34	24	4	6	88	42	52
ICI Alkali	34	20	9	5	86	45	49
Barnton	34	22	3	9	108	55	47
Lostock Gralam	34	22	3	9	102	66	47
Linotype	34	19	5	10	94	54	43
Warrington Town	34	15	7	12	70	65	37
Wilmslow Albion	34	13	9	12	53	47	35
Norley United	34	15	5	14	78	72	35
Runcorn Athletic	34	15	3	16	68	75	33
Crewe Alexandra "A"	34	11	5	18	56	79	27
Whitchurch Alport	34	10	5	19	77	94	25
Sandbach Ramblers	34	11	2	21	58	83	24
Crewe Rolls Royce	34	7	9	18	69	85	23
Knutsford	34	8	3	23	63	120	19
Congleton Town Reserves	34	6	6	22	50	93	18
Hartford	34	7	4	23	49	126	18
Moulton YC	34	7	3	24	43	95	17

1962-63

	P	W	D	L	F	A	Pts
Lostock Gralam	32	25	1	6	141	63	51
Linotype	32	21	4	7	84	51	46
Nantwich	32	18	6	8	92	54	42
ICI Alkali	32	19	4	9	68	45	42
Warrington Town	32	18	5	9	87	51	41
Middlewich Athletic	32	15	10	7	82	51	40
Knutsford	32	17	6	9	74	62	40
Whitchurch Alport	32	15	5	12	71	60	35
Wilmslow Albion	32	13	6	13	52	54	32
Barnton	32	11	7	14	78	64	29
Moulton YC	32	13	3	16	76	89	29
Sandbach Ramblers	32	11	2	19	47	81	24
Norley United	32	10	3	19	65	87	23
Hartford	32	10	3	19	67	99	23
Crewe Rolls Royce	32	8	6	18	60	114	22
Crewe Alexandra "A"	32	5	6	21	38	83	16
Congleton Town Reserves	32	4	2	26	45	120	10

Runcorn Athletic resigned and disbanded in February 1963 and their record was deleted. Crewe Rolls Royce also left the league.

1963-64

	P	W	D	L	F	A	Pts
Nantwich	30	22	6	2	80	29	50
Lostock Gralam	30	21	3	6	106	43	45
Sandbach Ramblers	30	21	3	6	82	42	45
Wilmslow Albion	30	20	4	6	70	27	44
Middlewich Athletic	30	16	8	6	72	47	40
ICI Alkali	30	12	10	8	57	51	34
Linotype	30	14	5	11	78	47	33
Barnton	30	13	7	10	67	48	33
Warrington Town	30	12	4	14	62	67	28
Hartford	30	9	8	13	50	68	26
Knutsford	30	9	7	14	56	71	25
Norley United	30	9	6	15	48	81	24
Whitchurch Alport	30	5	6	19	59	91	16
Crewe Alexandra "A"	30	6	4	20	44	102	16
Moulton YC	30	4	3	23	46	115	11
Congleton Town Reserves	30	2	6	22	21	68	10

Congleton Town disbanded their reserve side. Mossley Athletic joined the league, sharing Congleton Town's Booth Street ground.

1964-65

	P	W	D	L	F	A	Pts
Middlewich Athletic	28	25	1	2	126	37	51
Nantwich	28	21	3	4	105	24	45
Barnton	28	20	3	5	78	32	43
Wilmslow Albion	28	17	3	8	84	28	37
Lostock Gralam	28	16	5	7	97	56	37
Sandbach Ramblers	28	14	8	6	83	51	36
Knutsford	28	13	6	9	94	53	32
Warrington Town	28	13	3	12	63	56	29
Linotype	28	9	4	15	47	67	22
Hartford	28	6	7	15	67	81	19
ICI Alkali	28	8	3	17	44	79	19
Whitchurch Alport	28	7	4	17	58	91	18
Norley United	28	6	3	19	48	98	15
Moulton YC	28	3	4	21	41	130	10
Mossley Athletic	28	3	1	24	23	175	7

Crewe Alexandra "A" resigned during the season and their record was deleted. Nantwich moved to the Manchester League and Hartford and Norley United both disbanded. Congleton Town Reserves rejoined after being re-formed and Mossley Athletic left as they had been sharing Congleton's ground and were unable to find a replacement. ICI Alkali changed their name to Winnington Park and Eastwood (Hanley) joined.

1965-66

	P	W	D	L	F	A	Pts
Lostock Gralam	24	24	0	0	119	15	48
Middlewich Athletic	24	19	3	2	107	38	41
Eastwood Hanley	24	14	5	5	81	26	33
Sandbach Ramblers	24	13	3	8	56	48	29
Linotype	24	12	4	8	61	46	28
Barnton	24	12	3	9	49	39	27
Wilmslow Albion	24	12	3	9	50	48	27
Warrington Town	24	10	2	12	62	61	22
Whitchurch Alport	24	6	5	13	48	81	17
Knutsford	24	6	4	14	41	90	16
Winnington Park	24	5	2	17	37	76	12
Moulton YC	24	2	4	18	42	84	8
Congleton Town Reserves	24	2	0	22	24	121	4

Wilmslow Albion left the league. Kidsgrove Athletic joined from the Staffordshire County League (North) and Alsager Technical College, Crosfields and Nantwich Reserves also joined.

1966-67

	P	W	D	L	F	A	Pts
Lostock Gralam	30	24	5	1	114	28	53
Eastwood Hanley	30	26	1	3	103	33	53
Middlewich Athletic	30	20	2	8	89	56	42
Sandbach Ramblers	30	16	4	10	76	47	36
Warrington Town	30	13	9	8	70	50	35
Barnton	30	15	4	11	89	59	34
Crosfields	30	15	2	13	94	63	32
Linotype	30	13	4	13	45	53	30
Nantwich Reserves	30	12	5	13	77	70	29
Alsager Technical College	30	11	7	12	53	55	29
Kidsgrove Athletic	30	12	4	14	71	74	28
Winnington Park	30	9	8	13	36	65	26
Whitchurch Alport	30	8	5	17	60	80	21
Knutsford	30	8	5	17	45	83	21
Congleton Town Reserves	30	2	4	24	31	118	8
Moulton YC	30	0	4	26	27	146	4

Macclesfield British Legion and Helsby BI joined the league.

1967-68

	P	W	D	L	F	A	Pts
Lostock Gralam	34	29	4	1	110	35	62
Barnton	34	23	3	8	110	48	49
Alsager Technical College	34	21	6	7	81	40	48
Middlewich Athletic	34	22	3	9	94	53	47
Sandbach Ramblers	34	19	7	8	85	46	45
Macclesfield British Legion	34	17	5	12	73	61	39
Eastwood Hanley	34	14	10	10	76	58	38
Kidsgrove Athletic	34	16	6	12	76	62	38
Whitchurch Alport	34	14	7	13	64	69	35
Warrington Town	34	12	10	12	63	60	34
Nantwich Reserves	34	12	9	13	59	58	33
Helsby BI	34	13	7	14	64	79	33
Knutsford	34	8	8	18	60	82	24
Linotype	34	9	4	21	45	69	22
Crosfields	34	5	9	20	46	84	19
Winnington Park	34	7	5	22	33	73	19
Congleton Town Reserves	34	4	6	24	35	122	14
Moulton YC	34	5	3	26	36	107	13

Sandbach Ramblers moved to the Cheshire League and were replaced by their reserves. Congleton Town joined from the Manchester League, replacing their reserves. Rylands joined from the Liverpool County Combination and English Electric and Northwich Victoria Reserves also joined. Nantwich Reserves left the league.

1968-69

Linotype	38	27	5	6	89	35	59
Kidsgrove Athletic	38	27	5	6	114	49	59
Barnton	38	26	6	6	107	43	58
Lostock Gralam	38	24	9	5	105	56	57
Alsager Technical College	38	19	10	9	75	53	48
Whitchurch Alport	38	21	3	14	94	74	45
Knutsford	38	20	5	13	86	74	45
Congleton Town	38	17	7	14	72	67	41
Sandbach Ramblers Reserves	38	16	7	15	78	79	39
English Electric	38	15	8	15	74	76	38
Middlewich Athletic	38	14	9	15	87	70	37
Crosfields	38	12	9	17	87	95	33
Rylands	38	12	6	20	71	86	30
Winnington Park	38	10	9	19	52	95	29
Helsby BI	38	9	9	20	70	109	27
Warrington Town	38	9	7	22	60	92	25
Eastwood Hanley	38	10	4	24	57	103	24
Moulton YC	38	9	5	24	63	102	23
Northwich Victoria Reserves	38	9	4	25	74	117	22
Macclesfield British Legion	38	7	7	24	53	94	21

Eastwood (Hanley) moved to the West Midlands Regional League and Macclesfield British Legion resigned after losing their ground-share at Macclesfield Town and being unable to find a replacement venue. Helsby BI, Northwich Victoria Reserves and Sandbach Ramblers Reserves also left the league and Cuddington, Hartford College and Milton United joined.

1969-70

Whitchurch Alport	34	25	5	4	90	41	55
Congleton Town	34	25	5	4	86	45	55
Kidsgrove Athletic	34	24	4	6	104	41	52
Milton United	34	23	6	5	95	40	52
Linotype	34	22	7	5	81	33	51
Lostock Gralam	34	21	3	10	88	58	45
Middlewich Athletic	34	13	12	9	71	53	38
English Electric	34	16	5	13	72	50	37
Alsager Technical College	34	13	5	16	68	68	31
Winnington Park	34	10	11	13	48	55	31
Barnton	34	12	6	16	54	74	30
Cuddington	34	9	8	17	51	68	26
Warrington Town	34	10	3	21	58	78	23
Rylands	34	9	5	20	52	82	23
Crosfields	34	9	4	21	69	105	22
Knutsford	34	5	6	23	47	87	16
Hartford College	34	4	5	25	44	118	13
Moulton YC	34	3	6	25	36	118	12

1970-71

Kidsgrove Athletic	34	26	4	4	115	27	56
Whitchurch Alport	34	23	6	5	107	48	52
Middlewich Athletic	34	24	3	7	114	42	51
Linotype	34	20	9	5	80	30	49
Alsager Technical College	34	20	8	6	90	43	48
English Electric	34	20	6	8	68	44	46
Cuddington	34	16	6	12	68	50	38
Congleton Town	34	15	7	12	91	63	37
Winnington Park	34	15	7	12	59	49	37
Milton United	34	15	6	13	74	53	36
Rylands	34	14	4	16	54	59	32
Barnton	34	7	12	15	62	84	26
Crosfields	34	10	5	19	60	94	25
Warrington Town	34	11	3	20	58	106	25
Moulton YC	34	7	5	22	37	117	19
Knutsford	34	4	8	22	41	114	16
Lostock Gralam	34	3	5	26	33	106	11
Hartford College	34	2	4	28	24	107	8

Crosfields left the league after losing their ground and Hartford College also left. Alsager joined from the Crewe & District League and Witton Albion Reserves also joined.

1971-72

Middlewich Athletic	34	25	8	1	117	44	58
Congleton Town	34	25	7	2	117	46	57
Kidsgrove Athletic	34	21	10	3	110	48	52
Linotype	34	18	7	9	66	45	43
Rylands	34	17	8	9	60	51	42
Milton United	34	16	9	9	90	49	41
Whitchurch Alport	34	15	8	11	71	64	38
Alsager Technical College	34	13	9	12	63	31	35
Cuddington	34	14	5	15	69	64	33
English Electric	34	12	7	15	67	68	31
Barnton	34	12	6	16	64	82	30
Alsager	34	11	6	17	68	74	28
Winnington Park	34	11	5	18	54	70	27
Warrington Town	34	10	7	17	52	76	27
Knutsford	34	10	6	18	55	90	26
Lostock Gralam	34	8	4	22	51	91	20
Moulton YC	34	5	3	26	46	130	13
Witton Albion Reserves	34	3	5	26	58	121	11

English Electric left the league and Runcorn Boys Club Old Boys joined.

1972-73

Middlewich Athletic	34	29	2	3	111	25	60
Linotype	34	24	7	3	88	28	55
Lostock Gralam	34	22	8	4	95	41	52
Congleton Town	34	22	7	5	104	43	51
Milton United	34	20	6	8	89	43	46
Rylands	34	17	7	10	76	41	41
Whitchurch Alport	34	18	5	11	82	48	41
Winnington Park	34	13	8	13	66	71	34
Alsager Technical College	34	13	7	14	62	64	33
Warrington Town	34	11	10	13	71	82	32
Kidsgrove Athletic	34	14	3	17	59	63	31
Alsager	34	9	9	16	68	65	27
Barnton	34	9	8	17	48	73	26
Knutsford	34	11	4	19	52	80	26
Runcorn Boys Club Old Boys	34	10	4	20	52	78	24
Witton Albion Reserves	34	7	5	22	27	81	19
Moulton YC	34	3	2	29	32	130	8
Cuddington	34	2	2	30	23	157	6

Cuddington left the league and Bramhall and Newton both joined. Alsager changed their name to Alsager Town.

1973-74

Congleton Town	36	23	7	6	100	46	53
Middlewich Athletic	36	24	4	8	86	35	52
Moulton YC	36	22	7	7	77	35	51
Whitchurch Alport	36	20	8	8	68	42	48
Rylands	36	20	5	11	79	58	45
Linotype	36	18	9	9	45	42	45
Kidsgrove Athletic	36	14	15	7	58	44	43
Lostock Gralam	36	16	6	14	58	53	36
Alsager Technical College	36	13	9	14	50	62	35
Bramhall	36	14	6	16	66	62	34
Milton United	36	13	8	15	52	62	34
Alsager Town	36	11	9	16	62	83	31
Knutsford	36	10	8	18	48	58	28
Newton	36	12	4	20	44	54	28
Runcorn Boys Club Old Boys	36	9	9	18	60	73	27
Winnington Park	36	8	10	18	40	71	26
Warrington Town	36	11	3	22	46	85	25
Witton Albion Reserves	36	6	10	20	44	68	22
Barnton	36	6	7	23	43	93	19

Lostock Gralam had 2 points deducted.
E.R.F. joined the league.

1974-75

Middlewich Athletic	38	30	5	3	114	30	65
Milton United	38	27	6	5	82	33	60
Congleton Town	38	23	11	4	78	27	57
Kidsgrove Athletic	38	22	7	9	78	51	51
Whitchurch Alport	38	22	6	10	71	42	50
Moulton YC	38	17	6	15	81	59	40
Knutsford	38	17	5	16	66	54	39
Warrington Town	38	15	9	14	61	66	39
Alsager Technical College	38	17	5	16	58	72	39
Alsager Town	38	16	5	17	56	70	37
E.R.F.	38	13	10	15	54	58	36
Lostock Gralam	38	13	9	16	57	53	35
Bramhall	38	12	10	16	56	69	34
Linotype	38	13	7	18	53	55	33
Newton	38	12	8	18	53	58	32
Rylands	38	10	8	20	63	97	28
Barnton	38	8	10	20	43	77	26
Witton Albion Reserves	38	8	7	23	44	91	23
Winnington Park	38	7	5	26	35	97	19
Runcorn Boys Club Old Boys	38	5	7	26	54	98	17

Middlewich Athletic moved to the Cheshire League and Lostock Gralam moved to the Central Cheshire League. Runcorn Boys Club Old Boys and Witton Albion Reserves also left the league.
Prescot Town joined from the Lancashire Combination.

A Second Division was formed containing 14 members:
Bramhall Reserves, Congleton Town Reserves, Crewe LMR, Davenham, Hartford College, Knutsford Reserves, Linotype Reserves, Lion FC, Norwes Gas, Radcliffe Juniors, Rolls Royce, Rylands Reserves, United Services Club (Sale) and Wilmslow Town.

1975-76

Relegated clubs are shown in *italics*.   Promoted clubs are shown in **bold**.

Division One

Congleton Town	32	22	7	3	71	28	51
Milton United	32	17	9	6	63	30	43
Rylands	32	16	9	7	51	32	41
Barnton	32	16	9	7	61	45	41
Warrington Town	32	16	6	10	60	44	38
Linotype	32	12	12	8	58	30	36
Prescot Town	32	12	12	8	56	45	36
Newton	32	15	6	11	59	51	36
Kidsgrove Athletic	32	11	8	13	50	50	30
Whitchurch Alport	32	9	11	12	49	44	29
Alsager Technical College	32	10	8	14	44	62	28
Knutsford	32	11	5	16	40	51	27
Bramhall	32	10	7	15	42	56	27
Moulton YC	32	10	6	16	40	66	26
E.R.F.	32	8	8	16	47	67	24
Alsager Town	32	7	7	18	41	63	21
Winnington Park	32	3	4	25	26	94	10

E.R.F. left the league.

Division Two

Lion FC	26	20	4	2	80	23	44
Radcliffe Juniors	26	14	9	3	75	45	37
United Services Club (Sale)	26	13	8	5	75	41	34
Linotype Reserves	26	13	8	5	47	33	34
Hartford College	26	16	1	9	67	51	33
Crewe LMR	26	13	7	6	54	48	33
Rylands Reserves	26	11	2	13	55	66	24
Rolls Royce	26	9	4	13	37	53	22
Wilmslow Town	26	8	4	14	52	70	20
Bramhall Reserves	26	8	4	14	33	46	20
Norwes Gas	26	4	11	11	44	63	19
Davenham	26	8	3	15	48	70	19
Knutsford Reserves	26	6	2	18	49	70	14
Congleton Town Reserves	26	3	5	18	33	70	11

Rylands Reserves left the league.
Ellesmere Port Town, Hanley Town and Irwin Rangers joined the league.

1976-77

Division One

Prescot Town	30	25	3	2	99	23	53
Congleton Town	30	19	7	4	66	25	45
Kidsgrove Athletic	30	19	4	7	69	33	42
Milton United	30	17	8	5	60	31	42
Warrington Town	30	16	4	10	61	37	36
Barnton	30	14	8	8	51	34	36
Whitchurch Alport	30	12	9	9	50	33	33
Bramhall	30	11	8	11	48	53	30
Moulton YC	30	10	7	13	46	48	27
Alsager Town	30	9	8	13	37	54	26
Alsager Technical College	30	9	6	15	57	61	24
Linotype	30	7	9	14	26	43	23
Newton	30	7	5	18	43	71	19
Rylands	30	8	3	19	44	82	19
Knutsford	30	6	5	19	36	68	17
Winnington Park	30	3	2	25	21	118	8

Division Two

Crewe LMR	30	25	3	2	95	27	53
United Services Club (Sale)	30	20	7	3	83	36	47
Rolls Royce	30	19	6	5	58	32	44
Hanley Town	30	19	5	6	79	36	43
Lion FC	30	17	8	5	67	30	42
Radcliffe Juniors	30	14	6	10	77	59	34
Congleton Town Reserves	30	14	5	11	58	50	33
Bramhall Reserves	30	13	3	14	54	52	29
Linotype Reserves	30	10	8	12	43	39	28
Ellesmere Port Town	30	9	6	15	53	66	24
Irwin Rangers	30	7	8	15	47	64	22
Norwes Gas	30	7	8	15	48	74	22
Davenham	30	6	9	15	46	68	21
Wilmslow Town	30	6	5	19	42	79	17
Knutsford Reserves	30	4	6	20	27	88	14
Hartford College	30	2	3	25	30	107	7

Knutsford Reserves and Hartford College left the league and Styal and ICI Macclesfield both joined.

1977-78

Division One

Congleton Town	30	20	4	6	67	34	44
Whitchurch Alport	30	16	9	5	65	35	41
Prescot Town	30	16	7	7	67	31	39
Alsager Town	30	15	7	8	73	50	37
Warrington Town	30	13	9	8	58	41	35
Linotype	30	12	9	9	39	33	33
Kidsgrove Athletic	30	14	5	11	49	51	33
Moulton YC	30	12	6	12	40	47	30
Newton	30	12	3	15	40	53	27
Bramhall	30	9	8	13	39	47	26
United Services Club (Sale)	30	9	7	14	45	57	25
Barnton	30	8	8	14	39	53	24
Milton United	30	9	5	16	41	54	23
Rylands	30	9	5	16	45	59	23
Crewe LMR	30	6	11	13	41	60	23
Alsager Technical College	30	7	3	20	35	78	17

Congleton Town, Prescot Town and Warrington Town all left to join the Cheshire League and Milton United left to join the Staffordshire County League (North). Northwich Victoria Reserves joined the league.
Crewe LMR changed their name to LMR Hunters.

Division Two

	P	W	D	L	F	A	Pts
Rolls Royce	30	23	6	1	73	22	52
Lion FC	30	22	3	5	81	26	47
Hanley Town	30	21	3	6	81	36	45
Radcliffe Juniors	30	17	6	7	88	54	40
Wilmslow Town	30	18	4	8	76	50	40
Bramhall Reserves	30	16	3	11	69	45	35
Congleton Town Reserves	30	13	9	8	59	48	35
Davenham	30	11	8	11	53	53	30
Ellesmere Port Town	30	11	7	12	50	68	29
Styal	30	12	3	15	46	56	27
Knutsford	30	8	7	15	55	63	23
Linotype Reserves	30	10	3	17	35	52	23
Norwes Gas	30	7	6	17	49	71	20
Irwin Rangers	30	7	5	18	43	73	19
Winnington Park	30	2	5	23	38	109	9
ICI Macclesfield	30	2	2	26	28	98	6

Davenham, Ellesmere Port Town, ICI Macclesfield and Wilmslow Town all left the league. Alsager Town Reserves and Kidsgrove Athletic Reserves both joined from the Crewe & District League and GEC Villa and Prescot BI Reserves also joined.

1978-79

Division One

	P	W	D	L	F	A	Pts
Kidsgrove Athletic	30	22	6	2	70	24	50
United Services Club (Sale)	30	17	7	6	77	41	41
Alsager Town	30	16	7	7	67	43	39
Rolls Royce	30	12	12	6	51	38	36
Hanley Town	30	14	7	9	57	48	35
Barnton	30	12	10	8	50	39	34
Whitchurch Alport	30	12	10	8	47	42	34
Linotype	30	10	12	8	40	35	32
Rylands	30	10	9	11	41	45	29
Bramhall	30	11	6	13	52	55	28
Congleton Town Reserves	30	9	6	15	48	66	24
Moulton YC	30	8	8	14	31	52	24
Newton	30	6	9	15	42	52	21
LMR Hunters	30	7	7	16	30	52	21
Alsager Technical College	30	7	4	19	26	52	18
Northwich Victoria Reserves	30	3	8	19	26	71	14

Newton changed their name to HB & H Newton and LMR Hunters changed their name to Crewe LMR. Congleton Town disbanded their reserve side.

Division Two

	P	W	D	L	F	A	Pts
Lion FC	24	19	3	2	66	21	41
Radcliffe Juniors	24	15	4	5	86	40	34
Linotype Reserves	24	12	5	7	39	32	29
Prescot BI Reserves	24	11	6	7	40	19	28
Winnington Park	24	11	5	8	42	44	27
Alsager Town Reserves	24	10	6	8	50	47	26
Bramhall Reserves	24	8	10	6	39	49	26
Knutsford	24	7	6	11	41	51	20
GEC Villa	24	7	6	11	42	57	20
Handforth Irwin	24	5	8	11	40	50	18
Kidsgrove Athletic Reserves	24	5	7	12	38	48	17
Norwes Gas	24	4	9	11	31	50	17
Styal	24	2	5	17	27	69	9

GEC Villa changed their name to Sandbach Ramblers. Willaston White Star joined from the Crewe & District League and Shell (Carrington), Mirrlees and Laporte also joined.

1979-80

Division One

	P	W	D	L	F	A	Pts
Barnton	30	21	5	4	63	27	47
Bramhall	30	17	7	6	61	37	41
Rylands	30	17	6	7	55	31	40
Lion FC	30	14	6	10	47	43	34
Whitchurch Alport	30	11	11	8	41	42	33
United Services Club (Sale)	30	13	6	11	49	39	32
Hanley Town	30	11	10	9	40	40	32
Linotype	30	10	10	10	36	35	30
Alsager Town	30	10	8	12	56	55	28
Alsager Technical College	30	9	9	12	38	42	27
Rolls Royce	30	10	7	13	38	46	27
Kidsgrove Athletic	30	8	10	12	46	39	26
HB & H Newton	30	5	14	11	28	35	24
Radcliffe Juniors	30	9	5	16	51	60	23
Crewe LMR	30	8	7	15	31	48	23
Moulton YC	30	4	5	21	34	94	13

Lion FC disbanded.

Division Two

	P	W	D	L	F	A	Pts
Prescot BI Reserves	30	20	5	5	67	25	45
Shell (Carrington)	30	16	7	7	60	40	39
Willaston White Star	30	14	10	6	58	42	38
Handforth Irwin	30	15	7	8	69	46	37
Kidsgrove Athletic Reserves	30	14	6	10	48	43	34
Winnington Park	30	13	8	9	50	47	34
Alsager Town Reserves	30	11	9	10	48	48	31
Knutsford	30	11	9	10	42	43	31
Mirrlees	30	10	8	12	51	54	28
Northwich Victoria Reserves	30	9	9	12	54	54	27
Sandbach Ramblers	30	8	11	11	42	46	27
Styal	30	11	5	14	40	51	27
Laporte	30	9	5	16	49	71	23
Linotype Reserves	30	7	7	16	36	59	21
Bramhall Reserves	30	8	4	18	38	63	20
Norwes Gas	30	4	10	16	42	62	18

Rolls Royce Reserves joined from the Crewe & District League and Pilkington Recreation also joined. Laporte left the league.

1980-81

Division One

	P	W	D	L	F	A	Pts
Rylands	30	20	5	5	83	40	45
Linotype	30	17	7	6	51	29	41
United Services Club (Sale)	30	17	5	8	53	36	39
Whitchurch Alport	30	16	4	10	50	38	36
Barnton	30	13	7	10	48	38	33
Alsager Town	30	11	10	9	44	47	32
Prescot BI Reserves	30	13	5	12	48	47	31
HB & H Newton	30	12	6	12	57	57	30
Kidsgrove Athletic	30	12	6	12	30	30	30
Shell (Carrington)	30	11	8	11	43	45	30
Bramhall	30	12	4	14	41	43	28
Hanley Town	30	10	7	13	39	44	27
Crewe LMR	30	10	5	15	44	44	25
Rolls Royce	30	7	6	17	31	51	20
Radcliffe Juniors	30	6	7	17	42	74	19
Alsager Technical College	30	5	4	21	37	79	14

Division Two

	P	W	D	L	F	A	Pts
Handforth Irwin	30	24	2	4	63	25	50
Northwich Victoria Reserves	30	18	7	5	70	26	43
Moulton YC	30	16	6	8	61	39	38
Mirrlees	30	15	6	9	69	41	36
Alsager Town Reserves	30	16	3	11	68	43	35
Linotype Reserves	30	14	7	9	41	43	35
Knutsford	30	12	8	10	40	35	32
Pilkington Recreation	30	11	6	13	45	44	28
Bramhall Reserves	30	9	9	12	52	62	27
Winnington Park	30	9	8	13	47	58	26
Styal	30	9	8	13	41	69	26
Norwes Gas	30	8	7	15	44	54	23
Willaston White Star	30	8	7	15	42	74	23
Kidsgrove Athletic Reserves	30	9	4	17	38	52	22
Sandbach Ramblers	30	8	6	16	48	65	22
Rolls Royce Reserves	30	3	8	19	35	74	14

Handforth Irwin and Willaston White Star both left the league.
Intex and Rylands Reserves joined the league.

1981-82

Division One

	P	W	D	L	F	A	Pts
Hanley Town	30	18	10	2	43	18	46
Barnton	30	16	8	6	53	24	40
Whitchurch Alport	30	15	10	5	65	39	40
Linotype	30	14	8	8	40	28	36
Rylands	30	12	9	9	38	29	33
United Services Club (Sale)	30	11	11	8	45	42	33
Mirrlees	30	14	4	12	52	55	32
Kidsgrove Athletic	30	12	7	11	35	35	31
Bramhall	30	10	9	11	47	42	29
Crewe LMR	30	8	10	12	36	45	26
Northwich Victoria Reserves	30	10	5	15	35	48	25
HB & H Newton	30	9	7	14	45	60	25
Prescot BI Reserves	30	6	11	13	31	48	23
Shell (Carrington)	30	7	7	16	40	61	21
Alsager Town	30	9	2	19	44	57	20
Rolls Royce	30	8	4	18	40	58	20

HB & H Newton moved to the North West Counties League and Crewe LMR also left the league.

Division Two

	P	W	D	L	F	A	Pts
Intex	30	19	9	2	73	21	47
Kidsgrove Athletic Reserves	30	18	9	3	64	32	45
Linotype Reserves	30	15	11	4	55	26	41
Radcliffe Juniors	30	13	10	7	75	51	36
Alsager Technical College	30	14	7	9	61	59	35
Bramhall Reserves	30	14	6	10	67	49	34
Pilkington Recreation	30	12	9	9	60	47	33
Norwes Gas	30	11	10	9	47	39	32
Alsager Town Reserves	30	14	4	12	42	43	32
Moulton YC	30	11	7	12	47	45	29
Knutsford	30	9	7	14	43	58	25
Rylands Reserves	30	7	8	15	40	67	22
Winnington Park	30	7	7	16	52	73	21
Sandbach Ramblers	30	5	7	18	42	74	17
Styal	30	5	6	19	33	62	16
Rolls Royce Reserves	30	5	5	20	35	90	15

Middlewich Athletic joined from the Cheshire League and Newcastle Town joined from the Staffordshire County League (North).
Rolls Royce Reserves left the league.

1982-83

Division One

	P	W	D	L	F	A	Pts
Barnton	28	17	6	5	52	24	40
Rylands	28	14	9	5	59	40	37
United Services Club (Sale)	28	13	9	6	47	31	35
Intex	28	14	5	9	64	50	33
Linotype	28	11	11	6	35	28	33
Bramhall	28	12	8	8	52	37	32
Shell (Carrington)	28	13	5	10	57	52	31
Hanley Town	28	10	8	10	44	44	28
Rolls Royce	28	10	8	10	43	50	28
Kidsgrove Athletic	28	11	5	12	49	43	27
Mirrlees	28	10	6	12	53	63	26
Whitchurch Alport	28	9	6	13	45	48	24
Alsager Town	28	6	12	10	33	44	24
Northwich Victoria Reserves	28	5	5	18	35	64	15
Prescot BI Reserves	28	2	3	23	26	76	7

Intex, Shell (Carrington), Mirrlees and Prescot BI all left the league.

Division Two

	P	W	D	L	F	A	Pts
Newcastle Town	30	26	3	1	102	18	55
Linotype Reserves	30	21	5	4	68	33	47
Sandbach Ramblers	30	17	6	7	65	38	40
Winnington Park	30	17	5	8	84	59	39
Middlewich Athletic	30	14	8	8	62	46	36
Pilkington Recreation	30	14	7	9	66	49	35
Norwes Gas	30	13	5	12	47	46	31
Kidsgrove Athletic Reserves	30	11	5	14	44	50	27
Alsager Town Reserves	30	10	7	13	54	65	27
Alsager Technical College	30	10	6	14	54	75	26
Knutsford	30	10	5	15	43	61	25
Styal	30	10	4	16	44	49	24
Bramhall Reserves	30	8	7	15	42	49	23
Moulton YC	30	7	6	17	42	83	20
Rylands Reserves	30	5	3	22	32	83	13
Radcliffe Juniors	30	3	6	21	38	84	12

Alsager Town Reserves and Alsager Technical College both moved to the Crewe & District League. Linotype Reserves, Norwes Gas, Kidsgrove Athletic Reserves, Bramhall Reserves, Moulton YC, Rylands Reserves and Radcliffe Juniors left the league.

The remaining 7 clubs were promoted to Division One and Division Two closed down.

1983-84

	P	W	D	L	F	A	Pts
Rylands	34	25	8	1	94	27	58
Barnton	34	21	8	5	78	26	50
Alsager Town	34	21	7	6	75	39	49
Newcastle Town	34	16	7	11	56	33	39
Linotype	34	16	7	11	48	36	39
Knutsford	34	16	6	12	47	38	38
United Services Club (Sale)	34	15	8	11	54	47	38
Hanley Town	34	17	4	13	48	43	38
Sandbach Ramblers	34	15	5	14	51	54	35
Winnington Park	34	13	8	13	62	60	34
Bramhall	34	12	9	13	56	49	33
Kidsgrove Athletic	34	11	10	13	51	41	32
Middlewich Athletic	34	10	8	16	46	56	28
Pilkington Recreation	34	10	7	17	52	66	27
Styal	34	10	7	17	34	58	27
Rolls Royce	34	9	6	19	47	72	24
Northwich Victoria Reserves	34	8	2	24	31	65	18
Whitchurch Alport	34	2	1	31	12	141	5

Rolls Royce left the league.

1984-85

Bramhall	32	23	8	1	85	25	54
Barnton	32	23	6	3	85	23	52
Newcastle Town	32	19	9	4	68	30	47
Rylands	32	19	6	7	67	30	44
Kidsgrove Athletic	32	16	9	7	53	40	41
Linotype	32	16	7	9	63	37	39
Alsager Town	32	15	6	11	67	45	36
Hanley Town	32	13	7	12	45	39	33
Middlewich Athletic	32	14	5	13	51	51	33
Knutsford	32	7	11	14	30	50	25
United Services Club (Sale)	32	8	8	16	38	47	24
Northwich Victoria Reserves	32	8	6	18	42	70	22
Styal	32	9	4	19	39	68	22
Pilkington Recreation	32	9	3	20	36	56	21
Sandbach Ramblers	32	8	5	19	39	81	21
Winnington Park	32	7	5	20	38	87	19
Whitchurch Alport	32	1	9	22	26	93	11

United Services Club (Sale) disbanded and Sandbach Ramblers also left the league. Grove United, Malpas and Manchester Polytechnic joined.

1985-86

Newcastle Town	34	27	4	3	76	23	58
Kidsgrove Athletic	34	24	6	4	107	38	54
Rylands	34	23	6	5	94	36	52
Linotype	34	24	4	6	80	35	52
Grove United	34	20	5	9	67	35	45
Alsager Town	34	18	7	9	50	35	43
Malpas	34	18	5	11	91	46	41
Bramhall	34	18	5	11	71	43	41
Barnton	34	13	12	9	52	41	38
Whitchurch Alport	34	10	7	17	49	62	27
Northwich Victoria Reserves	34	11	3	20	52	88	25
Hanley Town	34	9	5	20	44	70	23
Styal	34	7	7	20	35	68	21
Pilkington Recreation	34	8	5	21	32	75	21
Winnington Park	34	6	9	19	36	88	21
Middlewich Athletic	34	7	4	23	35	89	18
Manchester Polytechnic	34	6	5	23	41	85	17
Knutsford	34	4	7	23	34	89	15

Middlewich Athletic moved to the North West Counties League and Northwich Victoria Reserves moved to the Lancashire League.
Alsager Town changed their name to Alsager United.
Poynton joined from the Lancashire & Cheshire League.

1986-87

Kidsgrove Athletic	32	23	6	3	91	25	52
Newcastle Town	32	19	10	3	52	23	48
Hanley Town	32	19	9	4	87	22	47
Linotype	32	20	6	6	53	30	46
Alsager United	32	20	6	6	56	34	46
Bramhall	32	19	4	9	70	46	42
Grove United	32	14	8	10	48	41	36
Rylands	32	15	5	12	64	42	35
Poynton	32	15	5	12	64	50	35
Barnton	32	10	11	11	49	38	31
Malpas	32	12	3	17	74	83	27
Whitchurch Alport	32	8	4	20	30	77	20
Manchester Polytechnic	32	6	7	19	39	66	19
Knutsford	32	6	6	20	31	86	18
Styal	32	6	5	21	34	72	17
Winnington Park	32	5	4	23	36	87	14
Pilkington Recreation	32	2	7	23	25	81	11

Newcastle Town moved to the North West Counties League and Manchester Polytechnic changed their name to Chorlton Town.

Division Two re-formed with the following 12 members:
Altrincham Reserves, Bollington Athletic, Bramhall Reserves, Chorlton Town Reserves, ICI Macclesfield, Leek Town Reserves, Linotype Reserves, Macclesfield College, Newcastle Town Reserves, Pelican Rovers, Poynton Reserves and Rylands Reserves.

1987-88

Division One

Kidsgrove Athletic	30	24	5	1	87	24	53
Alsager United	30	23	1	6	67	25	47
Hanley Town	30	21	4	5	90	34	46
Rylands	30	19	6	5	71	22	44
Grove United	30	19	3	8	59	24	41
Linotype	30	17	4	9	58	36	38
Barnton	30	17	4	9	60	46	38
Knutsford	30	12	3	15	48	54	27
Poynton	30	10	5	15	45	63	25
Bramhall	30	7	8	15	43	64	22
Chorlton Town	30	7	7	16	46	69	21
Malpas	30	8	5	17	50	70	21
Winnington Park	30	7	5	18	38	63	19
Pilkington Recreation	30	6	5	19	24	64	17
Whitchurch Alport	30	6	5	19	28	73	17
Styal	30	2	0	28	23	106	4

Alsager United disbanded for a season before re-forming in 1989 when they joined the Crewe & District League.

Division Two

Leek Town Reserves	**22**	**19**	**2**	**1**	**69**	**13**	**40**
Altrincham Reserves	**22**	**19**	**1**	**2**	**77**	**21**	**39**
Linotype Reserves	22	14	3	5	59	32	31
ICI Macclesfield	22	12	5	5	54	39	29
Bollington Athletic	22	12	2	8	52	47	26
Newcastle Town Reserves	22	10	3	9	40	33	23
Macclesfield College	22	9	3	10	43	42	21
Pelican Rovers	22	6	5	11	35	52	17
Chorlton Town Reserves	22	4	5	13	23	49	13
Rylands Reserves	22	2	5	15	25	62	9
Poynton Reserves	22	3	3	16	33	72	9
Bramhall Reserves	22	2	3	17	22	70	7

Rylands Reserves left the league. Garswood United joined from the Liverpool County Combination and Wilmslow Albion joined from the Lancashire & Cheshire Amateur League. Kidsgrove Athletic Reserves and Knutsford Reserves also joined.

1988-89

Division One

Barnton	28	18	8	2	59	24	44
Grove United	28	17	6	5	56	27	40
Linotype	28	16	7	5	48	24	39
Knutsford	28	13	9	6	34	23	35
Kidsgrove Athletic	28	12	7	9	56	51	31
Altrincham Reserves	28	13	4	11	64	43	30
Leek Town Reserves	28	12	4	12	44	44	28
Bramhall	28	11	5	12	60	54	27
Chorlton Town	28	9	8	11	46	41	26
Hanley Town	28	8	10	10	31	39	26
Rylands	28	10	4	14	44	43	24
Poynton	28	9	4	15	29	45	22
Winnington Park	28	6	8	14	29	57	20
Malpas	28	6	5	17	41	80	17
Pilkington Recreation	28	4	3	21	18	64	11

Division Two

Wilmslow Albion	28	21	5	2	66	22	47
Macclesfield College	28	16	7	5	68	42	39
Whitchurch Alport	28	17	4	7	78	48	38
Bollington Athletic	28	15	8	5	72	44	38
ICI Macclesfield	28	14	7	7	70	44	35
Garswood United	28	13	5	10	57	45	31
Linotype Reserves	28	13	5	10	52	47	31
Kidsgrove Athletic Reserves	28	11	7	10	65	63	29
Styal	28	11	5	12	58	56	27
Knutsford Reserves	28	12	2	14	37	47	26
Bramhall Reserves	28	7	6	15	45	62	20
Newcastle Town Reserves	28	8	3	17	41	58	19
Chorlton Town Reserves	28	6	6	16	32	66	18
Poynton Reserves	28	4	5	19	26	65	13
Pelican Rovers	28	3	3	22	33	91	9

Kidsgrove Athletic Reserves left the league. Rylands Reserves and Beechams both joined. Pelican Rovers changed their name to Trafford Town.

3 points were awarded for a win from the next season onwards.

1989-90

Division One

Grove United	30	19	8	3	58	21	65
Linotype	30	19	6	5	75	32	63
Bramhall	30	19	5	6	61	28	62
Chorlton Town	30	19	5	6	55	34	62
Barnton	30	15	3	12	61	34	48
Winnington Park	30	14	6	10	40	30	48
Altrincham Reserves	30	13	5	12	65	53	44
Kidsgrove Athletic	30	14	2	14	54	66	44
Wilmslow Albion	30	12	6	12	50	48	42
Rylands	30	13	2	15	45	50	41
Knutsford	30	9	9	12	34	38	36
Hanley Town	30	10	4	16	44	55	34
Malpas	30	9	6	15	38	56	33
Pilkington Recreation	30	8	4	18	32	66	28
Leek Town Reserves	30	7	5	18	30	62	26
Poynton	30	1	2	27	17	86	5

Altrincham Reserves moved to the Lancashire League, Kidsgrove Athletic moved to the North West Counties League and Leek Town Reserves also left the league.

Division Two

Garswood United	28	21	4	3	78	33	67
Linotype Reserves	28	17	6	5	59	32	57
Whitchurch Alport	28	17	4	7	94	47	55
Styal	28	15	5	8	80	48	50
ICI Macclesfield	28	13	6	9	71	63	45
Bollington Athletic	28	14	3	11	46	51	45
Chorlton Town Reserves	28	11	5	12	48	46	38
Macclesfield College	28	10	6	12	39	45	36
Bramhall Reserves	28	10	5	13	53	55	35
Knutsford Reserves	28	9	8	11	38	56	35
Beechams	28	10	3	15	67	76	33
Newcastle Town Reserves	28	8	9	11	39	50	33
Alsager Technical College	28	6	6	16	60	71	24
Rylands Reserves	28	6	5	17	29	77	23
Poynton Reserves	28	4	3	21	29	80	15

Trafford Town disbanded early in the season. Their record was deleted and they were replaced by Alsager Technical College. At the end of the season, North Trafford joined as a newly formed club and Middlewich Athletic, Garswood United Reserves, Grove United Reserves, Pilkington Recreation Reserves and Wilmslow Albion Reserves also joined. ICI Macclesfield changed their name to ICI Pharmaceuticals.

1990-91

Division One

Linotype	30	17	6	7	71	30	57
Bramhall	30	17	3	10	56	33	54
Knutsford	30	15	5	10	46	40	50
Whitchurch Alport	30	14	8	8	51	46	50
Chorlton Town	30	14	5	11	51	48	47
Barnton	30	13	7	10	61	47	46
Wilmslow Albion	30	13	7	10	50	43	46
Rylands	30	12	7	11	47	47	43
Garswood United	30	12	5	13	51	51	41
Grove United	30	11	6	13	45	47	39
Poynton	30	11	6	13	47	62	39
Winnington Park	30	10	7	13	38	47	37
Hanley Town	30	9	9	12	33	38	36
Styal	30	10	5	15	48	61	35
Malpas	*30*	*8*	*6*	*16*	*40*	*62*	*30*
Pilkington Recreation	*30*	*6*	*4*	*20*	*37*	*70*	*22*

Division Two

Newcastle Town Reserves	34	26	5	3	104	36	83
North Trafford	34	25	5	4	106	37	80
Middlewich Athletic	34	21	9	4	91	31	72
Knutsford Reserves	34	19	5	10	80	50	62
Beechams	34	19	4	11	104	65	61
Linotype Reserves	34	17	6	11	80	59	57
ICI Pharmaceuticals	34	15	6	13	84	66	51
Pilkington Recreation Reserves	34	14	6	14	60	72	48
Rylands Reserves	34	13	7	14	53	62	46
Wilmslow Albion Reserves	34	13	6	15	79	74	45
Chorlton Town Reserves	34	13	6	15	72	84	45
Garswood United Reserves	34	12	2	20	61	84	38
Bollington Athletic	34	10	6	18	57	92	36
Macclesfield College	34	10	5	19	60	88	35
Bramhall Reserves	34	10	3	21	46	89	33
Alsager Technical College	34	8	5	21	56	102	29
Grove United Reserves	34	7	5	22	54	98	26
Poynton Reserves	34	6	5	23	48	106	23

Pilkington Recreation Reserves and Macclesfield College both left the league and Alsager Technical College were expelled for persistent poor administration. Alsager joined from the Crewe & District League and Broadheath Central also joined.

1991-92

Division One

Grove United	30	23	2	5	74	21	71
Knutsford	30	18	6	6	47	29	60
Linotype	30	18	5	7	67	40	59
North Trafford	30	16	7	7	56	37	55
Barnton	30	15	4	11	60	48	49
Hanley Town	30	14	6	10	42	36	48
Garswood United	30	14	4	12	48	42	46
Poynton	30	14	4	12	57	45	46
Bramhall	30	13	6	11	62	56	45
Rylands	30	11	6	13	50	43	39
Whitchurch Alport	30	10	5	15	38	57	35
Newcastle Town Reserves	30	9	5	16	41	48	32
Chorlton Town	30	8	8	14	41	52	32
Wilmslow Albion	30	6	7	17	41	46	25
Winnington Park	30	5	7	18	40	67	22
Styal	*30*	*4*	*2*	*24*	*33*	*100*	*14*

North Trafford moved to the North West Counties League.

Division Two

Broadheath Central	32	24	4	4	85	31	76
Beechams	32	23	4	5	78	24	73
ICI Pharmaceuticals	32	20	5	7	93	43	65
Pilkington Recreation	32	17	7	8	69	46	58
Alsager	32	16	5	11	48	42	53
Middlewich Athletic	32	14	8	10	54	46	50
Malpas	32	14	5	13	68	60	47
Bramhall Reserves	32	13	8	11	55	58	47
Linotype Reserves	32	13	5	14	60	72	44
Rylands Reserves	32	13	5	14	59	74	44
Garswood United Reserves	32	11	7	14	60	47	40
Knutsford Reserves	32	10	9	13	40	42	39
Poynton Reserves	32	11	6	15	40	62	39
Chorlton Town Reserves	32	9	3	20	45	77	30
Bollington Athletic	32	7	7	18	36	78	28
Wilmslow Albion Reserves	32	4	7	21	38	77	19
Grove United Reserves	32	3	5	24	38	87	14

Beechams changed their name to The Beeches. Grove United Reserves left the league and Littlemoor, The Beeches Reserves and Warrington Town Reserves all joined.

1992-93

Division One

Grove United	30	22	4	4	87	28	70
Winnington Park	30	19	5	6	67	32	62
Chorlton Town	30	18	4	8	68	49	58
Barnton	30	15	9	6	57	49	54
Knutsford	30	16	5	9	59	45	53
The Beeches	30	15	5	10	62	44	50
Linotype	30	14	6	10	57	51	48
Wilmslow Albion	30	11	6	13	61	65	39
Hanley Town	30	10	6	14	39	43	36
Whitchurch Alport	30	10	4	16	46	59	34
Rylands	30	9	6	15	41	57	33
Broadheath Central	30	9	6	15	55	72	33
Poynton	30	9	5	16	47	61	32
Garswood United	30	5	9	16	48	69	24
Bramhall	*30*	*7*	*4*	*19*	*42*	*69*	*25*
Newcastle Town Reserves	30	6	6	18	28	61	24

Newcastle Town Reserves left the league.

Division Two

Malpas	34	28	5	1	119	35	89
Middlewich Athletic	34	25	5	4	90	49	80
Pilkington Recreation	34	20	7	7	83	51	67
Littlemoor	34	18	4	12	88	63	58
Bollington Athletic	34	16	5	13	71	65	53
ICI Pharmaceuticals	34	16	4	14	80	67	52
The Beeches Reserves	34	14	10	10	71	64	52
Warrington Town Reserves	34	11	12	11	63	58	45
Alsager	34	12	7	15	59	59	43
Knutsford Reserves	34	11	10	13	45	53	43
Chorlton Town Reserves	34	11	6	17	65	77	39
Linotype Reserves	34	9	12	13	50	61	39
Rylands Reserves	34	11	6	17	56	77	39
Poynton Reserves	34	9	9	16	52	66	36
Garswood United Reserves	34	8	12	14	41	63	36
Styal	34	7	10	17	52	67	31
Bramhall Reserves	34	8	5	21	41	100	29
Wilmslow Albion Reserves	34	4	7	23	53	104	19

Bramhall Reserves and Knutsford Reserves both left the league and Lostock Gralam and Grove United Reserves both joined.
ICI Pharmaceuticals changed their name to AFC Zeneca.

1993-94

Division One

Linotype	30	21	7	2	66	18	70
Chorlton Town	30	21	5	4	96	39	68
Grove United	30	20	5	5	68	28	65
The Beeches	30	16	8	6	75	50	56
Rylands	30	16	7	7	56	36	55
Garswood United	30	13	11	6	71	52	50
Barnton	30	14	7	9	60	43	49
Broadheath Central	30	11	9	10	57	54	42
Knutsford	30	10	10	10	80	58	40
Poynton	30	11	6	13	51	50	39
Malpas	30	9	5	16	50	78	32
Winnington Park	30	8	5	17	45	86	29
Whitchurch Alport	30	7	6	17	46	54	27
Middlewich Athletic	30	5	7	18	43	62	22
Wilmslow Albion	30	4	4	22	27	103	16
Hanley Town	30	1	4	25	28	108	7

Winnington Park disbanded and Hanley Town left in order to regroup in junior football.

Division Two

Bollington Athletic	32	24	2	6	88	41	74
Bramhall	32	19	8	5	84	34	65
Linotype Reserves	32	18	6	8	68	41	60
AFC Zeneca	32	17	8	7	75	51	59
Warrington Town Reserves	32	16	6	10	68	43	54
Styal	32	15	6	11	75	57	51
Chorlton Town Reserves	32	15	5	12	78	58	50
Pilkington Recreation	32	12	10	10	77	48	46
Littlemoor	32	12	9	11	74	60	45
Garswood United Reserves	32	12	7	13	65	64	43
The Beeches Reserves	32	13	4	15	68	77	43
Poynton Reserves	32	10	6	16	54	78	36
Grove United Reserves	32	10	4	18	53	79	34
Lostock Gralam	32	11	1	20	66	96	34
Alsager	32	8	9	15	67	66	33
Rylands Reserves	32	9	6	17	52	81	33
Wilmslow Albion Reserves	32	1	3	28	37	165	6

Cheadle Heath Nomads, Chester Nomads, Whitchurch Alport Reserves and Bollington Athletic Reserves all joined. Wilmslow Albion Reserves left the league.

1994-95

Division One

Knutsford	30	22	5	3	88	35	71
Bramhall	30	18	9	3	83	42	63
Grove United	30	17	7	6	69	38	58
Garswood United	30	18	4	8	71	40	58
Chorlton Town	30	15	6	9	59	55	50
Linotype	30	12	12	6	69	52	48
Barnton	30	12	7	11	71	64	43
Broadheath Central	30	11	8	11	43	52	41
The Beeches	30	9	8	13	51	60	35
Poynton	30	8	9	13	42	42	33
Whitchurch Alport	30	8	7	15	51	79	31
Wilmslow Albion	30	9	4	17	50	79	31
Rylands	30	6	8	16	32	69	26
Middlewich Athletic	30	6	7	17	53	73	25
Malpas	30	7	4	19	36	64	25
Bollington Athletic	*30*	*5*	*9*	*16*	*51*	*75*	*24*

Chorlton Town had 1 point deducted.
Middlewich Athletic moved to the North West Counties League.

Division Two

Cheadle Heath Nomads	34	29	1	4	110	42	88
Warrington Town Reserves	34	28	3	3	114	16	87
Littlemoor	34	24	3	7	81	49	75
Linotype Reserves	34	18	8	8	84	44	62
Lostock Gralam	34	19	4	11	98	46	61
Pilkington Recreation	34	16	7	11	78	53	55
Chester Nomads	34	15	6	13	69	68	51
Alsager	34	14	7	13	66	61	49
Styal	34	13	10	11	61	62	49
The Beeches Reserves	34	14	2	18	65	79	44
Whitchurch Alport Reserves	34	11	7	16	43	71	40
Bollington Athletic Reserves	34	10	5	19	61	94	35
Chorlton Town Reserves	34	10	4	20	52	82	34
Garswood United Reserves	34	9	6	19	55	79	33
Grove United Reserves	34	9	6	19	38	62	33
Poynton Reserves	34	6	12	16	48	81	30
AFC Zeneca	34	6	9	19	52	95	27
Rylands Reserves	34	2	6	26	27	118	12

Bollington Athletic Reserves left the league.

1995-96

Division One

Garswood United	30	24	4	2	89	25	76
Barnton	30	21	4	5	96	37	67
Grove United	30	20	3	7	65	35	63
Bramhall	30	16	6	8	83	42	54
Knutsford	30	13	7	10	69	48	46
Linotype	30	12	9	9	56	47	45
Chorlton Town	30	11	10	9	53	52	43
Warrington Town Reserves	30	9	12	9	60	43	39
Wilmslow Albion	30	11	6	13	46	52	39
Rylands	30	9	7	14	42	68	34
Broadheath Central	30	8	9	13	38	59	33
Cheadle Heath Nomads	30	9	5	16	46	64	32
Poynton	30	7	7	16	39	57	28
Whitchurch Alport	30	6	9	15	30	57	27
Malpas	30	6	8	16	35	98	26
The Beeches	*30*	*3*	*4*	*23*	*35*	*98*	*13*

Garswood United moved to the North West Counties League.
Warrington Town Reserves changed their name to Warrington Borough.

Division Two

Bollington Athletic	30	23	4	3	89	25	73
AFC Zeneca	30	21	4	5	78	41	67
Alsager	30	21	4	5	62	27	67
Pilkington Recreation	30	19	4	7	79	39	61
Lostock Gralam	30	17	5	8	72	44	56
Littlemoor	30	18	2	10	75	48	56
Chester Nomads	30	14	7	9	66	54	49
Poynton Reserves	30	10	7	13	53	52	37
Garswood United Reserves	30	11	3	16	48	76	36
The Beeches Reserves	30	11	2	17	43	72	35
Linotype Reserves	30	9	7	14	50	58	34
Chorlton Town Reserves	30	9	5	16	55	64	32
Grove United Reserves	30	9	3	18	37	68	30
Whitchurch Alport Reserves	30	5	7	18	39	72	22
Styal	30	4	7	19	55	79	19
Rylands Reserves	30	2	3	25	24	110	9

The Beeches Reserves left the league after the first team was relegated into the same division.
Hanley Town and Bollington Athletic Reserves joined.

1996-97

Division One

Barnton	30	26	3	1	105	17	81
Linotype	30	20	6	4	76	32	66
Grove United	30	19	4	7	66	27	61
Wilmslow Albion	30	17	6	7	60	42	57
Bramhall	30	18	2	10	75	28	56
Knutsford	30	14	6	10	59	34	48
Poynton	30	13	3	14	60	61	42
AFC Zeneca	30	12	4	14	62	79	40
Chorlton Town	30	11	6	13	50	44	39
Cheadle Heath Nomads	30	11	6	13	60	64	39
Whitchurch Alport	30	11	5	14	40	45	38
Bollington Athletic	30	10	6	14	50	50	36
Rylands	30	7	9	14	41	62	30
Warrington Borough	30	8	3	19	46	93	27
Broadheath Central	*30*	*4*	*6*	*20*	*33*	*75*	*18*
Malpas	*30*	*0*	*3*	*27*	*16*	*146*	*3*

Division Two

Lostock Gralam	30	24	4	2	113	34	76
The Beeches	30	22	3	5	93	30	69
Pilkington Recreation	30	21	2	7	88	35	65
Linotype Reserves	30	15	7	8	69	46	52
Alsager	30	14	7	9	58	38	49
Grove United Reserves	30	15	4	11	64	56	49
Garswood United Reserves	30	11	11	8	68	50	44
Chester Nomads	30	12	7	11	61	57	43
Littlemoor	30	10	4	16	63	77	34
Chorlton Town Reserves	30	10	4	16	63	90	34
Poynton Reserves	30	7	12	11	44	50	33
Hanley Town	30	8	9	13	40	54	33
Whitchurch Alport Reserves	30	7	7	16	43	76	28
Bollington Athletic Reserves	30	7	4	19	56	89	25
Rylands Reserves	30	5	5	20	37	121	20
Styal	30	5	4	21	48	105	19

Grove United Reserves and Whitchurch Alport Reserves both left the league and Padgate St. Oswalds joined.

1997-98

Division One

Barnton	30	23	4	3	95	30	73
Knutsford	30	22	4	4	91	27	70
Linotype	30	20	6	4	62	30	66
Poynton	30	14	10	6	69	48	52
Bollington Athletic	30	13	7	10	54	61	46
The Beeches	30	13	5	12	57	54	44
Warrington Borough	30	11	7	12	51	50	40
Chorlton Town	30	11	4	15	51	58	37
Rylands	30	10	7	13	46	61	37
Bramhall	30	11	4	15	63	79	37
Lostock Gralam	30	10	5	15	47	61	35
Cheadle Heath Nomads	30	10	4	16	52	74	34
Whitchurch Alport	30	8	8	14	37	51	32
AFC Zeneca	30	8	4	18	42	67	28
Grove United	*30*	*5*	*8*	*17*	*40*	*74*	*23*
Wilmslow Albion	30	5	5	20	48	80	20

Middlewich Athletic joined from the North West Counties League, having changed their name to Middlewich Town. Garswood United also joined from the North West Counties League. Wilmslow Albion moved to the Manchester League and Bramhall also left.

Division Two

Garswood United Reserves	28	19	5	4	52	24	62
Pilkington Recreation	28	18	4	6	92	35	58
Padgate St. Oswalds	28	16	8	4	87	38	56
Chester Nomads	28	15	6	7	49	37	51
Linotype Reserves	28	12	11	5	59	36	47
Malpas	28	13	6	9	60	49	45
Styal	28	13	5	10	66	65	44
Alsager	28	11	5	12	48	44	38
Poynton Reserves	28	10	7	11	55	51	37
Hanley Town	28	9	6	13	58	70	33
Rylands Reserves	28	10	2	16	45	62	32
Broadheath Central	28	8	6	14	52	65	30
Littlemoor	28	7	2	19	48	85	23
Chorlton Town Reserves	28	5	5	18	37	78	20
Bollington Athletic Reserves	28	3	4	21	40	109	13

Alsager and Hanley Town both moved to the Midland League.
Crewe, Ellesmere Port United, Trafford Reserves and Walker Sports all joined the league.

1998-99

Division One

Barnton	30	26	2	2	97	11	80
Linotype	30	20	3	7	72	41	63
Garswood United	30	19	4	7	85	40	61
Knutsford	30	14	10	6	47	35	52
The Beeches	30	15	6	9	48	45	51
Chorlton Town	30	14	8	8	60	46	50
Poynton	30	13	10	7	65	47	49
Rylands	30	14	4	12	69	57	46
Middlewich Town	30	11	7	12	41	40	40
Pilkington Recreation	30	11	7	12	60	61	40
Bollington Athletic	30	10	5	15	48	79	35
Cheadle Heath Nomads	30	9	6	15	45	62	33
Whitchurch Alport	30	9	0	21	35	61	27
AFC Zeneca	30	7	5	18	42	84	26
Warrington Borough	*30*	*5*	*2*	*23*	*52*	*82*	*17*
Lostock Gralam	*30*	*2*	*3*	*25*	*46*	*121*	*9*

The Beeches and AFC Zeneca both left the league.

Division Two

Padgate St. Oswalds	32	22	6	4	86	24	72
Grove United	32	20	7	5	95	41	67
Trafford Reserves	32	19	8	5	92	34	65
Garswood United Reserves	32	20	4	8	98	47	64
Linotype Reserves	32	17	10	5	56	34	61
Walker Sports	32	17	6	9	84	55	57
Rylands Reserves	32	15	3	14	68	66	48
Malpas	32	15	2	15	79	83	47
Ellesmere Port United	32	15	1	16	58	60	46
Broadheath Central	32	14	3	15	70	55	45
Chester Nomads	32	11	9	12	60	54	42
Crewe	32	11	5	16	69	83	38
Poynton Reserves	32	8	2	22	55	84	26
Chorlton Town Reserves	32	8	2	22	45	102	26
Styal	32	7	5	20	64	140	26
Littlemoor	32	7	4	21	47	96	25
Bollington Athletic Reserves	32	6	3	23	43	111	21

Bollington Athletic Reserves, Ellesmere Port United and Walker Sports all left the league. Cheadle Heath Nomads Reserves and Flixton Reserves both joined.

1999-2000

Division One

Barnton	26	20	4	2	59	16	64
Middlewich Town	26	14	6	6	49	38	48
Poynton	26	15	1	10	55	42	46
Linotype	26	13	4	9	39	36	43
Knutsford	26	10	11	5	43	30	41
Chorlton Town	26	11	4	11	45	43	37
Garswood United	26	9	7	10	35	36	34
Padgate St. Oswalds	26	9	6	11	27	32	33
Grove United	26	8	7	11	42	44	31
Bollington Athletic	26	7	8	11	32	54	29
Cheadle Heath Nomads	26	8	4	14	39	49	28
Rylands	26	7	7	12	35	50	28
Whitchurch Alport	26	6	6	14	39	41	24
Pilkington Recreation	26	5	5	16	25	53	20

Division Two

Trafford Reserves	28	22	2	4	90	29	68
Crewe	28	20	5	3	77	25	65
Malpas	28	19	4	5	64	33	61
Broadheath Central	28	19	1	8	77	42	58
Lostock Gralam	28	16	4	8	69	45	52
Cheadle Heath Nomads Reserves	28	12	4	12	59	70	40
Chester Nomads	28	11	4	13	57	48	37
Warrington Borough	28	11	3	14	62	61	36
Linotype Reserves	28	10	5	13	39	46	35
Chorlton Town Reserves	28	7	6	15	37	62	27
Poynton Reserves	28	7	5	16	46	70	26
Styal	28	7	5	16	51	75	26
Rylands Reserves	28	6	6	16	44	72	24
Littlemoor	28	7	2	19	35	78	23
Garswood United Reserves	28	5	6	17	42	88	21

Flixton Reserves were expelled just before the end of the season and their record was deleted: 29 10 4 15 55 62 34
Golborne Sports joined from the Warrington & District League. Kidsgrove Athletic Reserves and Pilkington Recreation Reserves also joined.

2000-01

Division One

Barnton	30	23	2	5	82	28	71
Poynton	30	17	8	5	77	45	59
Middlewich Town	30	18	3	9	50	33	57
Pilkington Recreation	30	18	3	9	65	48	57
Knutsford	30	15	10	5	52	29	55
Cheadle Heath Nomads	30	14	7	9	51	38	49
Linotype	30	13	7	10	58	40	46
Grove United	30	14	4	12	63	59	46
Rylands	30	11	8	11	44	51	41
Padgate St. Oswalds	30	8	11	11	42	63	35
Garswood United	30	11	1	18	48	64	34
Trafford Reserves	30	8	5	17	40	68	29
Crewe	30	8	4	18	36	55	28
Chorlton Town	30	8	3	19	48	87	27
Bollington Athletic	*30*	*7*	*5*	*18*	*54*	*64*	*26*
Whitchurch Alport	*30*	*4*	*5*	*21*	*39*	*77*	*17*

Division Two

	P	W	D	L	F	A	Pts
Broadheath Central	26	21	3	2	75	27	66
Styal	26	20	3	3	74	26	63
Golborne Sports	26	15	5	6	85	41	50
Warrington Borough	26	11	7	8	44	34	40
Chester Nomads	26	11	6	9	47	42	39
Rylands Reserves	26	11	5	10	44	42	38
Lostock Gralam	26	10	6	10	57	59	36
Cheadle Heath Nomads Reserves	26	10	6	10	54	64	36
Malpas	26	8	10	8	60	45	34
Linotype Reserves	26	9	3	14	47	55	30
Pilkington Recreation Reserves	26	7	5	14	58	63	26
Poynton Reserves	26	5	9	12	46	56	24
Garswood United Reserves	26	7	3	16	43	82	24
Littlemoor	26	0	3	23	31	129	3

Chorlton Town Reserves resigned during the season and their record was deleted when it stood as follows: 10 1 1 8 7 33 4
Kidsgrove Athletic Reserves also resigned during the season and their record at the time was deleted: 15 4 3 8 35 39 15
Crosfields and Daten both joined from the Warrington & District League and Middlewich Town Reserves joined from the Crewe & District League. Littlemoor left the league.

2001-02

Division One

	P	W	D	L	F	A	Pts
Barnton	28	18	7	3	65	25	61
Rylands	28	15	7	6	65	39	52
Cheadle Heath Nomads	28	15	7	6	58	35	52
Knutsford	28	15	6	7	45	25	51
Linotype	28	14	4	10	47	40	46
Styal	28	12	8	8	55	45	44
Crewe	28	12	7	9	50	59	43
Pilkington Recreation	28	10	9	9	37	40	39
Padgate St. Oswalds	28	10	6	12	48	58	36
Poynton	28	8	7	13	39	52	31
Broadheath Central	28	8	5	15	36	50	29
Middlewich Town	28	5	10	13	40	40	25
Chorlton Town	28	7	4	17	40	62	25
Garswood United	28	5	8	15	39	61	23
Trafford Reserves	*28*	*5*	*7*	*16*	*39*	*62*	*22*

Grove United left the league.

Division Two

	P	W	D	L	F	A	Pts
Crosfields	30	20	6	4	99	42	66
Daten	30	19	9	2	100	44	66
Golborne Sports	30	19	8	3	83	37	65
Malpas	30	16	4	10	73	52	52
Whitchurch Alport	30	14	9	7	75	40	51
Lostock Gralam	30	13	8	9	54	48	47
Bollington Athletic	30	12	8	10	58	48	44
Chester Nomads	30	13	4	13	52	54	43
Warrington Borough	30	13	4	13	50	57	43
Linotype Reserves	30	10	5	15	61	73	35
Pilkington Recreation Reserves	30	9	8	13	55	82	35
Garswood United Reserves	30	9	7	14	49	58	34
Poynton Reserves	30	7	11	12	52	60	32
Rylands Reserves	30	5	4	21	32	84	19
Cheadle Heath Nomads Reserves	30	5	4	21	45	107	19
Middlewich Town Reserves	30	4	5	21	36	88	17

Chester Nomads moved to the West Cheshire League.
Barnton Reserves and Crewe Reserves both joined the league.

2002-03

Division One

	P	W	D	L	F	A	Pts
Barnton	30	21	6	3	61	18	69
Middlewich Town	30	17	8	5	66	25	59
Poynton	30	17	6	7	62	38	57
Styal	30	17	5	8	60	41	56
Knutsford	30	15	9	6	52	29	54
Linotype	30	14	10	6	69	33	52
Rylands	30	13	8	9	52	44	47
Daten	30	12	9	9	59	42	45
Crosfields	30	11	8	11	50	59	41
Crewe	30	11	6	13	56	59	39
Pilkington Recreation	30	9	6	15	39	55	33
Broadheath Central	30	8	8	14	40	57	32
Cheadle Heath Nomads	30	7	6	17	35	63	27
Garswood United	30	6	7	17	36	67	25
Padgate St. Oswalds	*30*	*5*	*2*	*23*	*26*	*89*	*17*
Chorlton Town	30	3	4	23	30	74	13

Chorlton Town left the league.

Division Two

	P	W	D	L	F	A	Pts
Golborne Sports	30	23	5	2	96	28	74
Bollington Athletic	30	20	5	5	92	39	65
Malpas	30	17	6	7	60	26	57
Linotype Reserves	30	18	2	10	65	54	56
Trafford Reserves	30	15	6	9	63	37	51
Warrington Borough	30	14	6	10	63	56	48
Middlewich Town Reserves	30	14	5	11	49	48	47
Lostock Gralam	30	12	8	10	52	52	44
Whitchurch Alport	30	12	7	11	70	51	43
Poynton Reserves	30	12	6	12	67	62	42
Pilkington Recreation Reserves	30	11	6	13	55	51	39
Crewe Reserves	30	8	7	15	45	72	31
Rylands Reserves	30	7	5	18	33	73	26
Barnton Reserves	30	4	6	20	32	74	18
Cheadle Heath Nomads Reserves	30	4	5	21	53	102	17
Garswood United Reserves	30	4	5	21	28	98	17

Linotype Reserves, Middlewich Town Reserves, Poynton Reserves, Pilkington Recreation Reserves, Crewe Reserves, Rylands Reserves, Barnton Reserves, Cheadle Heath Nomads Reserves and Garswood United Reserves all left to join the new Mid Cheshire League Reserve Division. Curzon Ashton Reserves and Cheadle Town Reserves both joined from the North West Counties League Reserve Division, Sidac Sports joined from the Warrington & District League and Gamesley joined from the Hope Valley League. Club AZ, Nantwich Town Reserves, Witton Albion Reserves and Winsford United Reserves also joined.

2003-04

Division One

	P	W	D	L	F	A	Pts
Middlewich Town	30	22	4	4	69	27	70
Poynton	30	19	7	4	70	42	64
Barnton	30	19	3	8	67	33	60
Linotype	30	17	6	7	67	43	57
Bollington Athletic	30	14	6	10	64	60	48
Crewe	30	13	9	8	56	52	48
Rylands	30	9	13	8	53	41	40
Daten	30	11	6	13	53	51	39
Knutsford	30	10	8	12	51	53	38
Garswood United	30	11	5	14	43	45	38
Golborne Sports	30	9	9	12	52	59	36
Crosfields	30	10	5	15	52	71	35
Pilkington Recreation	30	10	3	17	56	76	33
Styal	30	8	8	14	49	61	32
Broadheath Central	*30*	*4*	*5*	*21*	*34*	*87*	*17*
Cheadle Heath Nomads	30	1	9	20	37	72	12

Linotype merged with Cheadle Heath Nomads to form Linotype & Cheadle Heath Nomads. Padgate St. Oswalds merged with Greenalls F.C. of the Warrington & District League, forming Greenalls Padgate St. Oswalds who continued to play in the Mid Cheshire League.

Division Two

Padgate St. Oswalds	24	16	2	6	57	31	50
Trafford Reserves	24	15	4	5	52	25	49
Sidac Sports	24	14	4	6	53	36	46
Curzon Ashton Reserves	24	12	5	7	57	43	41
Gamesley	24	12	5	7	42	28	41
Nantwich Town Reserves	24	12	2	10	65	55	38
Warrington Borough	24	10	5	9	39	33	35
Whitchurch Alport	24	10	3	11	39	36	33
Witton Albion Reserves	24	6	8	10	28	35	26
Malpas	24	5	9	10	36	41	24
Club AZ	24	6	5	13	34	45	23
Lostock Gralam	24	5	4	15	31	72	19
Cheadle Town Reserves	24	3	4	17	25	78	13

Winsford United Reserves resigned during the season and their record was deleted when it stood as follows: 23 1 1 21 16 99 4

Ashton Town Reserves, Glossop North End Reserves and Maine Road Reserves all joined from the North West Counties League – Reserve Division, Penketh & Sankey Eagle joined from the Warrington & District League and Billinge joined from the St. Helens Combination.

2004-05

Division One

Barnton	30	20	8	2	69	23	68
Middlewich Town	30	18	6	6	56	32	60
Crosfields	30	16	6	8	49	40	54
Greenalls Padgate St. Oswalds	30	13	8	9	50	40	47
Garswood United	30	13	6	11	42	49	45
Styal	30	12	6	12	68	56	42
Trafford Reserves	30	11	8	11	42	43	41
Knutsford	30	11	8	11	44	50	41
Poynton	30	11	7	12	50	58	40
Linotype & Cheadle Heath Nomads	30	11	5	14	55	48	38
Bollington Athletic	30	11	3	16	58	71	36
Pilkington Recreation	30	10	6	14	40	53	36
Rylands	30	9	7	14	43	59	34
Daten	30	8	8	14	53	54	32
Golborne Sports	*30*	*6*	*9*	*15*	*37*	*54*	*27*
Crewe	30	6	7	17	31	57	25

Division Two

Penketh & Sankey Eagle	30	22	5	3	73	30	71
Witton Albion Reserves	30	22	4	4	86	35	70
Club AZ	30	18	6	6	67	29	60
Broadheath Central	30	17	7	6	78	39	58
Gamesley	30	15	7	8	81	49	52
Billinge	30	14	4	12	65	53	46
Curzon Ashton Reserves	30	13	5	12	64	44	44
Maine Road Reserves	30	12	5	13	64	63	41
Malpas	30	11	8	11	38	54	41
Warrington Borough	30	9	11	10	53	49	38
Glossop North End Reserves	30	9	8	13	43	59	35
Lostock Gralam	30	10	5	15	46	78	35
Whitchurch Alport	30	6	8	16	40	64	26
Ashton Town Reserves	30	7	4	19	39	77	25
Nantwich Town Reserves	30	6	2	22	43	86	20
Cheadle Town Reserves	30	3	3	24	25	96	12

Sidac Sports left the league just before the start of the season. Penketh & Sankey Eagle changed their name to Eagle Sports and Warrington Borough changed their name to Warrington Town Reserves. Ashton Town Reserves and Nantwich Town Reserves both left the league. Monk Sports and Fearnhead both joined from the Warrington & District League and Woodley Sports Reserves also joined.

2005-06

Division One

Middlewich Town	30	21	6	3	83	20	69
Witton Albion Reserves	30	17	8	5	66	37	59
Knutsford	30	15	7	8	65	46	52
Greenalls Padgate St. Oswalds	30	13	8	9	55	47	47
Styal	30	12	10	8	53	42	46
Garswood United	30	12	8	10	55	38	44
Crosfields	30	11	11	8	49	42	41
Linotype & Cheadle Heath Nomads	30	10	9	11	46	52	39
Poynton	30	10	7	13	45	54	37
Trafford Reserves	30	10	7	13	45	54	37
Bollington Athletic	30	9	9	12	50	74	36
Pilkington Recreation	30	7	11	12	46	62	32
Barnton	30	7	9	14	42	77	30
Daten	30	7	7	16	42	51	28
Rylands	30	7	7	16	29	55	28
Eagle Sports	*30*	*6*	*8*	*16*	*38*	*58*	*26*

Crosfields had 3 points deducted.
Bollington Athletic moved to the East Cheshire League.

Division Two

Gamesley	30	19	5	6	96	37	62
Woodley Sports Reserves	30	16	9	5	81	44	57
Crewe	30	17	5	8	65	38	56
Golborne Sports	30	15	9	6	69	45	54
Warrington Town Reserves	30	15	7	8	40	25	52
Broadheath Central	30	14	8	8	67	52	50
Club AZ	30	14	5	11	68	60	47
Maine Road Reserves	30	14	4	12	61	63	46
Curzon Ashton Reserves	30	13	6	11	74	51	45
Whitchurch Alport	30	11	7	12	55	53	40
Monk Sports	30	9	6	15	53	76	33
Glossop North End Reserves	30	8	7	15	42	65	31
Lostock Gralam	30	8	6	16	48	83	30
Billinge	30	8	5	17	42	68	29
Malpas	30	7	7	16	44	69	28
Fearnhead	30	3	2	25	30	106	11

Cheadle Town Reserves left at the start of the season and Glossop North End Reserves moved to the North West Counties League – Reserve Division. Tarporley Victoria joined from the Chester & District League and Stalybridge Celtic Reserves and Congleton Town Reserves also joined.

2006-07

Division One

Middlewich Town	30	25	2	3	78	20	77
Knutsford	30	20	3	7	55	32	63
Greenalls Padgate St. Oswalds	30	18	5	7	61	38	59
Styal	30	16	7	7	53	34	55
Pilkington Recreation	30	16	7	7	59	45	55
Trafford Reserves	30	16	4	10	48	37	52
Crosfields	30	12	6	12	38	36	42
Woodley Sports Reserves	30	12	6	12	48	54	42
Barnton	30	11	8	11	52	45	41
Linotype & Cheadle Heath Nomads	30	11	6	13	41	47	39
Garswood United	30	10	5	15	43	51	35
Gamesley	30	9	6	15	53	57	33
Poynton	30	6	6	18	39	71	26
Witton Albion Reserves	30	6	6	18	39	59	24
Rylands	30	4	7	19	24	62	16
Daten	*30*	*4*	*2*	*24*	*30*	*73*	*14*

Rylands had 3 points deducted.

Division Two

Curzon Ashton Reserves	30	18	7	5	74	38	61
Stalybridge Celtic Reserves	30	18	7	5	74	38	61
Club AZ	30	18	6	6	62	39	60
Warrington Town Reserves	30	16	8	6	58	32	56
Broadheath Central	30	15	8	7	83	45	53
Golborne Sports	30	16	5	9	83	45	53
Crewe	30	13	5	12	59	59	44
Monk Sports	30	13	4	13	48	70	43
Maine Road Reserves	30	11	7	12	53	62	40
Eagle Sports	30	12	4	14	47	59	40
Tarporley Victoria	30	9	10	11	47	47	37
Whitchurch Alport	30	11	1	18	43	54	34
Lostock Gralam	30	6	6	18	34	63	24
Billinge	30	6	5	19	32	73	23
Malpas	30	4	10	16	45	81	22
Congleton Town Reserves	30	5	5	20	38	75	20

Fearnhead resigned during the season and their record was deleted when it stood as follows:

	22	5	0	17	38	80	15

Grappenhall Sports joined from the Warrington & District League and F.C. United of Manchester Reserves also joined the league.

The League changed its name to become the "Cheshire League".

CHESHIRE LEAGUE

2007-08

Division One

Styal	32	22	6	4	83	41	72
Middlewich Town	32	21	6	5	91	35	69
Pilkington Recreation	32	20	4	8	77	52	64
Greenalls Padgate St. Oswalds	32	19	5	8	75	48	62
Curzon Ashton Reserves	32	18	7	7	80	46	61
Garswood United	32	19	3	10	72	58	60
Crosfields	32	18	5	9	71	45	59
Stalybridge Celtic Reserves	32	16	8	8	75	55	56
Knutsford	32	13	4	15	54	61	43
Witton Albion Reserves	32	12	5	15	60	68	41
Barnton	32	10	6	16	46	64	36
Gamesley	32	11	3	18	51	75	36
Linotype & Cheadle Heath Nomads	32	9	6	17	56	70	33
Woodley Sports Reserves	32	8	6	18	47	64	30
Trafford Reserves	32	4	6	22	49	86	18
Poynton	*32*	*4*	*6*	*22*	*42*	*91*	*18*
Rylands	32	3	4	25	29	99	13

Woodley Sports Reserves changed their name to Woodley.
Crosfields and Rylands merged to form Crosfields-Rylands and Witton Albion Reserves were expelled.

Division Two

FC United of Manchester Reserves	32	21	6	5	82	29	69
Club AZ	**32**	**19**	**5**	**8**	**81**	**42**	**62**
Billinge	**32**	**17**	**7**	**8**	**58**	**42**	**58**
Warrington Town Reserves	32	17	5	10	65	44	56
Broadheath Central	32	17	5	10	69	59	56
Tarporley Victoria	32	17	4	11	69	52	55
Whitchurch Alport	32	12	13	7	44	34	49
Golborne Sports	32	14	6	12	67	62	48
Crewe	32	13	7	12	56	64	46
Maine Road Reserves	32	12	5	15	70	68	41
Grappenhall Sports	32	11	7	14	62	72	40
Daten	32	10	5	17	54	74	35
Malpas	32	10	4	18	49	74	34
Lostock Gralam	32	8	6	18	43	79	30
Eagle Sports	32	8	5	19	44	69	29
Monk Sports	32	11	1	20	58	85	28
Congleton Town Reserves	32	8	3	21	46	68	27

Monk Sports had 6 points deducted. FC United of Manchester Reserves left.
Moore United joined from the Warrington & District League and Denton Town joined from the Lancashire & Cheshire League.

2008-09

Division One

Woodley	30	22	5	3	99	32	71
Middlewich Town	30	20	5	5	71	27	65
Club AZ	30	18	6	6	61	24	60
Crosfields-Rylands	30	17	5	8	61	44	56
Stalybridge Celtic Reserves	30	15	6	9	65	46	51
Styal	30	14	5	11	52	55	47
Pilkington Recreation	30	14	4	12	66	62	46
Trafford Reserves	30	12	7	11	51	41	43
Greenalls Padgate St. Oswalds	30	12	6	12	53	57	42
Curzon Ashton Reserves	30	13	0	17	43	57	39
Billinge	30	9	7	14	39	58	34
Garswood United	30	9	6	15	35	51	33
Linotype & Cheadle Heath Nomads	30	7	7	16	34	67	28
Gamesley	30	6	9	15	36	55	27
Knutsford	30	5	6	19	40	82	21
Barnton	*30*	*4*	*2*	*24*	*39*	*87*	*14*

Curzon Ashton Reserves moved to the Lancashire League – West Division.

Division Two

Golborne Sports	**32**	**22**	**4**	**6**	**84**	**35**	**70**
Eagle Sports	**32**	**20**	**5**	**7**	**97**	**52**	**65**
Moore United	32	19	7	6	69	36	64
Lostock Gralam	32	19	6	7	81	42	63
Tarporley Victoria	32	17	8	7	72	36	59
Warrington Town Reserves	32	17	8	7	55	33	59
Whitchurch Alport	32	13	9	10	59	46	48
Grappenhall Sports	32	14	5	13	69	57	47
Poynton	32	13	8	11	59	50	47
Daten	32	14	3	15	59	57	45
Crewe	32	13	6	13	58	57	45
Denton Town	32	10	3	19	59	107	33
Monk Sports	32	8	5	19	52	73	29
Congleton Town Reserves	32	7	7	18	50	91	28
Maine Road Reserves	32	9	0	23	46	71	27
Malpas	32	8	3	21	46	98	27
Broadheath Central	32	4	3	25	34	108	15

Broadheath Central withdrew from senior football. New Mills Reserves joined from the North West Counties League – Reserve Division.

2009-10

Division One

Club AZ	28	20	4	4	59	37	64
Woodley	28	16	7	5	67	42	55
Middlewich Town	28	15	5	8	49	35	50
Knutsford	28	14	5	9	61	46	47
Gamesley	28	14	5	9	57	46	47
Eagle Sports	28	13	5	10	56	44	44
Linotype & Cheadle Heath Nomads	28	12	5	11	40	46	41
Trafford Reserves	28	11	5	12	54	49	38
Greenalls Padgate St. Oswalds	28	11	5	12	48	45	38
Crosfields-Rylands	28	11	4	13	46	40	37
Billinge	28	8	6	14	31	40	30
Pilkington Recreation	28	8	3	17	36	55	27
Styal	28	8	3	17	54	81	27
Golborne Sports	28	7	4	17	35	57	25
Garswood United	28	6	6	16	28	58	24

Stalybridge Celtic Reserves resigned during the season and their record was deleted when it stood as:

	11	3	4	4	13	15	13

Crosfields-Rylands changed their name to Rylands and Woodley changed their name to Northwich Villa. Trafford Reserves left the league.

Division Two

Lostock Gralam	30	21	3	6	76	45	66
Tarporley Victoria	30	17	6	7	61	40	57
Denton Town	30	16	5	9	63	38	53
Crewe	30	16	5	9	62	43	53
Moore United	30	15	5	10	55	45	50
Maine Road Reserves	30	15	3	12	53	49	48
Grappenhall Sports	30	14	5	11	62	56	47
Monk Sports	30	13	5	12	64	54	44
Whitchurch Alport	30	11	6	13	36	48	39
Barnton	30	11	5	14	60	68	38
Warrington Town Reserves	30	10	7	13	53	55	37
Daten	30	9	8	13	43	58	35
Congleton Town Reserves	30	10	3	17	53	60	33
Poynton	30	9	6	15	55	64	33
New Mills Reserves	30	8	8	14	44	60	32
Malpas	30	1	8	21	32	89	11

New Mills Reserves moved to the North West Counties League – Reserve
Division and Warrington Town Reserves also left nthe league.
Runcorn Town Reserves joined from the West Cheshire League and
Rudheath Social joined from Sunday football.

2010-11

Division One

Greenalls Padgate St. Oswalds	30	17	8	5	67	34	59
Pilkington Recreation	30	18	5	7	68	44	59
Eagle Sports	30	18	1	11	73	40	55
Middlewich Town	30	15	7	8	57	37	52
Gamesley	30	14	6	10	61	61	48
Lostock Gralam	30	14	3	13	60	57	45
Rylands	30	11	11	8	54	41	44
Knutsford	30	12	7	11	56	51	43
Styal	30	12	4	14	56	73	37
Northwich Villa	30	10	6	14	55	60	36
Garswood United	30	10	6	14	37	47	36
Golborne Sports	30	10	6	14	48	64	36
Club AZ	30	10	5	15	40	45	35
Billinge	30	9	8	13	45	58	35
Tarporley Victoria	30	8	6	16	39	77	30
Linotype & Cheadle Heath Nomads	30	4	7	19	45	72	19

Styal had 3 points deducted.
Northwich Villa moved to the North West Counties League – Division One
and Club AZ moved to the East Cheshire League.

Division Two

Denton Town	26	18	5	3	76	30	59
Grappenhall Sports	26	17	4	5	84	42	55
Whitchurch Alport	26	17	4	5	56	38	55
Crewe	26	12	9	5	55	35	45
Rudheath Social	26	14	3	9	58	42	45
Moore United	26	12	4	10	53	45	40
Runcorn Town Reserves	26	11	3	12	54	60	33
Poynton	26	9	4	13	42	63	31
Monk Sports	26	10	5	11	52	48	29
Daten	26	7	5	14	42	56	26
Congleton Town Reserves	26	8	2	16	49	66	26
Malpas	26	6	7	13	46	63	25
Barnton	26	6	4	16	35	70	22
Maine Road Reserves	26	4	3	19	45	89	15

Runcorn Town Reserves had 3 points deducted and Monk Sports had 6
points deducted.

Monk Sports withdrew from senior football. Sandbach United joined from
the Staffordshire County Senior League and Whaley Bridge joined from the
Hope Valley League.

2011-12

Division One

Knutsford	30	23	3	4	68	23	72
Greenalls Padgate St. Oswalds	30	20	3	7	72	41	63
Eagle Sports	30	18	5	7	74	32	59
Denton Town	30	14	4	12	67	55	46
Gamesley	30	14	4	12	67	57	46
Linotype & Cheadle Heath Nomads	30	13	7	10	73	70	46
Lostock Gralam	30	13	5	12	65	63	44
Middlewich Town	30	12	7	11	48	52	43
Pilkington Recreation	30	12	7	11	55	63	43
Styal	30	11	8	11	44	44	41
Billinge	30	11	5	14	50	54	38
Rylands	30	10	7	13	40	45	37
Grappenhall Sports	30	9	6	15	61	84	33
Garswood United	30	7	8	15	36	58	29
Golborne Sports	*30*	*7*	*6*	*17*	*49*	*74*	*27*
Tarporley Victoria	*30*	*3*	*1*	*26*	*23*	*77*	*10*

Division Two

Whaley Bridge	24	17	2	5	71	31	53
Crewe	24	15	6	3	65	28	51
Rudheath Social	24	15	5	4	62	21	50
Poynton	24	14	6	4	70	41	48
Sandbach United	24	13	2	9	64	46	41
Runcorn Town Reserves	24	11	4	9	55	51	37
Whitchurch Alport	24	10	4	10	40	45	34
Maine Road Reserves	24	10	1	13	50	64	31
Congleton Town Reserves	24	7	6	11	56	80	27
Malpas	24	7	5	12	34	56	26
Moore United	24	5	3	16	41	64	18
Daten	24	5	2	17	37	60	17
Barnton	24	2	4	18	25	83	10

Whitchurch Alport moved to the Mercian Regional League and Congleton
Town Reserves also left the league. Egerton joined from the Altrincham &
District League, Penlake joined from the Warrington & District League and
Congleton Vale also joined.

2012-13

Division One

Knutsford	30	23	3	4	77	29	72
Eagle Sports	30	20	5	5	68	38	65
Whaley Bridge	30	19	5	6	83	42	62
Garswood United	30	16	5	9	64	47	53
Crewe	30	16	4	10	65	45	52
Rylands	30	15	4	11	49	42	49
Gamesley	30	12	7	11	76	47	43
Middlewich Town	30	12	7	11	52	67	43
Greenalls Padgate St. Oswalds	30	12	4	14	56	47	40
Denton Town	30	12	1	17	50	76	37
Styal	30	10	6	14	60	73	36
Linotype & Cheadle Heath Nomads	30	10	5	15	64	61	35
Pilkington Recreation	30	10	4	16	44	61	34
Billinge	30	10	1	19	50	68	31
Lostock Gralam	*30*	*8*	*5*	*17*	*47*	*74*	*29*
Grappenhall Sports	*30*	*1*	*2*	*27*	*33*	*121*	*5*

Division Two

Barnton	26	21	2	3	101	50	65
Rudheath Social	26	21	0	5	83	31	63
Poynton	26	18	4	4	76	39	58
Runcorn Town Reserves	26	17	4	5	82	47	55
Maine Road Reserves	26	15	3	8	70	56	48
Sandbach United	26	12	4	10	69	60	40
Golborne Sports	26	10	1	15	53	80	31
Penlake	26	9	3	14	58	75	30
Tarporley Victoria	26	9	2	15	45	59	29
Malpas	26	8	4	14	48	69	28
Congleton Vale	26	8	3	15	38	61	27
Egerton	26	8	2	16	55	79	26
Moore United	26	5	1	20	46	78	16
Daten	26	3	3	20	42	82	12

Runcorn Town Reserves left the league. Barnton Wanderers joined from the Crewe & District League, Sale Town joined from the Altrincham & District League and Warrington Town Reserves also joined.

Division One was renamed the Premier Division and Division Two was renamed Division One for the next season.

2013-14

Premier Division

Garswood United	30	20	5	5	70	25	65
Eagle Sports	30	18	7	5	56	28	61
Whaley Bridge	30	18	6	6	72	28	60
Rudheath Social	30	19	3	8	66	38	60
Barnton	30	17	6	7	92	48	57
Knutsford	30	16	8	6	65	33	56
Crewe	30	16	3	11	67	41	51
Rylands	30	15	4	11	60	40	49
Greenalls Padgate St. Oswalds	30	13	6	11	57	59	45
Linotype & Cheadle Heath Nomads	30	13	4	13	67	56	43
Gamesley	30	11	6	13	44	46	39
Billinge	30	8	5	17	41	71	29
Styal	30	7	5	18	34	65	26
Denton Town	30	4	4	22	34	111	16
Pilkington Recreation	30	3	5	22	37	94	14
Middlewich Town	*30*	*3*	*1*	*26*	*28*	*107*	*10*

Division One

Poynton	30	23	5	2	88	31	71
Sandbach United	30	21	1	8	92	44	64
Congleton Vale	30	18	5	7	75	46	59
Malpas	30	18	3	9	84	56	57
Warrington Town Reserves	30	17	4	9	84	60	55
Lostock Gralam	30	16	3	11	73	58	51
Tarporley Victoria	30	13	5	12	69	56	44
Daten	30	13	5	12	49	55	44
Penlake	30	13	3	14	73	83	42
Golborne Sports	30	12	5	13	50	60	41
Grappenhall Sports	30	12	4	14	63	71	40
Maine Road Reserves	30	10	2	18	52	62	32
Egerton	30	9	4	17	58	83	31
Moore United	*30*	*7*	*1*	*22*	*40*	*80*	*22*
Sale Town	*30*	*6*	*2*	*22*	*61*	*107*	*20*
Barnton Wanderers	30	3	6	21	36	95	15

Poynton and Sale Town each had 3 points deducted.

A new Division Two was formed with the following 10 founder members:

Altrincham Reserves, Cheadle Town Reserves (from the Staffordshire County Senior League), Cuddington (Crewe & District League), FC Woodford, West Didsbury & Chorlton Reserves (both from the Altrincham & District League), Irlam Reserves, Mersey Valley (evolved from Sale Town from the Cheshire League – Division One), Moore United (relegated from the Cheshire League – Division One), Witton Albion Reserves (Lancashire League – West Division) and Wythenshawe Town (Manchester League).

2014-15

Premier Division

Linotype & Cheadle Heath Nomads	30	19	9	2	83	35	66
Knutsford	30	19	3	8	93	46	60
Eagle Sports	30	19	3	8	73	38	60
Crewe	30	18	5	7	73	40	59
Whaley Bridge	30	15	8	7	60	37	53
Poynton	30	13	7	10	75	63	46
Garswood United	30	14	4	12	68	57	46
Rudheath Social	30	10	8	12	56	54	38
Rylands	30	9	10	11	63	55	37
Gamesley	30	11	4	15	69	72	37
Sandbach United	30	10	4	16	68	76	34
Styal	30	10	4	16	49	95	34
Greenalls Padgate St. Oswalds	30	6	10	14	47	61	28
Denton Town	30	8	2	20	48	94	26
Billinge	*30*	*8*	*4*	*18*	*60*	*83*	*25*
Pilkington Recreation	*30*	*7*	*3*	*20*	*40*	*119*	*24*

Billinge had 3 points deducted.

Division One

Congleton Vale	22	19	1	2	73	32	58
Malpas	22	16	3	3	61	36	51
Middlewich Town	22	10	4	8	54	48	34
Egerton	22	10	0	12	50	53	30
Daten	22	8	5	9	40	43	29
Grappenhall Sports	22	8	5	9	44	52	29
Tarporley Victoria	22	9	1	12	49	60	28
Golborne Sports	22	8	3	11	44	56	27
Maine Road Reserves	22	7	3	12	43	44	24
Penlake	22	7	3	12	59	66	24
Warrington Town Reserves	*22*	*5*	*7*	*10*	*46*	*61*	*22*
Lostock Gralam	*22*	*4*	*7*	*11*	*44*	*56*	*19*

Division Two

Wythenshawe Town	18	18	0	0	74	9	54
Altrincham Reserves	18	11	2	5	49	31	35
Mersey Valley	18	9	3	6	47	33	30
Irlam Reserves	18	9	3	6	42	31	30
FC Woodford	18	8	5	5	35	25	29
Cuddington	18	7	1	10	40	55	22
West Didsbury & Chorlton Reserves	18	5	6	7	38	47	21
Witton Albion Reserves	18	4	2	12	27	49	14
Moore United	18	3	3	12	22	65	12
Cheadle Town Reserves	18	2	3	13	29	58	9

2015-16

Premier Division

Knutsford	30	20	5	5	68	29	65
Linotype & Cheadle Heath Nomads	30	20	1	9	77	40	61
Whaley Bridge	30	16	5	9	67	45	53
Sandbach United	30	16	4	10	69	44	52
Greenalls Padgate St. Oswalds	30	14	6	10	59	54	48
Congleton Vale	30	14	5	11	55	44	47
Crewe	30	14	2	14	54	57	44
Gamesley	30	12	5	13	64	68	41
Rudheath Social	30	13	2	15	44	54	41
Poynton	30	12	3	15	63	58	39
Eagle Sports	30	12	3	15	47	50	39
Malpas	30	10	8	12	57	73	38
Garswood United	30	9	7	14	47	48	34
Rylands	30	9	6	15	36	55	33
Denton Town	30	9	4	17	62	98	31
Styal	30	5	4	21	38	90	19

Sandbach United moved to the North West Counties League and Gamesley resigned.

Division One

Wythenshawe Town	20	14	3	3	65	18	45
Altrincham Reserves	20	13	4	3	55	25	43
Billinge	20	12	4	4	65	34	40
Middlewich Town	20	10	3	7	53	38	33
Golborne Sports	20	8	5	7	48	47	29
Pilkington Recreation	20	9	2	9	34	65	29
Daten	20	7	3	10	39	49	24
Grappenhall Sports	20	5	5	10	33	65	20
Egerton	20	5	2	13	38	56	17
Tarporley Victoria	20	4	5	11	26	46	17
Maine Road Reserves	20	4	2	14	25	38	14

Penlake withdrew from senior football shortly after the start of the season.

Division Two

AFC Macclesfield	22	20	1	1	88	23	61
Halebank	22	14	4	4	99	44	46
Warrington Town Reserves	22	15	1	6	90	39	46
FC St. Helens	22	14	3	5	55	44	45
Lostock Gralam	22	12	5	5	49	45	41
Mersey Valley	22	12	1	9	76	50	37
West Didsbury/Chorlton Reserves	22	7	2	13	44	54	23
Cheadle Town Reserves	22	6	5	11	39	59	23
Cuddington	22	7	0	15	45	76	21
Unicorn Athletic	22	5	2	15	45	99	17
Moore United	22	2	6	14	33	70	12
Litherland REMYCA Reserves	22	3	0	19	31	91	9

Litherland REMYCA Reserves left the league and nine clubs joined: Broadheath Central (from the Altrincham & District League), Deva Christleton (Chester & Wirral League), Ford Motors (West Cheshire League), Orford, Windle Labour (both from the Warrington & District League), Sandbach United Reserves (Cheshire League – Reserve Division), Winstanley Warriors (Wigan & District League), AFC Denton and Barnton Reserves (both newly formed clubs).

NORTH WEST COUNTIES LEAGUE 1982-2016

Formation

For almost 50 years, the best non-League clubs in the North West played in either the Cheshire County League or the Lancashire Combination. There were few transfers between the two leagues, only 10 clubs moving from Lancashire to Cheshire from 1920 to 1968 with 5 going in the opposite direction.

Generally speaking, the two competitions were of roughly equal status although the Cheshire League probably became slightly the stronger after the Second World War. However the formation of the Northern Premier League (NPL) in 1968 not only added an extra layer above the two older leagues, it also fundamentally changed the relationship between them. Instead of being roughly equal, the Cheshire League very quickly became the more senior, the Lancashire Combination rapidly declining in strength as the movements of its clubs very clearly shows.

In 1968, the Lancashire Combination lost 5 of its 22 clubs to the new NPL, theoretically still leaving 17 strong clubs to continue in the competition. Yet by the start of the 1970-71 season, 12 of those 17 had left, 3 more to the NPL and 7 to the Cheshire League. After 1970, no Lancashire Combination club was good enough to be promoted to the NPL but the Cheshire League had another 8 clubs good enough to be promoted. To a large extent, the Cheshire League made up its losses in this period by recruiting from the Lancashire Combination, taking 5 clubs between 1970 and 1977 and 8 more to help to form its new Second Division in 1978. The very fact that 8 Lancashire Combination clubs preferred Division Two of the Cheshire League shows that they recognised that in effect their own competition had become a feeder to its neighbour.

It therefore made perfect sense when in 1982, the management committees of the Cheshire League and the Lancashire Combination decided to recognise the position formally and merge the two competitions. A three division structure was put in place and 57 of the 58 clubs in the two leagues applied to join the new North West Counties League, the exception being Middlewich Athletic of Division Two of the Cheshire League who applied initially but then withdrew their application and rejoined the Mid Cheshire League instead. A points system was devised to decide which division of the new league the 57 clubs should play in and the results of this were recorded on 3rd June 1982.

The scoring system was as follows. The previous two seasons, that is 1980-81 and 1981-82, were considered and for each of those two seasons, the top team in Division One of the Cheshire League was awarded 40 points, the second team 39, and so on down the league table. The top teams of the Lancashire Combination and Cheshire League Division Two were each awarded 20 points, the second team 19 and so on down the league tables. Champions and runners-up in the Lancashire Combination and Cheshire League Division Two were awarded 5 bonus points each.

Having calculated the points, the three divisions were split as follows:

Division One – Included all clubs with ground grades of A to C with 35 points or more. The number of clubs was made up to 20 by adding the necessary number of D graded clubs with the most points.

Division Two – Included all remaining A to D clubs, all E clubs and the number of clubs was made up to 20 by adding the necessary number of F graded clubs with the most points.

Division Three – Included all remaining F graded clubs and all G graded clubs. The number was made even by electing new applicants.

The exceptions were that any club whose pitch size failed to meet the standards laid down was not considered for Division One and any club not playing on their own ground (i.e. ground-sharing) was also not considered for Division One. The results of all these deliberations are shown below.

However Hyde United and Chorley did not take up their places in the North West Counties League as they were later elected to the NPL. Their places were taken by Lancaster City who dropped down from the NPL due to financial difficulties and Penrith who were elected from the Northern League. Division Three was made up to 18 clubs by the election of Newton from the Mid Cheshire League where they had been known as HB&H Newton.

Meanwhile across the Pennines, the Midland League and Yorkshire League were also merging to form the Northern Counties (East) League and thus the second layer of the non-League pyramid covering most of the Northern half of the country was then in place.

Grading system for North West Counties League, 1982.

Club	Ground Grade	Points Awarded				Previous League	NWLC Division	See Notes
		1980-81	1981-82	Bonus	Total			
Hyde United	A	39	40		79	CL – 1	1	N
Chorley	A	35	39		74	CL – 1	1	N
Stalybridge Celtic	A	36	31		67	CL – 1	1	
Horwich RMI	A	32	25		57	CL – 1	1	
Winsford United	B	38	37		75	CL – 1	1	
Prescot Cables	B	33	32		65	CL – 1	1	
Burscough	B	25	38		63	CL – 1	1	
Leek Town	B	31	26		57	CL – 1	1	
Accrington Stanley	B	20	28	5	53	CL – 1	1	
Rhyl	B	14	19	5	38	CL – 2	1	
Kirkby Town	B	22	14		36	CL – 2	2	G
Curzon Ashton	C	29	33		62	CL – 1	1	
Ashton United	C	30	22		52	CL – 1	1	
St. Helens Town	C	28	23		51	CL – 1	1	
Droylsden	C	23	21		44	CL – 1	2	P
Congleton Town	C	11	20	5	36	CL – 2	1	
Leyland Motors	C	18	17		35	CL – 2	1	
Nantwich Town	D	40	27		67	CL – 1	1	
Formby	D	37	29		66	CL – 1	1	

| Club | Ground Grade | Points Awarded | | | | Previous League | NWLC Division | See Notes |
		1980-81	1981-82	Bonus	Total			
Glossop	D	19	35	5	59	CL – 1	1	
Bootle	D	34	24		58	CL – 1	1	
Darwen	D	24	34		58	CL – 1	1	
Fleetwood Town	D	27	30		57	CL – 1	2	
Ellesmere Port & Neston	A	0	7		7	CL – 2	2	
Great Harwood Town	B	18	15		33	Lancs.	2	P
Ford Motors	C	12	9		21	CL – 2	2	
Salford	C	6	5		11	CL – 2	2	
Skelmersdale United	C	4	6		10	CL – 2	2	
Padiham	D	17	11		28	Lancs.	2	
Atherton Laburnum Rovers	D	16	10		26	CL – 2	2	
Chadderton	D	11	14		25	Lancs.	2	
Radcliffe Borough	D	10	15		25	CL – 2	2	
Eastwood Hanley	D	5	12		17	CL – 2	2	
Rossendale United	E	26	36		62	CL – 1	2	
Caernarfon Town	E	15	20	5	40	Lancs.	2	
Irlam Town	E	9	18		27	CL – 2	2	
Lytham	E	13	10		23	Lancs.	2	
New Mills	E	21	2		23	CL – 2	2	
Prescot BI	E	15	8		23	CL – 2	2	
Wren Rovers	F	20	17	5	42	Lancs.	2	
Maghull	F	13	16		29	CL – 2	3	
Clitheroe	F	12	16		28	Lancs.	3	
Vulcan Newton	F	14	12		26	Lancs.	3	
Nelson	F	4	18		22	Lancs.	3	
Warrington Town	F	8	13		21	CL – 2	3	
Bacup Borough	F	7	7		14	Lancs.	3	
Oldham Dew	F	0	9		9	Lancs.	3	
Atherton Collieries	F	3	4		7	CL – 2	3	
Ashton Town	F	2	3		5	CL – 2	3	
Colne Dynamoes	G	19	19	10	48	Lancs.	3	
Blackpool Mechanics	G	5	13		18	Lancs.	3	
Wigan Rovers	G	9	8		17	Lancs.	3	
Whitworth Valley	G	10	6		16	Lancs.	3	
Daisy Hill	G	8	5		13	Lancs.	3	

Club	Ground Grade	Points Awarded				Previous League	NWLC Division	See Notes
		1980-81	1981-82	Bonus	Total			
Ashton Athletic	G	6	3		9	Lancs.	3	
Prestwich Heys	G	7	1		8	CL – 2	3	
Bolton ST	G	0	4		4	Lancs.	3	

Notes:

N – Elected to the Northern Premier League instead.
G – Groundsharing at Prescot Cables.
P – Under-sized pitch.

In the tables below, clubs promoted to the Northern Premier League are shown in **bold** type, those promoted within the North West Counties League are in ***bold italics*** and those relegated within the North West Counties League are in *italics*.

1982-83

Division One

Burscough	38	26	7	5	93	45	59
Rhyl	38	23	11	4	76	30	57
Horwich RMI	38	22	10	6	77	35	54
Stalybridge Celtic	38	17	15	6	60	32	49
Winsford United	38	18	10	10	72	48	46
Darwen	38	17	12	9	68	46	46
Lancaster City	38	17	11	10	69	54	45
Congleton Town	38	13	14	11	52	35	40
Penrith	38	17	6	15	68	61	40
Accrington Stanley	38	13	12	13	56	55	38
Leek Town	38	14	9	15	42	44	37
Curzon Ashton	38	14	8	16	46	47	36
Ashton United	38	13	10	15	55	69	36
Bootle	38	14	6	18	55	79	32
Prescot Cables	38	9	13	16	50	60	31
Formby	38	10	8	20	48	68	28
Leyland Motors	38	7	10	21	34	74	24
Glossop	38	6	11	21	29	67	23
St. Helens Town	38	5	10	23	29	80	20
Nantwich Town	*38*	*6*	*5*	*27*	*43*	*93*	*17*

Bootle had 2 points deducted for fielding an ineligible player.
Netherfield joined the league after being relegated from the Northern Premier League.

Division Two

Radcliffe Borough	*38*	*33*	*4*	*1*	*110*	*25*	*70*
Caernarfon Town	*38*	*28*	*7*	*3*	*85*	*27*	*63*
Wren Rovers	38	23	7	8	84	38	53
Eastwood Hanley	38	23	7	8	81	42	53
Kirkby Town	38	22	3	13	80	60	47
Irlam Town	38	17	8	13	79	52	42
Chadderton	38	18	6	14	55	51	42
Rossendale United	38	15	10	13	75	68	40
Ford Motors	38	18	4	16	61	59	40
Ellesmere Port & Neston	38	17	5	16	56	68	39
Skelmersdale United	38	13	11	14	70	63	37
Fleetwood Town	38	12	8	18	54	80	32
Atherton Laburnum Rovers	38	11	9	18	52	70	31
Lytham	38	11	5	22	54	71	27
Great Harwood Town	38	8	10	20	54	76	26
Salford	38	10	6	22	43	86	26
Droylsden	38	11	5	22	49	71	25
Prescot BI	38	10	5	23	46	81	25
Padiham	*38*	*8*	*6*	*24*	*41*	*74*	*22*
New Mills	38	7	4	27	39	106	18

Droylsden had 2 points deducted.
Kirkby Town disbanded and New Mills also left the league

Division Three

Colne Dynamoes	*34*	*25*	*5*	*4*	*95*	*37*	*55*
Warrington Town	*34*	*24*	*6*	*4*	*83*	*33*	*54*
Clitheroe	34	22	7	5	87	35	51
Prestwich Heys	34	18	11	5	70	37	47
Vulcan Newton	34	13	10	11	70	65	36
Blackpool Mechanics	34	11	13	10	67	56	35
Bacup Borough	34	14	7	13	53	45	35
Atherton Collieries	34	12	11	11	55	57	35
Whitworth Valley	34	13	9	12	54	65	35
Nelson	34	7	16	11	49	56	30
Daisy Hill	34	10	10	14	47	58	30
Maghull	34	10	9	15	56	61	29
Ashton Town	34	12	5	17	53	73	29
Newton	34	8	12	14	59	62	28
Oldham Dew	34	10	8	16	48	61	28
Bolton ST	34	9	6	19	50	84	24
Wigan Rovers	34	5	7	22	35	72	17
Ashton Athletic	34	3	8	23	18	92	14

Wigan Rovers moved to the West Lancashire League – Division Two.
Urmston Town joined from the Manchester League and Cheadle Town also joined.

1983-84

Division One

Stalybridge Celtic	38	26	8	4	81	30	60
Penrith	38	23	9	6	88	39	55
Radcliffe Borough	38	26	3	9	79	41	55
Burscough	38	22	8	8	87	47	52
Curzon Ashton	38	21	5	12	74	51	47
Lancaster City	38	21	3	14	76	56	43
Accrington Stanley	38	17	8	13	67	60	42
St. Helens Town	38	17	7	14	69	55	41
Congleton Town	38	18	5	15	64	50	41
Prescot Cables	38	17	6	15	72	45	40
Leek Town	38	14	10	14	56	64	38
Winsford United	38	12	12	14	49	54	36
Formby	38	14	7	17	48	61	35
Caernarfon Town	38	11	12	15	46	55	34
Glossop	38	11	11	16	38	61	33
Bootle	38	11	7	20	46	69	27
Leyland Motors	38	9	9	20	44	79	27
Netherfield	38	5	11	22	27	73	21
Ashton United	*38*	*7*	*9*	*22*	*47*	*86*	*19*
Darwen	*38*	*2*	*2*	*34*	*29*	*111*	*6*

Bootle and Lancaster City each had 2 points deducted and Ashton United had 4 points deducted.

Division Two

Fleetwood Town	34	24	8	2	73	24	56
Eastwood Hanley	34	21	6	7	69	35	48
Irlam Town	34	19	8	7	67	41	46
Warrington Town	34	18	7	9	65	45	43
Droylsden	34	19	5	10	59	42	43
Colne Dynamoes	34	16	9	9	55	37	41
Ellesmere Port & Neston	34	12	10	12	49	38	34
Chadderton	34	14	6	14	56	46	34
Atherton Laburnum Rovers	34	11	11	12	37	41	33
Wren Rovers	34	11	10	13	45	47	32
Skelmersdale United	34	13	6	15	60	63	32
Ford Motors	34	9	9	16	38	53	27
Prescot BI	34	9	9	16	50	66	27
Lytham	34	13	3	18	56	81	27
Rossendale United	34	10	6	18	53	84	26
Great Harwood Town	34	5	12	17	36	60	22
Salford	34	5	11	18	24	60	21
Nantwich Town	34	8	2	24	44	73	18

Lytham had 2 points deducted.
Prescot BI left the league.

Division Three

Clitheroe	34	22	7	5	79	29	51
Padiham	34	19	8	7	58	34	46
Ashton Town	34	19	7	8	54	42	45
Oldham Dew	34	17	9	8	63	37	43
Daisy Hill	34	19	3	12	54	40	41
Maghull	34	16	8	10	60	50	40
Blackpool Mechanics	34	17	5	12	70	49	39
Atherton Collieries	34	14	9	11	54	50	37
Vulcan Newton	34	15	8	11	64	54	36
Prestwich Heys	34	15	5	14	61	59	33
Whitworth Valley	34	11	8	15	45	53	30
Bolton ST	34	10	10	14	49	64	30
Bacup Borough	34	11	9	14	65	60	27
Nelson	34	8	10	16	49	55	26
Cheadle Town	34	9	8	17	39	67	26
Urmston Town	34	7	9	18	35	67	23
Newton	34	8	4	22	33	63	20
Ashton Athletic	34	4	3	27	30	89	11

Prestwich Heys and Vulcan Newton each had 2 points deducted and Bacup Borough had 4 points deducted.
Colwyn Bay joined from the Welsh League (North) and Kirkby Town also joined. Vulcan Newton left the league.

Division Two

Clitheroe	34	19	13	2	70	33	51
Irlam Town	34	21	9	4	60	24	51
Warrington Town	34	17	14	3	59	29	48
Ashton United	34	17	7	10	56	55	41
Droylsden	34	15	10	9	51	47	40
Wren Rovers	34	15	9	10	53	41	39
Great Harwood Town	34	17	4	13	49	44	38
Chadderton	34	13	9	12	47	46	35
Colne Dynamoes	34	9	14	11	45	40	32
Atherton Laburnum Rovers	34	13	6	15	42	43	32
Nantwich Town	34	13	5	16	50	47	31
Ford Motors	34	11	8	15	44	45	30
Skelmersdale United	34	11	8	15	39	56	30
Rossendale United	34	10	9	15	51	53	29
Salford	34	11	5	18	46	64	27
Darwen	34	7	6	21	32	62	20
Padiham	34	8	5	21	42	74	19
Ellesmere Port & Neston	34	5	7	22	34	67	15

Padiham and Ellesmere Port & Neston each had 2 points deducted.

Division Three

Kirkby Town	34	26	5	3	83	30	57
Colwyn Bay	34	22	10	2	75	32	54
Newton	34	16	10	8	56	33	42
Urmston Town	34	14	10	10	42	39	38
Blackpool Mechanics	34	15	7	12	61	48	37
Lytham	34	14	7	13	54	45	35
Atherton Collieries	34	13	8	13	44	44	34
Ashton Town	34	13	7	14	62	56	33
Oldham Dew	34	11	10	13	51	44	32
Bolton ST	34	12	8	14	55	73	32
Maghull	34	12	7	15	56	51	31
Cheadle Town	34	12	7	15	46	62	31
Bacup Borough	34	11	8	15	54	59	30
Ashton Athletic	34	12	6	16	45	61	30
Daisy Hill	34	10	9	15	51	61	27
Whitworth Valley	34	10	7	17	51	71	27
Nelson	34	9	4	21	43	80	22
Prestwich Heys	34	7	4	23	35	75	16

Daisy Hill and Prestwich Heys each had 2 points deducted.
Oldham Dew changed their name to Oldham Town.
Ashton Town and Urmston Town both moved to the Manchester League.
Lytham also left the league and Huyton Town joined.

1984-85

Division One

Radcliffe Borough	38	24	10	4	67	33	58
Caernarfon Town	38	23	9	6	73	40	55
Burscough	38	23	7	8	81	46	53
Stalybridge Celtic	38	21	10	7	89	40	52
Eastwood Hanley	38	20	12	6	72	42	52
Curzon Ashton	38	21	6	11	85	60	48
Winsford United	38	20	7	11	58	37	47
Fleetwood Town	38	18	8	12	84	57	44
Leek Town	38	16	11	11	52	38	43
Congleton Town	38	13	11	14	43	46	37
Leyland Motors	38	13	8	17	52	67	34
St. Helens Town	38	12	9	17	64	75	33
Prescot Cables	38	13	7	18	64	68	31
Bootle	38	10	11	17	34	48	31
Accrington Stanley	38	11	8	19	45	59	30
Glossop	38	8	11	19	46	70	27
Formby	38	9	9	20	41	79	25
Netherfield	38	7	9	22	42	80	23
Lancaster City	38	8	5	25	46	90	21
Penrith	38	4	4	30	36	99	12

Formby and Prescot Cables each had 2 points deducted.

1985-86

Division One

Clitheroe	38	20	14	4	61	30	54
Congleton Town	38	22	10	6	51	29	54
Eastwood Hanley	38	22	9	7	68	45	53
Stalybridge Celtic	38	21	10	7	62	39	52
Fleetwood Town	38	21	10	7	70	34	50
Irlam Town	38	16	14	8	66	45	46
Leek Town	38	20	6	12	64	44	46
Curzon Ashton	38	18	9	11	52	50	45
Burscough	38	15	10	13	45	35	40
St. Helens Town	38	15	8	15	65	55	38
Accrington Stanley	38	13	11	14	62	60	37
Leyland Motors	38	13	8	17	62	67	34
Winsford United	38	14	6	18	55	68	34
Radcliffe Borough	38	12	9	17	48	49	33
Bootle	38	11	7	20	46	54	29
Penrith	38	9	8	21	46	63	26
Netherfield	38	8	10	20	38	76	26
Glossop	38	7	10	21	37	69	24
Prescot Cables	38	5	9	24	33	68	19
Formby	38	5	8	25	35	86	18

Fleetwood Town had 2 points deducted.

ivision Two

Kirkby Town	34	24	7	3	85	30	55
Rossendale United	34	20	8	6	81	36	48
Wren Rovers	34	18	8	8	60	46	44
Warrington Town	34	17	9	8	62	48	43
Colwyn Bay	34	17	8	9	74	53	42
Chadderton	34	15	12	7	66	48	42
Colne Dynamoes	34	15	9	10	59	43	39
Great Harwood Town	34	13	10	11	38	45	36
Skelmersdale United	34	14	5	15	58	53	33
Droylsden	34	13	7	14	48	56	33
Atherton Laburnum Rovers	34	12	6	16	49	61	30
Lancaster City	34	10	9	15	57	66	29
Ellesmere Port & Neston	34	9	9	16	45	61	27
Ashton United	34	11	5	18	46	64	25
Darwen	34	8	8	18	48	57	24
Salford	34	9	4	21	38	72	22
Ford Motors	34	5	10	19	36	64	20
Nantwich Town	34	5	8	21	31	78	18

Ashton United had 2 points deducted.

Division Three

Blackpool Mechanics	28	22	2	4	77	33	44
Oldham Town	28	14	9	5	56	29	37
Maghull	28	15	6	7	62	36	36
Daisy Hill	28	13	7	8	62	45	33
Atherton Collieries	28	13	7	8	48	37	33
Bolton ST	28	12	7	9	42	34	29
Cheadle Town	28	9	10	9	42	26	28
Bacup Borough	28	10	8	10	36	40	28
Padiham	28	8	10	10	44	45	26
Prestwich Heys	28	10	6	12	53	66	26
Newton	28	7	10	11	43	48	24
Whitworth Valley	28	7	8	13	42	48	22
Huyton Town	28	7	7	14	41	71	21
Nelson	28	7	7	14	36	65	19
Ashton Athletic	28	1	6	21	24	85	8

Blackpool Mechanic, Bolton ST and Nelson all had 2 points deducted.
Ashton Athletic and Prestwich Heys both moved to the Manchester League and Bolton ST and Huyton Town also left. Flixton and Ashton Town both joined from the Manchester League, Flixton from the Premier Division and Ashton Town from Division One.

Division Two

Droylsden	34	20	8	6	79	42	48
Warrington Town	34	16	13	5	48	34	45
Ashton United	34	19	6	9	73	45	44
Wren Rovers	34	18	8	8	65	39	44
Colwyn Bay	34	17	9	8	61	43	43
Darwen	34	15	8	11	45	47	38
Chadderton	34	14	9	11	52	47	37
Colne Dynamoes	34	14	8	12	57	44	36
Skelmersdale United	34	13	10	11	52	53	36
Ellesmere Port & Neston	34	15	5	14	68	54	35
Formby	34	13	7	14	54	55	33
Blackpool Mechanics	34	12	8	14	56	64	32
Lancaster City	34	12	7	15	55	53	31
Prescot Cables	34	12	6	16	46	48	28
Great Harwood Town	34	9	8	17	36	59	24
Oldham Town	34	7	9	18	38	57	23
Atherton Laburnum Rovers	34	8	5	21	32	61	21
Salford	34	1	8	25	17	89	10

Prescot Cables and Great Harwood Town each had 2 points deducted.
The 10 clubs in bold italics above were all promoted to Division One.

Division Three

Atherton Collieries	24	16	4	4	46	22	36
Flixton	24	15	5	4	58	29	35
Maghull	24	14	2	8	44	29	30
Nelson	24	12	6	6	37	29	30
Newton	24	11	5	8	42	36	27
Ford Motors	24	9	8	7	38	27	26
Bacup Borough	24	10	6	8	27	27	26
Cheadle Town	24	9	5	10	33	44	23
Daisy Hill	24	6	7	11	21	42	17
Padiham	24	4	8	12	35	39	16
Nantwich Town	24	5	6	13	26	42	16
Ashton Town	24	4	9	11	29	39	15
Whitworth Valley	24	3	5	16	17	48	11

Daisy Hill and Ashton Town each had 2 points deducted.
All Division Three clubs were promoted to Division Two along with newcomers Maine Road (from the Manchester League), Newcastle Town (from the Mid Cheshire League) and Vauxhall GM (from the West Cheshire League). Division Three then closed down.

1986-87

Division One

Stalybridge Celtic	38	25	8	5	74	39	58
Accrington Stanley	38	19	15	4	63	32	53
Clitheroe	38	20	12	6	76	47	52
Kirkby Town	38	22	4	12	71	48	48
Bootle	38	19	10	9	52	38	48
St. Helens Town	38	19	9	10	65	37	47
Winsford United	38	19	8	11	55	39	46
Fleetwood Town	38	16	13	9	61	49	45
Penrith	38	16	10	12	62	59	42
Rossendale United	38	14	11	13	66	59	39
Congleton Town	38	13	11	14	38	39	37
Burscough	38	11	11	16	58	54	33
Leyland Motors	38	13	7	18	52	56	33
Eastwood Hanley	38	10	11	17	40	50	31
Radcliffe Borough	38	11	8	19	46	57	30
Leek Town	38	9	12	17	42	55	30
Netherfield	38	12	5	21	45	73	29
Irlam Town	38	4	13	21	36	74	21
Curzon Ashton	38	4	12	22	35	78	20
Glossop	38	5	8	25	33	87	18

The 12 clubs in bold type above, plus Droylsden and Lancaster City from Division Two, left to become founder members of the Northern Premier League's new Division One.

1987-88

Division One

Colne Dynamoes	34	24	7	3	71	14	55
Rossendale United	34	24	7	3	68	23	55
Clitheroe	34	18	10	6	51	20	46
Colwyn Bay	34	20	7	7	60	42	45
St. Helens Town	34	18	6	10	61	36	42
Ellesmere Port & Neston	34	17	5	12	55	48	39
Darwen	34	14	10	10	55	45	38
Warrington Town	34	16	5	13	68	47	37
Kirkby Town	34	11	13	10	57	54	35
Burscough	34	14	7	13	45	51	35
Leyland Motors	34	10	11	13	53	53	31
Prescot Cables	34	10	11	13	34	45	29
Bootle	34	12	5	17	43	61	29
Formby	34	6	10	18	32	63	22
Salford	34	8	6	20	33	66	22
Skelmersdale United	34	4	11	19	34	64	19
Atherton Laburnum Rovers	34	4	7	21	31	78	15
Glossop	34	5	4	25	30	71	14

Colwyn Bay and Prescot Cables each had 2 points deducted.
Kirkby Town changed their name to Knowsley United.

Division Two

	P	W	D	L	F	A	Pts
Ashton United	42	32	6	4	107	30	70
Flixton	42	27	10	5	94	38	64
Wren Rovers	42	26	9	7	92	51	61
Newcastle Town	42	26	7	9	81	39	59
Maine Road	42	23	4	15	74	48	50
Maghull	42	18	11	13	73	66	47
Vauxhall GM	42	15	16	11	58	50	46
Atherton Collieries	42	20	6	16	63	63	46
Whitworth Valley	42	15	12	15	50	60	42
Ashton Town	42	17	8	17	64	70	40
Oldham Town	42	13	11	18	44	51	37
Cheadle Town	42	13	11	18	47	62	35
Chadderton	42	13	9	20	55	71	35
Great Harwood Town	42	14	8	20	52	66	34
Blackpool Mechanics	42	12	10	20	57	77	34
Nelson	42	12	10	20	49	76	34
Ford Motors	42	12	9	21	59	70	33
Daisy Hill	42	12	8	22	55	66	32
Padiham	42	10	14	18	53	76	32
Newton	42	10	12	20	47	84	30
Nantwich Town	42	8	13	21	41	68	29
Bacup Borough	42	8	8	26	38	71	22

Ashton Town, Bacup Borough, Cheadle Town, Great Harwood Town, Newton and Padiham all had 2 points deducted. Whitworth Valley moved to the Manchester League, Ford Motors moved to the Liverpool County Combination and Nelson moved to the West Lancashire League.

1988-89

Division One

	P	W	D	L	F	A	Pts
Rossendale United	34	24	8	2	84	27	56
Knowsley United	34	21	8	5	85	43	50
St. Helens Town	34	20	8	6	60	25	48
Colwyn Bay	34	19	9	6	77	45	47
Darwen	34	19	9	6	64	36	47
Warrington Town	34	16	10	8	47	37	42
Flixton	34	15	8	11	61	44	38
Leyland Motors	34	15	8	11	53	44	38
Bootle	34	14	4	16	49	54	32
Burscough	34	11	10	13	40	51	32
Ellesmere Port & Neston	34	9	12	13	36	42	30
Clitheroe	34	8	12	14	38	41	28
Skelmersdale United	34	8	9	17	39	68	25
Atherton Laburnum Rovers	34	9	6	19	47	74	24
Prescot Cables	34	7	9	18	36	60	23
Salford	34	7	8	19	33	70	22
Ashton United	34	7	6	21	37	72	18
Formby	34	3	4	27	24	77	10

Ashton United had 2 points deducted.
Ellesmere Port & Neston disbanded.

Division Two

	P	W	D	L	F	A	Pts
Vauxhall GM	34	25	8	1	68	17	58
Maine Road	34	22	7	5	96	40	51
Chadderton	34	20	9	5	71	29	49
Wren Rovers	34	19	10	5	77	45	48
Nantwich Town	34	20	4	10	66	28	44
Newcastle Town	34	15	10	9	53	37	40
Great Harwood Town	34	16	6	12	52	40	38
Maghull	34	12	13	9	46	44	37
Bacup Borough	34	11	12	11	55	57	34
Daisy Hill	34	12	6	16	36	49	30
Atherton Collieries	34	9	11	14	52	58	29
Padiham	34	9	10	15	39	57	28
Glossop	34	10	7	17	42	60	27
Cheadle Town	34	10	7	17	46	67	27
Oldham Town	34	6	11	17	46	66	23
Blackpool Mechanics	34	9	5	20	46	72	23
Ashton Town	34	4	11	19	31	68	19
Newton	34	1	5	28	23	111	7

Daisy Hill changed their name to Westhoughton Town.

3 points were awarded for a win from the next season.

1989-90

Division One

	P	W	D	L	F	A	Pts
Warrington Town	34	22	6	6	69	31	72
Knowsley United	34	21	6	7	68	45	69
Colwyn Bay	34	16	12	6	79	50	60
Vauxhall GM	34	16	9	9	50	42	57
Clitheroe	34	17	6	11	48	47	57
Darwen	34	15	9	10	40	34	54
Nantwich Town	34	13	5	16	50	52	44
St. Helens Town	34	10	13	11	50	48	43
Ashton United	34	11	10	13	39	45	43
Prescot Cables	34	10	11	13	49	54	41
Bootle	34	11	8	15	44	58	41
Flixton	34	11	7	16	37	47	40
Leyland Motors	34	10	7	17	55	64	37
Atherton Laburnum Rovers	34	8	13	13	43	58	37
Skelmersdale United	34	8	11	15	48	59	35
Salford	34	8	11	15	31	47	35
Burscough	34	8	12	14	38	41	33
Chadderton	34	7	12	15	39	55	33

Burscough had 3 points deducted.
Penrith and Eastwood Hanley joined after relegation from the Northern Premier League. Prescot Cables changed their name to Prescot, Leyland Motors changed their name to Leyland DAF-SGL and Salford changed their name to Salford City.

Division Two

	P	W	D	L	F	A	Pts
Maine Road	30	22	4	4	84	35	70
Bacup Borough	30	21	5	4	76	30	68
Blackpool Mechanics	30	17	6	7	59	30	57
Wren Rovers	30	16	7	7	72	38	55
Great Harwood Town	30	16	6	8	52	29	54
Cheadle Town	30	13	8	9	54	45	47
Maghull	30	13	6	11	40	43	45
Atherton Collieries	30	12	7	11	34	38	43
Oldham Town	30	11	5	14	47	51	38
Ashton Town	30	9	7	14	42	57	34
Padiham	30	9	6	15	44	53	33
Formby	30	7	7	16	33	57	28
Newcastle Town	30	8	4	18	38	65	28
Glossop	30	8	3	19	34	58	27
Westhoughton Town	30	8	3	19	36	62	27
Newton	30	5	6	19	29	83	21

Wren Rovers changed their name to Blackpool Rovers. Bradford Park Avenue joined from the Central Midlands League, Bamber Bridge joined from the Preston & District League. Castleton Gabriels joined from the Manchester League and Kidsgrove Athletic joined from the Mid Cheshire League. Padiham moved to the West Lancashire League and Newton moved to the West Cheshire League.

1990-91

Division One

Knowsley United	36	25	8	3	95	37	83
Colwyn Bay	36	22	10	4	85	32	76
Ashton United	36	20	7	9	80	45	67
Eastwood Hanley	36	16	12	8	42	29	60
Vauxhall GM	36	15	10	11	42	36	55
Prescot	36	13	12	11	57	55	51
Flixton	36	14	7	15	48	72	49
St. Helens Town	36	13	9	14	52	47	48
Maine Road	36	13	9	14	58	61	48
Skelmersdale United	36	12	11	13	56	49	47
Nantwich Town	36	13	8	15	43	56	47
Leyland DAF-SGL	36	12	10	14	51	53	46
Bootle	36	10	9	17	55	64	39
Bacup Borough	36	9	12	15	38	47	39
Clitheroe	36	10	8	18	50	63	38
Darwen	36	9	11	16	44	62	38
Penrith	36	10	8	18	41	65	38
Atherton Laburnum Rovers	36	9	11	16	42	68	38
Salford City	*36*	*6*	*10*	*20*	*30*	*68*	*28*

Leyland DAF-SGL left.

Division Two

Great Harwood Town	*34*	*27*	*5*	*2*	*81*	*22*	*86*
Blackpool Rovers	*34*	*25*	*4*	*5*	*84*	*33*	*78*
Bradford Park Avenue	*34*	*20*	*9*	*5*	*72*	*41*	*69*
Bamber Bridge	34	20	6	8	78	46	66
Blackpool Mechanics	34	18	7	9	51	30	61
Newcastle Town	34	16	12	6	48	30	60
Cheadle Town	34	17	3	14	55	54	54
Glossop	34	12	10	12	47	42	46
Burscough	34	12	8	14	39	51	44
Westhoughton Town	34	11	10	13	50	64	43
Castleton Gabriels	34	11	9	14	42	47	42
Chadderton	34	10	6	18	51	61	36
Maghull	34	9	8	17	37	54	35
Kidsgrove Athletic	34	7	10	17	37	65	31
Ashton Town	34	9	2	23	43	86	29
Oldham Town	34	8	4	22	35	66	27
Formby	34	5	9	20	46	63	24
Atherton Collieries	34	6	4	24	37	78	22

Blackpool Rovers and Oldham Town each had 1 point deducted.
Squires Gate and Holker Old Boys both joined from the West Lancashire League.

1991-92

Division One

Ashton United	**34**	**24**	**5**	**5**	**61**	**31**	**77**
Great Harwood Town	**34**	**22**	**8**	**4**	**68**	**38**	**74**
Eastwood Hanley	34	18	9	7	54	35	63
Blackpool Rovers	34	16	7	11	73	57	55
Prescot	34	15	6	13	48	43	51
Penrith	34	15	5	14	57	58	50
Skelmersdale United	34	11	11	12	48	52	44
Flixton	34	11	9	14	46	50	42
Clitheroe	34	11	9	14	44	55	42
Darwen	34	10	11	13	56	55	41
Atherton Laburnum Rovers	34	11	8	15	38	45	41
Nantwich Town	34	11	10	13	44	49	40
Vauxhall GM	34	10	10	14	42	51	40
Bacup Borough	34	9	11	14	41	45	38
St. Helens Town	34	9	9	16	49	55	36
Maine Road	34	9	9	16	40	60	36
Bradford Park Avenue	34	10	5	19	57	68	35
Bootle	*34*	*9*	*8*	*17*	*41*	*61*	*35*

Nantwich Town had 3 points deducted.
Vauxhall GM moved to the West Cheshire League.

Division Two

Bamber Bridge	*34*	*25*	*3*	*6*	*97*	*39*	*78*
Newcastle Town	*34*	*23*	*6*	*5*	*69*	*26*	*75*
Blackpool Mechanics	*34*	*20*	*9*	*5*	*75*	*34*	*69*
Burscough	*34*	*19*	*7*	*8*	*82*	*46*	*64*
Formby	34	17	5	12	49	39	56
Glossop	*34*	*15*	*9*	*10*	*61*	*44*	*54*
Salford City	*34*	*14*	*9*	*11*	*57*	*41*	*51*
Castleton Gabriels	34	14	9	11	54	43	51
Cheadle Town	34	15	6	13	53	50	51
Kidsgrove Athletic	*34*	*14*	*7*	*13*	*44*	*45*	*49*
Chadderton	*34*	*14*	*6*	*14*	*50*	*48*	*48*
Oldham Town	34	11	8	15	49	62	41
Atherton Collieries	34	12	4	18	51	64	40
Squires Gate	34	11	5	18	45	60	38
Holker Old Boys	34	10	6	18	37	53	36
Maghull	34	7	2	25	38	90	23
Ashton Town	34	4	7	23	47	101	19
Westhoughton Town	34	5	4	25	34	106	19

Glossop changed their name to Glossop North End. Stantondale joined from the Liverpool County Combination, North Trafford joined from the Mid Cheshire League, Burnley Bank Hall and Nelson both joined from the West Lancashire League, K Chell joined from the West Midland Regional League, Irlam Town joined from the Northern Premier League and Ellesmere Port Town joined as a new club.

1992-93

Division One

Atherton Laburnum Rovers	42	33	7	2	75	25	106
Bamber Bridge	**42**	**24**	**11**	**7**	**81**	**37**	**83**
Chadderton	42	24	11	7	99	64	83
Prescot	42	20	12	10	68	44	72
Newcastle Town	42	20	8	14	70	57	68
Bradford Park Avenue	42	19	8	15	54	43	65
Clitheroe	42	17	8	17	61	40	59
St. Helens Town	42	16	11	15	79	62	59
Salford City	42	15	13	14	58	61	58
Burscough	42	16	10	16	58	68	58
Flixton	42	14	15	13	50	42	57
Blackpool Rovers	42	16	9	17	66	64	57
Nantwich Town	42	14	15	13	60	60	57
Penrith	42	15	11	16	62	67	56
Bacup Borough	42	14	13	15	66	59	55
Glossop North End	42	16	9	17	70	67	54
Darwen	42	14	10	18	54	61	52
Eastwood Hanley	42	14	10	18	45	57	52
Maine Road	42	12	9	21	55	63	45
Kidsgrove Athletic	42	9	8	25	53	94	35
Skelmersdale United	42	7	10	25	45	84	31
Blackpool Mechanics	*42*	*2*	*4*	*36*	*27*	*137*	*10*

Glossop North End had 3 points deducted.
Rossendale United joined after relegation from the Northern Premier League.

Division Two

Maghull	34	21	9	4	77	26	72
Bootle	*34*	*20*	*8*	*6*	*89*	*49*	*68*
Oldham Town	34	20	6	8	79	47	66
Ellesmere Port Town	34	16	9	9	65	46	57
Stantondale	34	16	9	9	59	49	57
Castleton Gabriels	34	15	10	9	61	48	55
North Trafford	34	14	9	11	67	63	51
Formby	34	14	9	11	49	49	51
Atherton Collieries	34	14	7	13	63	67	49
Burnley Bank Hall	34	14	4	16	87	77	46
Westhoughton Town	34	14	3	17	65	75	42
Cheadle Town	34	12	7	15	44	48	40
Squires Gate	34	11	5	18	56	73	38
K Chell	34	10	8	16	52	72	38
Holker Old Boys	34	8	13	13	57	60	37
Ashton Town	34	8	8	18	51	74	32
Nelson	34	7	7	20	47	82	28
Irlam Town	34	4	5	25	47	110	17

Cheadle Town and Westhoughton Town both had 3 points deducted.
Burnley Bank Hall left and Haslingden joined from the West Lancashire League.

1993-94

Division One

Atherton Laburnum Rovers	**42**	**25**	**13**	**4**	**83**	**34**	**88**
Rossendale United	42	25	9	8	76	46	84
Burscough	42	22	13	7	107	50	79
Nantwich Town	42	22	11	9	80	54	77
Eastwood Hanley	42	22	11	9	75	52	77
Bootle	42	21	10	11	77	61	73
Penrith	42	20	11	11	62	44	71
Blackpool Rovers	42	19	10	13	64	57	67
Clitheroe	42	19	9	14	75	58	66
Kidsgrove Athletic	42	16	10	16	70	61	58
St. Helens Town	42	14	13	15	60	55	55
Prescot	42	14	13	15	46	47	55
Maine Road	42	14	13	15	58	64	55
Newcastle Town	42	14	10	18	66	67	52
Bradford Park Avenue	42	12	12	18	54	79	48
Darwen	42	12	8	22	38	61	44
Glossop North End	42	12	8	22	58	86	44
Salford City	42	11	10	21	50	67	43
Chadderton	42	10	8	24	49	85	38
Bacup Borough	42	9	9	24	57	85	36
Skelmersdale United	42	8	8	26	55	92	32
Flixton	42	9	5	28	35	90	32

Division Two

Haslingden	34	26	5	3	117	39	83
North Trafford	*34*	*24*	*2*	*8*	*95*	*36*	*74*
Holker Old Boys	*34*	*23*	*3*	*8*	*75*	*40*	*72*
Stantondale	34	20	8	6	88	45	68
Castleton Gabriels	34	19	6	9	55	46	63
Nelson	34	16	8	10	75	52	56
Atherton Collieries	34	15	9	10	58	40	54
Maghull	34	15	8	11	70	46	53
Ellesmere Port Town	34	14	8	12	62	63	50
Formby	34	12	11	11	59	50	47
Oldham Town	34	13	6	15	61	68	45
Cheadle Town	34	11	9	14	69	62	42
Blackpool Mechanics	34	10	5	19	50	69	35
Westhoughton Town	34	9	3	22	53	100	30
Ashton Town	34	7	8	19	42	91	29
Irlam Town	34	8	4	22	41	73	28
K Chell	34	4	6	24	35	97	18
Squires Gate	34	1	9	24	20	108	12

North Trafford changed their name to Trafford and Westhoughton Town changed their name to Daisy Hill. Ellesmere Port Town and K Chell both disbanded. Tetley Walker joined from the Warrington & District League.

1994-95

Division One

Bradford Park Avenue	**42**	**30**	**4**	**8**	**96**	**43**	**94**
Clitheroe	42	27	9	6	104	49	90
St. Helens Town	42	27	8	7	86	42	89
Trafford	42	27	5	10	98	50	86
Newcastle Town	42	24	7	11	75	57	79
Glossop North End	42	23	8	11	88	59	77
Blackpool Rovers	42	22	7	13	81	64	73
Burscough	42	19	15	8	102	65	72
Prescot	42	16	8	18	47	47	56
Penrith	42	16	7	19	72	72	55
Chadderton	42	15	7	20	56	70	52
Maine Road	42	14	9	19	68	81	51
Eastwood Hanley	42	14	8	20	75	81	50
Holker Old Boys	42	13	11	18	63	72	50
Kidsgrove Athletic	42	14	8	20	66	78	50
Nantwich Town	42	14	7	21	85	83	49
Darwen	42	14	5	23	65	82	47
Rossendale United	42	12	11	19	60	82	47
Bootle	42	11	10	21	46	68	43
Skelmersdale United	42	10	7	25	67	118	37
Salford City	42	9	9	24	45	85	36
Bacup Borough	*42*	*3*	*6*	*33*	*35*	*132*	*15*

Mossley joined the league following their relegation from the Northern Premier League.

Division Two

Flixton	*30*	*21*	*6*	*3*	*98*	*32*	*69*
Oldham Town	30	20	6	4	83	34	66
Tetley Walker	30	18	5	7	75	46	59
Atherton Collieries	30	18	4	8	67	41	58
Stantondale	30	18	3	9	58	43	57
Nelson	30	13	8	9	64	44	47
Haslingden	30	14	4	12	76	64	46
Blackpool Mechanics	30	12	8	10	72	57	44
Maghull	30	11	8	11	58	46	41
Formby	30	11	6	13	57	53	39
Cheadle Town	30	10	7	13	48	52	37
Castleton Gabriels	30	9	9	12	56	75	36
Daisy Hill	30	6	8	16	53	73	26
Ashton Town	30	6	2	22	39	92	20
Irlam Town	30	5	3	22	30	98	18
Squires Gate	30	2	5	23	30	114	11

Irlam Town left the league.
Middlewich Athletic joined from the Mid Cheshire League, Vauxhall GM joined from the West Cheshire League and Ramsbottom United joined from the Manchester League.

1995-96

Division One

Flixton	42	28	8	6	85	30	92
Newcastle Town	42	26	7	9	88	42	85
Trafford	42	26	5	11	89	45	83
Mossley	42	24	8	10	87	59	80
Burscough	42	23	8	11	77	40	77
Bootle	42	23	5	14	74	55	74
Clitheroe	42	20	12	10	63	44	72
St. Helens Town	42	19	13	10	71	53	70
Nantwich Town	42	20	7	15	64	59	67
Prescot	42	17	11	14	70	66	62
Holker Old Boys	42	19	4	19	77	72	61
Glossop North End	42	15	15	12	55	48	60
Kidsgrove Athletic	42	15	9	18	61	64	54
Eastwood Hanley	42	12	15	15	60	57	51
Maine Road	42	12	14	16	60	71	50
Chadderton	42	14	8	20	52	69	50
Blackpool Rovers	42	11	9	22	49	74	42
Penrith	42	9	12	21	57	69	39
Darwen	42	9	10	23	57	77	37
Salford City	42	10	5	27	49	93	35
Rossendale United	42	6	10	26	32	114	28
Skelmersdale United	*42*	*5*	*3*	*34*	*45*	*121*	*18*

Prescot changed their name to Prescot Cables.

1996-97

Division One

Trafford	42	29	7	6	99	38	94
Newcastle Town	42	27	7	8	71	31	88
Clitheroe	42	23	14	5	75	36	83
Penrith	42	23	10	9	75	49	79
Burscough	42	22	9	11	68	48	75
Eastwood Hanley	42	20	10	12	64	51	70
Mossley	42	20	8	14	79	58	68
Blackpool Rovers	42	17	16	9	70	47	67
Prescot Cables	42	17	11	14	68	60	62
Vauxhall GM	42	14	15	13	70	69	57
Nantwich Town	42	14	11	17	74	74	53
Bootle	*42*	*15*	*8*	*19*	*62*	*73*	*53*
Glossop North End	42	14	11	17	56	67	53
St. Helens Town	42	14	6	22	65	79	48
Atherton Collieries	42	12	9	21	63	85	45
Kidsgrove Athletic	42	10	14	18	53	73	44
Rossendale United	42	11	9	22	51	76	42
Chadderton	42	10	11	21	49	80	41
Holker Old Boys	42	10	9	23	60	80	39
Maine Road	42	9	11	22	49	85	38
Darwen	42	9	10	23	49	82	37
Salford City	42	8	12	22	53	82	36

Penrith moved to the Northern League and Eastwood Hanley disbanded. Atherton Laburnum Rovers and Warrington Town joined after relegation from the Northern Premier League.

Division Two

Vauxhall GM	*34*	*28*	*4*	*2*	*112*	*25*	*88*
Atherton Collieries	*34*	*25*	*5*	*4*	*90*	*44*	*80*
Tetley Walker	34	22	7	5	76	35	73
Castleton Gabriels	34	19	5	10	77	52	62
Nelson	34	17	9	8	78	55	60
Cheadle Town	34	17	5	12	67	49	56
Haslingden	34	15	9	10	69	45	54
Maghull	34	16	3	15	55	42	51
Oldham Town	34	14	8	12	75	74	50
Middlewich Athletic	34	12	7	15	45	74	43
Daisy Hill	34	12	4	18	46	66	40
Ramsbottom United	34	11	6	17	60	65	39
Formby	34	10	7	17	59	76	37
Stantondale	34	11	4	19	47	75	37
Blackpool Mechanics	34	8	8	18	56	74	32
Ashton Town	34	8	3	23	53	102	27
Squires Gate	34	5	7	22	37	82	22
Bacup Borough	34	4	3	27	35	102	15

Garswood United joined from the Mid Cheshire League, Leek County School Old Boys joined from the Midland League and Colne joined as a new club.

Division Two

Ramsbottom United	*38*	*27*	*6*	*5*	*100*	*34*	*87*
Haslingden	*38*	*27*	*6*	*5*	*90*	*32*	*87*
Garswood United	38	26	5	7	90	38	83
Tetley Walker	38	24	5	9	105	58	77
Castleton Gabriels	38	22	8	8	78	39	74
Leek County School Old Boys	38	22	7	9	67	49	73
Formby	38	21	6	11	86	57	69
Maghull	38	17	7	14	52	50	58
Cheadle Town	38	15	8	15	59	63	53
Skelmersdale United	38	14	10	14	72	66	52
Nelson	38	14	10	14	64	72	52
Stantondale	38	11	12	15	59	69	45
Middlewich Athletic	38	13	6	19	54	65	45
Squires Gate	38	12	4	22	44	79	40
Daisy Hill	38	10	5	23	47	76	35
Bacup Borough	38	9	6	23	48	83	33
Ashton Town	38	6	14	18	53	77	32
Blackpool Mechanics	38	7	5	26	48	88	26
Oldham Town	38	6	7	25	48	113	25
Colne	38	6	5	27	35	91	23

Woodley Sports joined from the Manchester League and Fleetwood Freeport joined as a new club.

1997-98

Division One

Kidsgrove Athletic	42	32	3	7	127	50	99
Burscough	**42**	**29**	**7**	**6**	**101**	**30**	**94**
Newcastle Town	42	23	16	3	82	32	85
Vauxhall GM	42	24	9	9	91	52	81
St. Helens Town	42	22	12	8	91	59	78
Clitheroe	42	21	10	11	72	51	73
Prescot Cables	42	19	11	12	72	57	68
Glossop North End	42	19	7	16	78	69	64
Mossley	42	16	14	12	67	52	62
Nantwich Town	42	17	6	19	71	79	57
Maine Road	42	15	10	17	56	70	55
Chadderton	*42*	*15*	*8*	*19*	*63*	*59*	*53*
Rossendale United	42	15	6	21	61	80	51
Blackpool Rovers	42	13	9	20	68	84	48
Atherton Laburnum Rovers	42	12	11	19	54	73	47
Haslingden	42	12	10	20	68	95	46
Ramsbottom United	42	12	9	21	58	85	45
Salford City	42	13	4	25	64	92	43
Warrington Town	42	10	10	22	56	72	40
Holker Old Boys	42	7	12	23	46	96	33
Darwen	*42*	*6*	*13*	*23*	*42*	*93*	*31*
Atherton Collieries	42	7	9	26	42	100	30

Workington joined after relegation from the Northern Premier League. Blackpool Rovers and Haslingden left the league.

1998-99

Division One

Workington	**40**	**27**	**9**	**4**	**86**	**28**	**90**
Mossley	40	27	7	6	91	38	88
Vauxhall GM	40	26	7	7	92	40	85
Newcastle Town	40	25	9	6	86	33	84
Kidsgrove Athletic	40	24	7	9	90	47	79
Prescot Cables	40	21	9	10	78	44	72
Skelmersdale United	40	21	8	11	82	48	71
St. Helens Town	40	22	5	13	77	58	71
Leek County School Old Boys	40	14	11	15	52	58	53
Salford City	40	15	7	18	63	73	52
Ramsbottom United	40	14	8	18	54	64	50
Clitheroe	40	14	6	20	68	58	48
Maine Road	40	14	6	20	50	71	48
Rossendale United	40	14	5	21	59	81	47
Nantwich Town	40	12	6	22	54	68	42
Glossop North End	40	12	6	22	53	81	42
Cheadle Town	40	12	6	22	56	97	42
Atherton Laburnum Rovers	40	10	9	21	45	73	39
Atherton Collieries	40	9	7	24	50	88	34
Bootle	40	9	7	24	41	84	34
Holker Old Boys	*40*	*4*	*3*	*33*	*21*	*116*	*15*

Vauxhall GM changed their name to Vauxhall Motors. Great Harwood Town joined after relegation from the Northern Premier League.

Division Two

Oldham Town	40	27	8	5	118	49	89
Skelmersdale United	*40*	*26*	*7*	*7*	*111*	*50*	*85*
Leek County School O.B.	*40*	*26*	*7*	*7*	*76*	*38*	*85*
Cheadle Town	*40*	*24*	*9*	*7*	*108*	*58*	*81*
Woodley Sports	40	22	7	11	118	56	73
Formby	40	22	7	11	90	63	73
Bootle	*40*	*19*	*15*	*6*	*82*	*60*	*72*
Garswood United	40	19	10	11	98	62	67
Tetley Walker	40	19	9	12	98	62	66
Castleton Gabriels	40	18	7	15	86	59	61
Maghull	40	16	10	14	67	62	58
Fleetwood Freeport	40	15	11	14	73	55	56
Nelson	40	17	5	18	69	76	56
Bacup Borough	40	13	8	19	58	83	47
Squires Gate	40	11	9	20	72	88	42
Daisy Hill	40	11	9	20	60	86	42
Middlewich Athletic	40	11	8	21	48	90	41
Colne	40	8	7	25	48	91	31
Ashton Town	40	6	6	28	73	137	24
Stantondale	40	4	4	32	50	146	16
Blackpool Mechanics	40	2	5	33	33	165	11

Middlewich Athletic reformed as Middlewich Town and moved to the Mid Cheshire League, Garswood United moved to the Mid Cheshire League and Stantondale also left.
Abbey Hey joined from the Manchester League and Curzon Ashton joined from the Northern Counties (East) League.

Division Two

Fleetwood Freeport	*36*	*21*	*8*	*7*	*102*	*34*	*71*
Abbey Hey	*36*	*20*	*6*	*10*	*70*	*35*	*66*
Squires Gate	36	17	14	5	53	31	65
Warrington Town	36	18	9	9	82	46	63
Woodley Sports	36	17	10	9	60	38	61
Castleton Gabriels	36	17	10	9	71	56	61
Formby	36	17	7	12	81	59	58
Darwen	36	13	12	11	64	53	51
Chadderton	36	11	17	8	42	38	50
Tetley Walker	36	14	8	14	62	64	50
Bacup Borough	36	11	14	11	47	61	47
Daisy Hill	36	12	9	15	51	63	45
Nelson	36	11	11	14	51	49	44
Curzon Ashton	36	12	7	17	56	58	43
Maghull	36	11	10	15	50	70	43
Colne	36	11	7	18	53	70	40
Ashton Town	36	11	6	19	35	59	39
Oldham Town	36	5	7	24	35	99	22
Blackpool Mechanics	36	4	6	26	40	122	18

Maghull moved to the West Cheshire League and Alsager joined from the Midland League.

1999-2000

Division One

Vauxhall Motors	42	29	7	6	101	32	94
Newcastle Town	42	26	7	9	82	35	85
Ramsbottom United	42	23	10	9	87	53	79
Mossley	42	23	10	9	80	50	79
Rossendale United	42	23	9	10	77	46	78
Skelmersdale United	42	22	9	11	91	53	75
Fleetwood Freeport	42	21	10	11	75	45	73
Prescot Cables	42	21	10	11	83	55	73
St. Helens Town	42	20	13	9	81	59	73
Clitheroe	42	21	7	14	75	49	70
Salford City	42	17	7	18	70	69	58
Atherton Collieries	42	16	6	20	58	68	54
Kidsgrove Athletic	42	14	9	19	47	66	51
Abbey Hey	42	14	8	20	50	75	50
Nantwich Town	42	13	9	20	60	73	48
Great Harwood Town	42	12	9	21	55	81	45
Glossop North End	42	10	11	21	52	73	41
Cheadle Town	42	8	13	21	49	85	37
Maine Road	42	9	10	23	59	100	37
Leek County School Old Boys	42	8	10	24	49	101	34
Bootle	42	6	8	28	29	90	26
Atherton Laburnum Rovers	42	4	12	26	51	103	24

Flixton joined after relegation from the Northern Premier League.

Division Two

Woodley Sports	34	24	6	4	85	29	78
Curzon Ashton	34	24	6	4	78	26	78
Nelson	34	21	8	5	77	31	71
Darwen	34	20	6	8	69	35	66
Bacup Borough	34	15	11	8	68	42	56
Squires Gate	34	16	7	11	70	49	55
Tetley Walker	34	16	4	14	56	70	52
Castleton Gabriels	34	15	6	13	67	67	51
Warrington Town	34	14	8	12	66	44	50
Chadderton	34	12	12	10	52	57	48
Formby	34	12	8	14	52	68	44
Alsager	34	11	8	15	48	64	41
Colne	34	12	2	20	44	70	38
Holker Old Boys	34	8	11	15	59	73	35
Blackpool Mechanics	34	9	6	19	49	74	33
Daisy Hill	34	7	5	22	41	75	26
Oldham Town	34	4	6	24	43	86	18
Ashton Town	34	5	2	27	30	94	17

Padiham joined from the West Lancashire League and Stone Dominoes joined from the Midland League.

2000-01

Division One

Rossendale United	42	29	5	8	114	44	92
Clitheroe	42	27	8	7	105	47	89
Ramsbottom United	42	28	4	10	85	44	88
St. Helens Town	42	26	9	7	98	40	87
Fleetwood Freeport	42	26	4	12	90	50	82
Kidsgrove Athletic	42	24	10	8	81	46	82
Salford City	42	23	10	9	87	41	79
Prescot Cables	42	24	5	13	94	54	77
Newcastle Town	42	20	7	15	69	45	67
Mossley	42	19	7	16	73	56	64
Curzon Ashton	42	18	9	15	67	66	63
Skelmersdale United	42	17	8	17	69	69	59
Woodley Sports	42	16	9	17	69	69	57
Abbey Hey	42	15	6	21	76	92	51
Maine Road	42	15	3	24	75	102	48
Nantwich Town	42	10	9	23	46	79	39
Atherton Collieries	42	11	6	25	43	88	39
Glossop North End	42	9	4	29	41	111	31
Great Harwood Town	42	7	9	26	44	93	30
Flixton	42	5	13	24	47	100	28
Leek County School Old Boys	42	5	12	25	39	89	27
Cheadle Town	42	5	9	28	42	129	24

Congleton Town and Winsford United joined after relegation from the Northern Premier League.

Division Two

Warrington Town	38	24	7	7	90	31	79
Tetley Walker	38	24	5	9	83	41	77
Atherton Laburnum Rovers	38	24	3	11	88	50	75
Nelson	38	21	11	6	89	44	74
Squires Gate	38	21	7	10	75	47	70
Blackpool Mechanics	38	21	6	11	85	47	69
Alsager	38	19	8	11	48	42	65
Padiham	38	20	4	14	83	71	64
Daisy Hill	38	18	6	14	78	80	60
Chadderton	38	17	7	14	68	58	58
Darwen	38	16	7	15	72	66	55
Formby	38	15	8	15	65	56	53
Stone Dominoes	38	15	6	17	62	63	51
Bacup Borough	38	13	9	16	59	60	48
Holker Old Boys	38	14	5	19	67	79	47
Bootle	38	11	8	19	70	76	41
Castleton Gabriels	38	10	7	21	52	90	37
Ashton Town	38	8	3	27	46	98	27
Colne	38	4	4	30	37	107	16
Oldham Town	38	3	3	32	38	149	12

Alsager changed their name to Alsager Town and Tetley Walker left the league. Stand Athletic joined from the Manchester League and Norton United joined from the Midland League.

2001-02

Division One

	P	W	D	L	F	A	Pts
Kidsgrove Athletic	44	31	9	4	125	47	102
Prescot Cables	44	29	10	5	110	42	97
Salford City	44	29	10	5	91	40	97
St. Helens Town	44	28	6	10	101	44	90
Newcastle Town	44	22	11	11	97	66	77
Clitheroe	44	22	10	12	73	53	76
Winsford United	44	19	12	13	72	71	69
Mossley	44	18	14	12	82	63	68
Skelmersdale United	44	19	5	20	87	89	62
Woodley Sports	44	16	12	16	58	65	60
Warrington Town	44	16	11	17	78	72	59
Ramsbottom United	44	15	10	19	75	73	55
Curzon Ashton	44	16	7	21	74	72	55
Fleetwood Freeport	44	13	13	18	70	86	52
Nantwich Town	44	12	15	17	63	90	51
Congleton Town	44	13	11	20	71	79	50
Atherton Collieries	44	13	8	23	66	91	47
Abbey Hey	44	12	11	21	62	101	47
Glossop North End	44	13	7	24	78	105	46
Atherton Laburnum Rovers	44	11	11	22	62	88	44
Flixton	44	11	9	24	61	112	42
Maine Road	44	8	7	29	68	115	31
Great Harwood Town	44	5	11	28	39	99	26

Fleetwood Freeport changed their name to Fleetwood Town.

2002-03

Division One

	P	W	D	L	F	A	Pts
Prescot Cables	42	30	6	6	110	38	96
Clitheroe	42	28	8	6	97	38	92
Mossley	42	27	7	8	100	41	88
Newcastle Town	42	23	12	7	83	52	81
Skelmersdale United	42	22	8	12	91	51	74
Nantwich Town	42	19	11	12	90	74	68
St. Helens Town	42	17	14	11	77	60	65
Congleton Town	42	19	8	15	72	62	65
Salford City	42	17	12	13	84	63	63
Fleetwood Town	42	17	9	16	73	70	60
Alsager Town	42	15	11	16	61	67	56
Squires Gate	42	13	12	17	58	71	51
Abbey Hey	42	12	13	17	56	73	49
Atherton Laburnum Rovers	42	11	12	19	65	86	45
Ramsbottom United	42	11	11	20	73	83	44
Warrington Town	42	11	11	20	48	66	44
Woodley Sports	42	11	9	22	62	85	42
Curzon Ashton	42	11	9	22	60	87	42
Atherton Collieries	42	11	7	24	52	85	40
Glossop North End	42	10	9	23	55	104	39
Flixton	42	10	8	24	44	112	38
Winsford United	42	10	7	25	48	91	37

Trafford joined after relegation from the Northern Premier League.

Division Two

	P	W	D	L	F	A	Pts
Stand Athletic	40	30	5	5	110	47	95
Alsager Town	40	24	9	7	77	31	81
Squires Gate	40	24	9	7	103	60	81
Stone Dominoes	40	25	3	12	71	40	78
Formby	40	21	14	5	76	39	77
Bootle	40	19	7	14	82	64	64
Norton United	40	19	7	14	56	51	64
Blackpool Mechanics	40	18	9	13	69	48	63
Nelson	40	18	9	13	73	63	63
Leek County School Old Boys	40	17	8	15	62	65	59
Darwen	40	15	10	15	77	73	55
Bacup Borough	40	13	13	14	52	66	52
Padiham	40	14	8	18	69	66	50
Colne	40	14	8	18	61	72	50
Chadderton	40	15	5	20	65	81	50
Ashton Town	40	13	6	21	65	85	45
Cheadle Town	40	10	8	22	66	85	38
Castleton Gabriels	40	10	3	27	61	95	33
Holker Old Boys	40	7	9	24	43	79	30
Daisy Hill	40	8	4	28	49	114	28
Oldham Town	40	7	4	29	50	113	25

Bootle and Formby both moved to the Liverpool County Combination.

Division Two

	P	W	D	L	F	A	Pts
Bacup Borough	34	25	2	7	91	32	77
Stone Dominoes	34	24	3	7	94	34	75
Maine Road	34	23	2	9	74	55	71
Padiham	34	20	5	9	69	42	65
Holker Old Boys	34	18	7	9	65	42	61
Great Harwood Town	34	15	7	12	64	61	52
Nelson	34	13	12	9	50	40	51
Darwen	34	14	7	13	59	64	49
Norton United	34	14	6	14	50	52	48
Colne	34	14	5	15	65	53	47
Ashton Town	34	12	9	13	49	53	45
Castleton Gabriels	34	10	8	16	43	60	38
Cheadle Town	34	10	8	16	39	56	38
Blackpool Mechanics	34	9	10	15	39	52	37
Leek County School Old Boys	34	8	9	17	46	57	33
Daisy Hill	34	7	5	22	42	93	26
Oldham Town	34	4	12	18	40	86	24
Chadderton	34	5	5	24	33	80	20

Stand Athletic resigned in mid-season and their record was deleted when it stood as follows: 12   5   4   3   24   17   19
Formby joined from the Liverpool County Combination and Eccleshall joined from the Midland League.

2003-04

Division One

Clitheroe	**42**	**29**	**5**	**8**	**88**	**55**	**92**
Mossley	**42**	**28**	**8**	**6**	**109**	**54**	**89**
Fleetwood Town	42	26	8	8	84	51	86
Woodley Sports	**42**	**26**	**5**	**11**	**99**	**56**	**83**
Warrington Town	**42**	**20**	**10**	**12**	**72**	**59**	**70**
Newcastle Town	42	21	6	15	94	67	69
Curzon Ashton	42	19	10	13	84	79	64
Skelmersdale United	42	19	6	17	79	64	63
Alsager Town	42	16	15	11	54	47	63
Stone Dominoes	42	18	8	16	57	60	62
Congleton Town	42	15	16	11	62	50	61
Atherton Laburnum Rovers	42	17	7	18	77	76	58
Nantwich Town	42	15	11	16	73	66	53
Bacup Borough	42	15	8	19	68	72	53
Salford City	42	14	11	17	62	66	53
Trafford	42	14	8	20	72	91	50
Ramsbottom United	42	12	12	18	71	92	48
Glossop North End	42	9	9	24	51	95	36
St. Helens Town	42	10	6	26	51	81	33
Squires Gate	42	7	12	23	52	83	33
Abbey Hey	42	7	8	27	46	90	29
Atherton Collieries	42	6	9	27	48	99	23

Mossley, Curzon Ashton, Nantwich Town and St. Helens Town all had 3 points deducted and Atherton Collieries had 4 points deducted.

Division Two

Colne	*38*	*26*	*6*	*6*	*102*	*41*	*84*
Maine Road	*38*	*23*	*5*	*10*	*99*	*58*	*74*
Formby	*38*	*21*	*9*	*8*	*86*	*48*	*72*
Great Harwood Town	*38*	*15*	*14*	*9*	*68*	*44*	*59*
Flixton	38	16	11	11	76	60	59
Darwen	38	17	11	10	81	67	59
Ashton Town	38	16	11	11	66	60	59
Winsford United	38	15	11	12	66	62	56
Holker Old Boys	38	15	8	15	82	76	53
Nelson	38	14	11	13	55	64	53
Leek County School Old Boys	38	14	8	16	72	63	50
Padiham	38	14	8	16	63	80	50
Oldham Town	38	13	9	16	69	74	48
Blackpool Mechanics	38	13	7	18	45	59	46
Norton United	38	11	12	15	66	72	45
Cheadle Town	38	12	9	17	55	69	45
Eccleshall	38	10	14	14	56	65	44
Chadderton	38	7	11	20	42	63	32
Daisy Hill	38	7	10	21	33	82	31
Castleton Gabriels	38	6	5	27	53	128	23

Darwen had 3 points deducted.
Cammell Laird joined from the West Cheshire League, Silsden joined from the West Riding County Amateur League and New Mills joined from the Manchester League.

2004-05

Division One

Fleetwood Town	**42**	**31**	**6**	**5**	**107**	**42**	**99**
Newcastle Town	42	28	8	6	94	51	92
St. Helens Town	42	21	13	8	75	48	76
Curzon Ashton	42	23	7	12	66	45	76
Ramsbottom United	42	22	9	11	70	47	75
Skelmersdale United	42	21	11	10	94	57	74
Alsager Town	42	19	11	12	65	47	68
Maine Road	42	20	7	15	76	69	67
Bacup Borough	42	19	8	15	52	47	65
Colne	42	18	10	14	75	61	64
Stone Dominoes	42	17	12	13	73	64	63
Trafford	42	16	8	18	69	59	56
Glossop North End	42	15	10	17	79	75	55
Abbey Hey	42	16	6	20	51	69	54
Atherton Laburnum Rovers	42	14	6	22	64	82	48
Nantwich Town	42	12	8	22	71	91	44
Squires Gate	42	12	8	22	38	64	44
Salford City	42	11	9	22	68	90	42
Congleton Town	42	9	7	26	54	88	34
Formby	42	8	8	26	47	99	32
Atherton Collieries	42	8	7	27	57	102	31
Great Harwood Town	*42*	*8*	*9*	*25*	*48*	*96*	*29*

Great Harwood Town had 4 points deducted.

Division Two

Cammell Laird	*36*	*27*	*6*	*3*	*142*	*34*	*87*
Silsden	*36*	*25*	*5*	*6*	*93*	*42*	*77*
Winsford United	36	23	7	6	72	28	76
Padiham	36	21	7	8	84	56	70
Norton United	36	17	12	7	63	40	60
Nelson	36	16	11	9	75	52	59
Ashton Town	36	13	8	15	61	62	47
Daisy Hill	36	12	10	14	61	68	46
New Mills	36	13	6	17	51	74	45
Blackpool Mechanics	36	12	9	15	49	67	42
Eccleshall	36	11	8	17	47	58	41
Cheadle Town	36	11	7	18	47	80	40
Oldham Town	36	10	12	14	54	56	39
Leek County School Old Boys	36	9	10	17	59	68	37
Holker Old Boys	36	10	7	19	65	81	37
Darwen	36	13	5	18	39	56	35
Chadderton	36	7	7	22	40	94	28
Flixton	36	14	6	16	72	79	27
Castleton Gabriels	36	4	5	27	32	111	17

Silsden, Norton United, Blackpool Mechanics and Oldham Town all had 3 points deducted, Darwen had 9 points deducted and Flixton had 21 points deducted.
FC United of Manchester joined as a new club.

2005-06
Division One

Cammell Laird	42	35	3	4	126	36	102
Skelmersdale United	42	28	7	7	119	48	91
Alsager Town	42	27	7	8	87	43	88
Nantwich Town	42	26	6	10	91	37	84
Salford City	42	23	10	9	79	46	79
Newcastle Town	42	21	9	12	97	52	72
Curzon Ashton	42	20	8	14	72	66	68
St. Helens Town	42	20	7	15	70	68	67
Colne	42	22	3	17	84	70	63
Maine Road	42	17	10	15	65	56	61
Abbey Hey	42	14	12	16	61	70	54
Congleton Town	42	15	8	19	50	63	53
Squires Gate	42	12	15	15	43	62	51
Silsden	42	16	8	18	76	75	50
Trafford	42	13	13	16	71	56	49
Glossop North End	42	12	11	19	62	78	47
Bacup Borough	42	13	8	21	44	62	47
Ramsbottom United	42	9	18	15	45	60	45
Atherton Collieries	42	7	9	26	43	93	30
Atherton Laburnum Rovers	42	7	8	27	40	115	29
Stone Dominoes	42	5	5	32	39	146	20
Formby	42	4	7	31	43	105	19

Trafford had 3 points deducted and Cammell Laird, Colne and Silsden all had 6 points deducted.

2006-07
Division One

FC United of Manchester	42	36	4	2	157	36	112
Curzon Ashton	42	31	6	5	116	38	99
Nantwich Town	42	29	8	5	108	41	95
Salford City	42	26	9	7	103	55	87
Trafford	42	24	11	7	94	46	83
Maine Road	42	22	7	13	79	58	73
Atherton Collieries	42	19	13	10	72	55	70
Ramsbottom United	42	19	7	16	78	63	64
Glossop North End	42	19	6	17	71	71	63
Congleton Town	42	18	8	16	75	62	62
Colne	42	16	13	13	75	70	61
Newcastle Town	42	16	10	16	70	63	58
Flixton	42	15	11	16	72	67	56
Silsden	42	16	6	20	66	79	54
Bacup Borough	42	11	13	18	50	65	46
Atherton Laburnum Rovers	42	11	9	22	65	106	42
Abbey Hey	42	10	10	22	44	83	40
Squires Gate	42	10	8	24	56	97	38
St. Helens Town	42	10	6	26	47	92	36
Nelson	42	7	6	29	41	113	27
Formby	42	6	4	32	43	111	22
Stone Dominoes	42	2	3	37	36	147	9

Division Two

FC United of Manchester	36	27	6	3	111	35	87
Flixton	36	24	7	5	93	37	79
Nelson	36	23	5	8	82	53	74
Winsford United	36	19	8	9	65	41	65
Padiham	36	19	5	12	76	52	62
Great Harwood Town	36	18	8	10	51	33	62
Ashton Town	36	17	7	12	59	57	58
Norton United	36	13	12	11	45	47	51
Blackpool Mechanics	36	13	10	13	48	51	49
Oldham Town	36	14	6	16	46	49	48
Eccleshall	36	13	7	16	50	64	46
New Mills	36	13	7	16	46	62	46
Chadderton	36	13	8	15	51	62	44
Cheadle Town	36	14	6	16	55	53	42
Holker Old Boys	36	11	8	17	58	74	41
Darwen	36	11	2	23	47	61	35
Leek County School Old Boys	36	7	7	22	51	82	28
Daisy Hill	36	7	6	23	38	75	27
Castleton Gabriels	36	2	3	31	38	122	1

Chadderton had 3 points deducted, Cheadle Town had 6 points deducted and Castleton Gabriels had 8 points deducted.

Great Harwood Town disbanded. Bootle joined from the Liverpool County Combination, Ashton Athletic joined from the Manchester League and Runcorn Linnets joined as a new club.

Division Two

Winsford United	34	23	7	4	82	35	76
Runcorn Linnets	34	24	4	6	77	35	76
Padiham	34	21	6	7	75	39	69
New Mills	34	21	6	7	74	42	69
Chadderton	34	18	7	9	59	35	61
Oldham Town	34	17	5	12	69	54	56
Darwen	34	14	10	10	56	45	52
Ashton Town	34	15	7	12	55	56	52
Leek County School Old Boys	34	14	8	12	51	52	50
Bootle	34	14	8	12	63	48	46
Eccleshall	34	12	6	16	45	46	42
Cheadle Town	34	9	8	17	41	60	35
Blackpool Mechanics	34	10	6	18	39	48	30
Holker Old Boys	34	6	11	17	47	81	29
Daisy Hill	34	7	8	19	38	78	29
Ashton Athletic	34	6	10	18	38	62	28
Norton United	34	6	7	21	37	73	25
Castleton Gabriels	34	5	4	25	38	95	19

Bootle had 4 points deducted and Blackpool Mechanics had 6 points deducted.

Kirkham & Wesham joined from the West Lancashire League.

2007-08

Division One

Team	P	W	D	L	F	A	Pts
Trafford	38	30	5	3	102	35	95
Salford City	38	26	6	6	75	35	84
Newcastle Town	38	24	7	7	95	45	79
Maine Road	38	20	8	10	75	45	68
Colne	38	19	11	8	69	45	68
Squires Gate	38	19	9	10	52	43	66
Glossop North End	38	20	5	13	72	46	65
Flixton	38	17	7	14	65	65	58
Congleton Town	38	17	6	15	73	60	57
Winsford United	38	16	8	14	60	47	56
Silsden	38	15	10	13	65	57	55
Runcorn Linnets	38	14	6	18	53	64	48
Formby	38	14	3	21	52	60	42
St. Helens Town	38	11	8	19	64	93	41
Atherton Collieries	38	10	10	18	44	67	40
Ramsbottom United	38	9	10	19	41	59	37
Abbey Hey	38	6	9	23	45	106	27
Bacup Borough	38	5	11	22	35	69	26
Atherton Laburnum Rovers	38	5	9	24	38	86	24
Nelson	38	5	8	25	42	90	23

Formby had 3 points deducted.
Alsager Town joined after relegation from the Northern Premier League.

2008-09

Premier Division

Team	P	W	D	L	F	A	Pts
AFC Fylde	42	33	5	4	122	35	104
New Mills	42	34	2	6	92	33	104
Newcastle Town	42	26	9	7	91	33	87
Congleton Town	42	26	8	8	85	44	86
Glossop North End	42	25	7	10	83	49	82
Ashton Athletic	42	18	7	17	67	68	61
Alsager Town	42	18	5	19	66	72	59
Bacup Borough	42	16	10	16	71	71	58
Silsden	42	16	10	16	62	67	58
Squires Gate	42	14	15	13	56	56	57
Runcorn Linnets	42	16	7	19	64	84	55
Atherton Laburnum Rovers	42	12	15	15	70	77	51
Maine Road	42	14	9	19	60	74	51
Ramsbottom United	42	13	12	17	56	72	50
Formby	42	15	3	24	57	67	48
St. Helens Town	42	14	4	24	64	97	46
Nelson	42	11	12	19	68	86	45
Colne	42	11	10	21	64	75	43
Winsford United	42	10	9	23	52	82	39
Abbey Hey	42	11	5	26	60	89	38
Flixton	42	9	14	19	58	86	41
Atherton Collieries	*42*	*7*	*8*	*27*	*42*	*93*	*29*

Ramsbottom United had 1 point deducted.

Division Two

Team	P	W	D	L	F	A	Pts
New Mills	*34*	*28*	*3*	*3*	*107*	*23*	*87*
Kirkham & Wesham	*34*	*24*	*5*	*5*	*88*	*31*	*77*
Ashton Athletic	*34*	*20*	*7*	*7*	*68*	*35*	*67*
Oldham Town	34	19	7	8	79	44	64
Chadderton	34	19	4	11	55	52	61
Bootle	34	18	6	10	86	53	60
Leek County School Old Boys	34	16	7	11	57	51	55
Norton United	34	13	11	10	47	52	50
Blackpool Mechanics	34	11	12	11	47	45	45
Stone Dominoes	34	12	8	14	60	59	44
Darwen	34	13	5	16	55	65	44
Padiham	34	11	8	15	50	48	41
Ashton Town	34	12	4	18	53	80	40
Cheadle Town	34	10	6	18	44	80	33
Eccleshall	34	8	6	20	41	69	30
Holker Old Boys	34	8	2	24	41	82	26
Castleton Gabriels	34	6	6	22	46	97	24
Daisy Hill	34	2	5	27	28	86	11

Cheadle Town had 3 points deducted.
Kirkham & Wesham changed their name to AFC Fylde, Blackpool Mechanics changed their name to AFC Blackpool and Castleton Gabriels changed their name to Rochdale Town.
Irlam and Wigan Robin Park both joined from the Manchester League and AFC Liverpool joined as a newly formed club.

Division One

Team	P	W	D	L	F	A	Pts
Bootle	*34*	*25*	*5*	*4*	*78*	*27*	*80*
Padiham	*34*	*22*	*7*	*5*	*93*	*41*	*73*
Stone Dominoes	34	23	2	9	85	51	71
AFC Liverpool	34	22	3	9	82	39	69
Wigan Robin Park	34	18	5	11	61	49	59
Oldham Town	34	16	5	13	60	54	53
Cheadle Town	34	16	6	14	54	44	52
Irlam	34	13	13	8	51	43	52
Holker Old Boys	34	14	8	12	59	61	50
Chadderton	34	14	6	14	60	54	48
Eccleshall	34	14	5	15	44	44	47
Norton United	34	12	6	16	63	60	42
Darwen	34	11	7	16	51	74	40
Leek County School Old Boys	34	7	10	17	51	72	31
AFC Blackpool	34	7	8	19	34	59	29
Rochdale Town	34	6	6	22	55	91	24
Daisy Hill	34	6	4	24	39	101	22
Ashton Town	34	4	8	22	35	91	20

Oldham Town changed their name to Oldham Borough. Barnoldswick Town joined from the West Lancashire League and Darwen moved to the West Lancashire League as AFC Darwen.

Division One was renamed the Premier Division and Division Two was renamed Division One.

2009-10

Premier Division

Newcastle Town	42	37	3	2	121	21	114
New Mills	42	27	9	6	108	38	90
Bootle	42	26	7	9	92	41	85
Ramsbottom United	42	24	9	9	92	69	81
Congleton Town	42	24	8	10	90	46	80
Maine Road	42	21	7	14	82	59	70
Glossop North End	42	19	12	11	74	49	69
Colne	42	19	10	13	70	65	67
St. Helens Town	42	20	6	16	74	75	66
Padiham	42	18	6	18	71	71	60
Runcorn Linnets	42	17	6	19	75	78	57
Bacup Borough	42	15	12	15	63	75	57
Squires Gate	42	15	8	19	61	74	53
Silsden	42	13	7	22	53	75	46
Formby	42	14	3	25	57	81	45
Flixton	42	12	8	22	54	85	44
Nelson	42	12	8	22	47	87	44
Alsager Town	42	11	7	24	60	79	40
Winsford United	42	11	7	24	53	79	40
Atherton Laburnum Rovers	42	10	7	25	53	96	37
Ashton Athletic	42	8	8	26	51	101	32
Abbey Hey	42	7	6	29	49	106	27

Nelson disbanded. Rossendale United joined the league after relegation from the Northern Premier League.

Division One

Stone Dominoes	32	21	6	5	81	37	69
Barnoldswick Town	32	20	7	5	66	27	67
Norton United	32	16	6	10	51	41	54
Chadderton	32	14	8	10	54	46	50
AFC Liverpool	32	15	4	13	60	43	49
Atherton Collieries	32	15	4	13	63	66	49
Holker Old Boys	32	13	8	11	50	50	47
Leek County School Old Boys	32	13	7	12	50	48	46
Eccleshall	32	13	7	12	43	45	46
Irlam	32	12	7	13	52	45	43
Daisy Hill	32	12	7	13	55	60	43
Wigan Robin Park	32	12	5	15	54	60	41
Ashton Town	32	11	7	14	62	73	40
Cheadle Town	32	9	9	14	46	57	33
AFC Blackpool	32	9	5	18	50	64	32
Oldham Borough	32	7	8	17	37	57	29
Rochdale Town	32	5	5	22	36	91	20

Cheadle Town had 3 points deducted.
AFC Darwen joined from the West Lancashire League and Runcorn Town joined from the West Cheshire League.

2010-11

Premier Division

New Mills	42	32	6	4	102	38	102
Ramsbottom United	42	29	4	9	101	45	91
Winsford United	42	26	5	11	99	50	83
Padiham	42	21	10	11	84	62	73
Colne	42	21	10	11	90	73	73
Bootle	42	21	9	12	78	56	72
Barnoldswick Town	42	19	12	11	81	58	69
Congleton Town	42	18	10	14	70	60	64
Squires Gate	42	18	10	14	74	70	64
Atherton Laburnum Rovers	42	19	6	17	75	72	63
Bacup Borough	42	17	10	15	68	55	61
Runcorn Linnets	42	16	8	18	68	77	56
Maine Road	42	15	9	18	69	64	54
Glossop North End	42	14	11	17	68	55	53
Flixton	42	13	9	20	78	91	48
Silsden	42	13	9	20	47	74	48
St. Helens Town	42	14	5	23	79	116	44
Formby	42	11	10	21	67	95	43
Stone Dominoes	42	12	6	24	60	90	42
Alsager Town	42	10	8	24	57	94	38
Rossendale United	42	6	11	25	63	106	28
Ashton Athletic	42	5	6	31	45	122	21

Rossendale United had 1 point deducted. The club disbanded at the end of the season.

Division One

AFC Blackpool	34	28	3	3	94	30	87
Runcorn Town	34	26	6	2	114	39	81
Holker Old Boys	34	19	6	9	77	42	63
AFC Liverpool	34	19	6	9	65	34	63
Atherton Collieries	34	18	6	10	70	44	60
Chadderton	34	18	6	10	64	48	60
Norton United	34	17	7	10	64	54	58
Wigan Robin Park	34	17	5	12	68	51	53
Irlam	34	14	5	15	63	69	47
Cheadle Town	34	13	7	14	54	62	46
Eccleshall	34	15	3	16	64	70	45
Leek County School Old Boys	34	11	9	14	54	58	42
AFC Darwen	34	9	10	15	38	69	37
Daisy Hill	34	6	8	20	47	90	26
Abbey Hey	34	6	6	22	48	72	24
Ashton Town	34	5	8	21	37	86	23
Oldham Borough	34	5	6	23	37	77	21
Rochdale Town	34	2	9	23	44	107	15

Runcorn Town, Wigan Robin Park and Eccleshall all had 3 points deducted. Northwich Villa joined from the Cheshire League and Nelson joined as a newly formed club.

2011-12
Premier Division

	P	W	D	L	F	A	Pts
Ramsbottom United	42	31	3	8	108	43	96
Runcorn Town	42	29	5	8	111	49	92
Bootle	42	24	13	5	87	43	84
Barnoldswick Town	42	26	5	11	73	38	83
Runcorn Linnets	42	22	10	10	70	62	76
Glossop North End	42	22	7	13	76	42	73
Winsford United	42	21	6	15	88	69	69
Colne	42	19	4	19	68	60	61
AFC Blackpool	42	17	10	15	67	64	61
Flixton	42	18	5	19	69	68	59
Congleton Town	42	18	5	19	56	64	59
Silsden	42	16	9	17	59	59	57
Alsager Town	42	16	9	17	63	65	57
Ashton Athletic	42	15	6	21	70	80	51
Padiham	42	14	9	19	51	65	51
Squires Gate	42	14	8	20	74	89	50
Bacup Borough	42	15	7	20	59	77	49
Maine Road	42	13	9	20	58	69	44
AFC Liverpool	42	13	6	23	60	73	42
Stone Dominoes	42	10	6	26	39	92	36
St. Helens Town	42	6	8	28	50	105	26
Atherton Laburnum Rovers	*42*	*5*	*6*	*31*	*36*	*116*	*21*

Bootle had 1 point deducted.
AFC Liverpool and Bacup Borough each had 3 points deducted.
Maine Road had 4 points deducted.
Stockport Sports joined following their relegation from the Northern Premier League and Flixton disbanded.

2012-13
Premier Division

	P	W	D	L	F	A	Pts
Padiham	42	26	10	6	92	45	88
Maine Road	42	28	3	11	99	57	87
Bootle	42	26	8	8	79	43	86
Runcorn Town	42	26	9	7	105	45	84
Winsford United	42	25	8	9	85	45	83
Runcorn Linnets	42	21	9	12	82	58	72
Congleton Town	42	20	9	13	85	55	69
Colne	42	19	10	13	93	60	67
Barnoldswick Town	42	19	9	14	77	57	66
AFC Blackpool	42	19	9	14	60	58	66
AFC Liverpool	42	18	6	18	69	64	60
Wigan Robin Park	42	17	5	20	66	71	56
Glossop North End	42	14	11	17	73	71	53
Norton United	42	16	7	19	69	83	52
Alsager Town	42	14	8	20	66	78	50
Stockport Sports	42	14	9	19	72	69	45
Bacup Borough	42	13	8	21	51	71	47
Silsden	42	11	6	25	58	98	39
St. Helens Town	42	9	9	24	54	91	36
Ashton Athletic	42	10	5	27	58	91	35
Squires Gate	42	8	6	28	47	95	30
Stone Dominoes	42	3	4	35	31	166	13

Runcorn Town and Norton United each had 3 points deducted and Stockport Sports had 6 points deducted.
Stone Dominoes withdrew from senior football.
Bacup Borough changed their name to Bacup & Rossendale Borough.

Division One

	P	W	D	L	F	A	Pts
Wigan Robin Park	*34*	*25*	*6*	*3*	*90*	*36*	*81*
Norton United	*34*	*24*	*8*	*2*	*110*	*43*	*80*
Abbey Hey	34	22	3	9	82	44	69
Atherton Collieries	34	15	7	12	69	52	52
Rochdale Town	34	14	10	10	72	57	52
Chadderton	34	13	10	11	53	51	49
Eccleshall	34	14	5	15	52	64	47
Cheadle Town	34	13	9	12	60	61	45
Holker Old Boys	34	12	9	13	53	64	45
Irlam	34	13	5	16	68	75	44
Formby	34	13	4	17	72	69	43
Daisy Hill	34	12	5	17	59	67	41
AFC Darwen	34	10	8	16	62	77	38
Oldham Borough	34	9	10	15	52	56	37
Nelson	34	9	5	20	40	83	32
Northwich Villa	34	7	10	17	51	86	31
Leek County School Old Boys	34	10	7	17	50	70	37
Ashton Town	34	6	9	19	49	89	27

Cheadle Town had 3 points deducted and Leek County School Old Boys had 7 points deducted.
West Didsbury & Chorlton joined from the Manchester League.

Division One

	P	W	D	L	F	A	Pts
Formby	34	28	2	4	117	42	86
Abbey Hey	*34*	*26*	*3*	*5*	*88*	*25*	*81*
West Didsbury & Chorlton	*34*	*22*	*4*	*8*	*79*	*43*	*70*
Atherton Collieries	34	21	6	7	78	47	69
AFC Darwen	34	20	3	11	79	57	63
Ashton Town	34	18	8	8	77	43	62
Cheadle Town	34	14	7	13	61	65	49
Oldham Borough	34	15	5	14	59	50	47
Rochdale Town	34	12	9	13	54	60	45
Nelson	34	11	9	14	64	76	42
Leek County School Old Boys	34	10	9	15	52	68	39
Chadderton	34	10	9	15	52	69	39
Atherton Laburnum Rovers	34	8	11	15	37	55	35
Irlam	34	9	6	19	47	72	33
Eccleshall	34	7	7	20	44	79	28
Daisy Hill	34	7	6	21	55	81	27
Holker Old Boys	34	7	2	25	31	74	23
Northwich Villa	34	6	4	24	38	106	22

Oldham Borough had 3 points deducted.
Hanley Town joined from the Staffordshire County Senior League, Widnes Vikings joined from the West Cheshire League and 1874 Northwich joined as a newly formed club. Northwich Villa changed their name to Northwich Flixton Villa.

2013-14

Premier Division

Norton United	42	32	4	6	101	38	100
Runcorn Linnets	42	29	8	5	103	39	95
Glossop North End	42	25	8	9	73	33	83
Maine Road	42	24	9	9	85	42	81
Runcorn Town	42	25	4	13	87	45	79
Ashton Athletic	42	23	5	14	78	50	74
AFC Liverpool	42	21	7	14	88	54	70
Bootle	42	21	7	14	87	57	70
Colne	42	20	4	18	71	67	64
Congleton Town	42	17	9	16	58	58	60
Stockport Sports	42	15	12	15	64	69	57
West Didsbury & Chorlton	42	15	8	19	52	66	53
AFC Blackpool	42	14	7	21	60	87	49
Winsford United	42	15	3	24	57	83	48
Silsden	42	13	8	21	52	70	47
Barnoldswick Town	42	12	7	23	59	89	43
St. Helens Town	42	11	10	21	55	89	43
Alsager Town	42	11	7	24	57	85	40
Squires Gate	42	12	4	26	51	89	40
Abbey Hey	42	9	13	20	47	86	40
Bacup & Rossendale Borough	42	9	12	21	38	68	39
Wigan Robin Park	*42*	*7*	*8*	*27*	*53*	*112*	*29*

2014-15

Premier Division

Glossop North End	40	33	3	4	100	23	102
Runcorn Linnets	40	28	8	4	89	39	92
1874 Northwich	40	26	8	6	90	35	86
Colne	40	25	5	10	86	47	80
Ashton Athletic	40	21	12	7	69	38	75
Squires Gate	40	17	16	7	62	42	67
Bootle	40	19	6	15	76	63	63
Congleton Town	40	17	9	14	68	57	60
AFC Liverpool	40	17	8	15	74	56	59
Silsden	40	16	8	16	55	62	56
Nelson	40	16	7	17	69	64	55
Winsford United	40	15	10	15	66	62	55
Runcorn Town	40	13	8	19	72	75	47
Abbey Hey	40	14	5	21	56	74	47
Maine Road	40	12	9	19	52	75	45
West Didsbury & Chorlton	40	13	4	23	57	84	43
Alsager Town	40	12	6	22	64	87	42
AFC Blackpool	40	7	9	24	37	81	30
Barnoldswick Town	40	7	6	27	45	98	27
St. Helens Town	*40*	*7*	*5*	*28*	*46*	*115*	*26*
Bacup & Rossendale Borough	*40*	*6*	*6*	*28*	*42*	*98*	*24*

Stockport Sports were expelled from the league on 2nd March 2015 and their record was deleted. They later disbanded.
Padiham joined following their relegation from the Northern Premier League. Bacup & Rossendale Borough changed their name to Bacup Borough.

Division One

Nelson	*36*	*29*	*2*	*5*	*135*	*51*	*89*
Formby	36	26	6	4	97	37	84
1874 Northwich	*36*	*26*	*6*	*4*	*79*	*28*	*84*
Hanley Town	36	23	4	9	86	55	73
Atherton Collieries	36	19	9	8	100	62	66
Holker Old Boys	36	17	9	10	80	60	60
Rochdale Town	36	17	4	15	95	78	55
Atherton Laburnum Rovers	36	17	3	16	66	66	54
AFC Darwen	36	15	7	14	64	64	51
Irlam	36	14	8	14	53	64	50
Cheadle Town	36	14	7	15	65	74	46
Ashton Town	36	11	11	14	57	61	44
Chadderton	36	12	8	16	58	71	41
Widnes Vikings	36	9	9	18	58	84	35
Leek County School Old Boys	36	8	5	23	55	93	29
Oldham Borough	36	7	7	22	45	90	28
Eccleshall	36	7	5	24	43	78	26
Daisy Hill	36	6	4	26	43	103	22
Northwich Flixton Villa	36	6	4	26	48	108	22

AFC Darwen and Widnes Vikings each had 1 point deducted and Chadderton, Cheadle Town and Northwich Flixton Villa each had 3 points deducted.
Leek County School Old Boys moved to the Staffordshire County Senior League and Formby disbanded. Cammell Laird 1907 joined from the Northern Premier League, Barnton joined from the Cheshire League and Litherland REMYCA joined from the Liverpool County Premier League. Widnes Vikings changed their name to Widnes.

Division One

Atherton Collieries	*36*	*31*	*3*	*2*	*129*	*26*	*96*
Cammell Laird 1907	*36*	*28*	*5*	*3*	*114*	*35*	*89*
AFC Darwen	*36*	*20*	*8*	*8*	*103*	*60*	*68*
Hanley Town	36	21	4	11	89	63	67
Holker Old Boys	36	18	6	12	79	50	60
Chadderton	36	18	6	12	68	56	60
Barnton	36	18	5	13	77	66	59
Daisy Hill	36	15	7	14	57	68	52
Litherland REMYCA	36	13	8	15	72	73	47
Cheadle Town	36	13	7	16	68	67	46
Northwich Flixton Villa	36	12	9	15	73	65	45
Atherton Laburnum Rovers	36	12	7	17	46	70	43
Rochdale Town	36	11	9	16	71	84	42
Irlam	36	11	8	17	51	64	41
Eccleshall	36	12	5	19	47	91	41
Widnes	36	10	5	21	62	101	35
Ashton Town	36	7	6	23	51	78	27
Oldham Borough	36	6	7	23	37	105	25
Wigan Robin Park	36	7	3	26	41	113	24

Oldham Borough and Wigan Robin Park both disbanded.
Whitchurch Alport joined from the Mercian Regional League and Stockport Town joined as a newly formed club. Northwich Flixton Villa changed their name to Northwich Manchester Villa.

2015-16

Premier Division

Colne	42	31	7	4	105	41	100
Runcorn Linnets	42	32	2	8	97	35	98
Atherton Collieries	42	25	9	8	113	66	84
1874 Northwich	42	24	6	12	89	62	78
West Didsbury & Chorlton	42	21	5	16	81	65	68
Congleton Town	42	19	10	13	79	65	67
Ashton Athletic	42	17	10	15	73	68	61
Bootle	42	17	10	15	75	75	61
Barnoldswick Town	42	17	8	17	77	69	59
Abbey Hey	42	16	11	15	67	66	59
Padiham	42	16	9	17	84	90	57
Maine Road	42	16	7	19	72	76	55
Runcorn Town	42	15	7	20	70	76	52
Winsford United	42	14	10	18	66	93	52
Cammell Laird 1907	42	14	8	20	71	83	50
Nelson	42	13	9	20	69	70	48
AFC Liverpool	42	11	15	16	86	92	48
AFC Darwen	42	12	7	23	82	111	43
Squires Gate	42	11	8	23	53	91	41
Alsager Town	*42*	*11*	*6*	*25*	*56*	*101*	*39*
Silsden	*42*	*9*	*11*	*22*	*57*	*88*	*38*
AFC Blackpool	*42*	*9*	*9*	*24*	*65*	*104*	*36*

New Mills joined after relegation from the Northern Premier League.

Division One

Hanley Town	*34*	*25*	*3*	*6*	*68*	*32*	*78*
Irlam	*34*	*24*	*5*	*5*	*73*	*27*	*77*
Barnton	*34*	*19*	*9*	*6*	*94*	*36*	*66*
Stockport Town	34	19	6	9	68	44	63
Bacup Borough	34	17	6	11	81	54	57
Cheadle Town	34	16	8	10	89	59	56
St. Helens Town	34	17	4	13	84	61	55
Holker Old Boys	34	16	7	11	73	62	55
Litherland REMYCA	34	16	6	12	63	51	54
Rochdale Town	34	14	5	15	66	77	47
Ashton Town	34	12	7	15	57	57	43
Daisy Hill	34	12	6	16	56	72	42
Widnes	34	10	5	19	67	77	35
Chadderton	34	9	8	17	43	53	35
Northwich Manchester Villa	34	10	4	20	48	77	34
Eccleshall	34	9	5	20	53	77	32
Atherton Laburnum Rovers	34	4	6	24	32	103	18
Whitchurch Alport	34	2	10	22	31	127	16

Rochdale Town moved to the Manchester League and Northwich Manchester Villa disbanded. Carlisle City joined from the Northern Alliance, Charnock Richard joined from the West Lancashire League, FC Oswestry Town joined from the Mercian Regional League, Prestwich Heys joined from the Manchester League, Sandbach United joined from the Cheshire League and City of Liverpool joined as a newly formed club.